THE IMPACT ROADMAP™

SCALE PROFIT WITH PURPOSE FOR PEOPLE AND PLANET
POWERED BY THE SUSTAINABLE DEVELOPMENT GOALS

NUPUR SAXENA

COPYRIGHT

The United Nations Sustainable Development Goals website:
https://www.un.org/sustainabledevelopment/

DEDICATION

To my loving and supportive parents Sunita & Vinod Saxena, who raised me to believe that anything is possible... And to all the IMPACT Game Changers™ out there, who are pushing the boundaries to bring the Sustainable Development Goals to life by 2030 for People and Planet.

This book is a humble contribution towards the preservation of our society and the planet's thriving health, sustainability, and beauty for the next generation... to my nephews Alexander, Tristan, and Sebastian.

'Never doubt that a small group of thoughtful, committed citizens can change the world; indeed, it's the only thing that ever has.'
– Margaret Mead, Anthropologist

CONTENTS

Score Your IMPACT:

Are you ready to Scale Profit with Purpose for People and Planet™?

To get the most out of this book, start by taking The IMPACT Roadmap Scorecard™. It will allow you to focus in on the areas of the book that are most beneficial to you.

The IMPACT Roadmap Scorecard™ is built on the 3 steps:
PLAN with PURPOSE™ – PERSUADE with PROMISE™ –
PROFIT with IMPACT™.

Be Part of the Solution. Start an IMPACT Revolution™.

www.splitsecondltd.com

THE CLOCK IS TICKING ...

So, you want to make a Profit? Have purpose? Make a lasting positive IMPACT on People and Planet?

Start with the end in mind.

Impossible?

Think again.

We are standing on the precipice of change. The decisions we make over the next decade will alter our fate for generations to come. Most people would rather forget 2020. A period in time so inconceivable, no one could have ever imagined its ripple effects. Yet, what if this was a wake-up call reminding us that if certain boundaries are crossed, there will be severe consequences. Perhaps this is even an opportunity to course-correct the next 'normal' which will put us on a more sustainable and just path.

For decades, most western countries have enjoyed whatever money could buy. Consumers have purchased and increased their consumption of goods and services without a second thought. Businesses have put shareholders first and prospered like never before, generating profit, delivering a return on investment and accumulating wealth for a select and powerful few. However, the single-minded pursuit of capitalism and consumerism comes at a price.

Monopoly, inequality, and the exploitation of people and planet have brought us face to face with our own existential crisis. We have tipped the socio-economic and environmental scales to the limit. The boundaries can no longer be pushed further without irreversible damage. Doing nothing is no longer an option.

Even though 90%[1] of larger organisations report their individual sustainable development vision, they tend to be managed within the corporate social responsibility (CSR) functions. This often results in various socio-economic and environmental agendas being siloed in one part of the business, with little connection to the company's commercial strategy and customers. It also deprioritises the sense of urgency. Yet it is this intersection of social entrepreneurship and profitability that will foster the longevity of any business, big or small, moving forward.

Brands and businesses are in a unique position to use their purpose for good. They can confront the social, political, economic and environmental challenges head on through their company ideology, strategy, innovation, and culture. *Putting purpose at the heart* has become a mantra for many businesses across all industry sectors. Yet what does this mean? What role does purpose play in value creation? Are purpose, sustainability, and profit mutually exclusive?

Purpose-driven companies grow six times[2] faster than their competitors, increase their market share and have a greater workforce and customer satisfaction. Coincidence? No. That's because 81%[3] of consumers feel that they must be able to trust a brand to do the right thing. As such, they use their spending power to connect with, and even advocate for, businesses that make authentic and meaningful contributions to the world.

Whether you are a start-up, want to scale up, or level-up as an entrepreneur or intrapreneur in a large corporate – we are all global citizens who must endeavour to redress the balance in order to live in a beautiful society, on a clean earth with an active economy. If ignored, it is an inevitable ticking time bomb.

Every second counts.

WAKE-UP CALL

Just over a hundred years ago, in the aftermath of World War I, the Spanish flu swept the world killing millions, followed by the Great Depression. Economic and political strife, along with the collapse of international trade, created the perfect storm for World War II. With so much hardship and fear of another Depression, consumerism was deemed to be the solution for economic survival.

Similarly, the cumulative domino-effect of the Covid-19 pandemic saw life as we knew it radically change overnight. Almost every aspect that we had taken for granted had been somehow altered. The social distancing measures, health, mobility, and economic repercussions have been felt on an unimaginable global scale. Was this another wake-up call for humanity?

The crisis caught the world off guard and lifted the veil on environmental and societal deficiencies. It exposed archaic economic, healthcare, and political systems that require major re-engineering for the 21st century. Or maybe it simply accelerated the macro trends that were already in motion. What lessons can we learn from history repeating itself?

The Power Shift

Since the last century, consumerism highlighted three distinct eras that shaped how we buy, sell and influence purchasing behaviours. These are the brand, retail, and consumer eras which defined who held the power in the market.

The **Brand Era** emerged in the 1950s following years of deprivation, rationing, institutional and functional trading. Manufacturers saw the commercial opportunity to pivot from the production of war-essential commodities to aspirational consumer goods brands. Television and media were the new key catalysts for engaging the middle-class. Limited TV channels and repetitive advertising led to communal conversations that made brands status symbols a cultural currency for decades.

Creative campaigns, brand innovation and marketing based on consumer desires gave manufacturers the power to invent household brands. Advertising reeled them in with style, selling the idea that mass consumption equalled happiness. Many brands conceived cultural and iconic traditions to entice consumers, such as the De Beers' 'A diamond is forever' engagement ring and 'The holidays are coming' Coca-Cola Santa Claus. This encouraged consumers to take a leap from the 'must be nice' to the 'must-have' purchase. Soon, manufacturers dominated the stock market and leveraged their brand power to impose their demands onto retailers with a 'one cannot afford not to stock my brand' approach.

The **Retail Era** was marked by global merchants, customer experience and the arrival of the internet in the early 1990s. This caused a power shift that unlocked an international marketplace. Retailers could no longer fight on price alone and the functional general store was no longer relevant. They had to deliver on quality, shopping experience and value to stand out as bricks-and-mortar environments while having a strong online offering as well. Retailers began to engage consumers and shoppers through their above-the-line (ATL) TV and media advertising and their in-store below-the-line (BTL) marketing campaigns.

With the advent of sales and customer data, retailers were able to anticipate customer behaviour. This fact-based insight led them to develop their own range of products and services that gave brands a run for their money. Store formats, customer engagement and tailored promotions – all increased their sales. Retailers began to call the shots with suppliers, demanding lucrative category partnerships which often created a level of friction. Retailers raised the stakes and also made their way onto the stock market. Brand suppliers had to collaborate to ensure their place in-store and find other routes-to-markets.

Then a radical disruptor shook the retail world. Amazon sold its first book in 1994[4] and went on to build the global empire that it is today. Retailers were clearly in the driver's seat and took a 'one cannot afford not to be stocked in my store' approach with brand suppliers.

The **Consumer Era** was the third shift that gave power to the people. For decades, brand owners and retailers had dictated the supply and demand terms. Together they drove consumption of goods and services, developed global distribution systems, and made shopping into a pastime. Consumers and shoppers were offered endless choice as to where they shopped, what they bought and their personal brand experiences. Shoppers became more promiscuous, so understanding and anticipating their behaviour became challenging. Ultimately, it became difficult to win customer loyalty.

With the rise of technology firms such as Apple, Amazon, YouTube, Google, Facebook and Instagram, consumers have a plethora of platforms to purchase from and share their own views, breaking with convention. A new generation of online influencers and social media celebrities have become the voices that champion brands and are brands in their own right.

Today, anyone can become an influencer marketing sensation. From the 8-year-old boy who made $26 million[5] by unboxing and playing with toys on his YouTube channel with 45 billion[6] views and rising, to a sports and comedy team that generated over $20 million[7], to anyone who feels brave enough to have their moment in the spotlight. One does not need to be a big corporation to launch a lucrative brand anymore. The consumer took a no-nonsense approach: *'one cannot afford not to offer me what I want, or I will create it myself'*.

Without a crystal ball, predicting what the future holds is anyone's guess. However, one thing for certain is that every seismic shift is underpinned in one or more of the macro trends. From globalisation, instant gratification, health, and wellbeing to personalisation, AI and 24/7 connectivity – the macro trends are always evolving and shaping all aspects of our lives. They identify the drivers of change, understand motivation, and provide a wider context that enable society and investors to hedge their bets on the next big thing.

However, there is one major factor that humanity has not had to consider until now – The Planet.

The Tipping Point

'We are the first generation to feel the effects of climate change and the last generation to be able to do something about it.'
– Barack Obama

We have hit a collective social, economic, and environmental tipping point. Times of upheaval always push the boundaries of uncertainty and instability. They disrupt and offer different paths at the crossroads of radical change.

As the business environment becomes more unpredictable and complex, organisations are put to the test by the marketplace, their customers, and their own operational and strategic resilience. The ability to absorb external shocks, stretch resources, recover, and even flourish under extenuating circumstances, must be part of their arsenal. Naturally it is a period of great diversification, experimentation of business models, digital revenue streams and other practices. Moving forward, to ensure our long-term survival, every business must take responsibility for urgent global challenges such as the climate crisis, rising inequality and socio-economic issues that ultimately affect us all.

The UN's Intergovernmental Panel on Climate Change (IPCC) 'code red' report says that we are set to pass the 1.5°C threshold by 2040. Human activity is the main catalyst for global warming. We are responsible for the melting icebergs, forest fires, warmer oceans, rising sea levels and intense heatwaves. Scientists have been warning us for decades that we are close to reaching an irreversible climate catastrophe. The undeniable evidence is clear: the greenhouse gas emissions are literally choking our planet and, ultimately, ourselves. The game has changed, and we must act with pace.

Businesses need to discard a one-size-fits-all approach and respond to the planet's alarm bell. Fossil fuels must be abandoned as a matter of urgency, instead, opting for renewal energy sources. Greener cities and environmental urban planning must become the norm. People must also embrace sustainable diets and reduce the consumption of meat and dairy and shop local. Brands and businesses must include sustainability and their genuine positive IMPACT in core business values and ethos aligned to the new conscious consumer. We must reframe the way we do business, treat people, and preserve the planet. Every action at the right time, in the right direction, with the right people can create an equilibrium for a sustainable present and future.

The Triple Bottom Line

Companies are structured to generate sales, maximise profit and deliver a return on investment. Today however, real success is measured by a *Triple Bottom Line* (TBL) with three key components: People, Planet, and Profit. This term was first coined by John Elkington in 1994[8], who believes that businesses should own all three metrics to measure social, environmental, and financial performances.

- **People:** How socially responsible is an organisation with its human capital?
- **Planet:** How environmentally responsible is it now and in the long-term?
- **Profit:** How do a company's activities IMPACT share value, People, and the Planet over time?

One of the great ironies is that the most profitable companies are not always those solely focused on generating a profit. Businesses that commit to and deliver all three components tend to win and lead the market. They take account of the overall cost, purpose, and IMPACT of doing business. This comes at a time when full transparency from organisations is expected because consumers are better informed and engaged with brands that go beyond the short-term gains. Sustainability and socio-economic practices are now front and centre on the global business stage.

Profit does not have to cost the earth. Period.

WINDOW OF OPPORTUNITY

'Our natural world is under greater pressure now than at any time in human history, and the future of the entire planet – on which every single one of us depends is in grave jeopardy. We still have an opportunity to reverse catastrophic biodiversity loss, but time is running out.'
– Sir David Attenborough

Some say that we live in the greatest time of humanity, armed with breakthroughs in health, wealth, technology, and education. Yet, despite appearances, the cracks are beginning to show in the form of mass fires, melting icebergs, rising sea levels, flooding, and unusual weather patterns. They are all direct results of excessive carbon emissions, 80%[9] of which are primarily generated by 20 countries alone. In addition to the climate crisis, the tension between the haves and have-nots, racial and gender inequality, political upheaval, and pollution have reached an untenable point. Mankind has become his own worst enemy.

Now close your eyes and imagine the year is 2030. The global population is winning the fight against climate change, enjoying cleaner air, pristine oceans, and protecting our natural resources. People are thriving in world peace and greater social equality, prospering in smart cities where circular economies have become *the* economy and living longer, healthier, happier lives. This is a world where we have unleashed our true human potential. Today, there is still a small window of opportunity to make it happen, but the clock is ticking.

Unlock $12 Trillion

Sustainability is no longer a choice, but an imperative. It sometimes conjures up notions of added cost and business transformation, but mission-driven organisations profit from its long-term potential. According to the *Business & Sustainable Development Commission* (BSDC) there is a very compelling case for the private sector to focus on four key economic sectors[10] to realise and unlock a $12 trillion a year sustainability opportunity:

- Food and Agriculture = $2.3 trillion

- Cities and urban mobility = $3.7 trillion
- Energy and material = $4.3 trillion
- Health and wellbeing = $1.8 trillion[11]

These incremental market opportunities will create 380 million jobs[12] by 2030 if sustainable business models are adopted. The choice is clear. Embrace a sustainable future that benefits all or suffer the consequences. Industry leaders are best placed to drive far-reaching change, generate sustainable value creation, and harness a new business model with infinite possibilities.

The private sector plays an indispensable role in unlocking the $12 trillion opportunity. It is a source of finance, goods, services, innovation, and technology that accelerate economic growth and employment. It is an extremely diverse sector, comprised of multinational corporations, dynamic small-and-medium-sized enterprises (SMEs) and social enterprises (SEs). In fact, SMEs generate over 50% of jobs globally, drive groundbreaking innovation. With over 5.6 million SMEs in the UK alone (vs. 7700 corporates) – they are the future to sustainable solutions.[13]

To seize these lucrative opportunities, organisations must implement and endorse social and sustainable practices to increase their shareholder value and be businesses for good. The risk of inaction is bleak. In order to gain critical mass behind these initiatives a collective global approach must be adopted, one that translates purpose into action. It must transcend all markets, industry sectors, politics and ideologies that culminate into a unified vision.

Embrace the Sustainable Development Goals (SDGs)

The global alarm clock was set in 2015 when the United Nations gave the world an ambitious and urgent mandate to step up and tackle the socio-economic and environmental emergency we are facing. One hundred and ninety-three nations committed to deliver the UN's Sustainable Development Goals (SDGs) by 2030, an international consensus that holds every global citizen accountable. These 17 SDGs will ensure that people are thriving in peace, prosperity and on a protected and healthy planet.

Source: The United Nations by permission (21.04.2022)

Although some advancements have been made in areas such as extreme poverty, access to electricity, labour productivity and employment rates, the progress pales in comparison to some of the other critical goals. Climate change, pollution and social inequalities still afflict 70%[14] of the global population which means that world targets are not on track to be met by the impending deadline. In order to drive radical change, extreme measures must be taken.

How are the Sustainable Development Goals relevant to the business world? The SDGs offer clear socio-economic and sustainability targets and a wealth of opportunities for organisations to aim for. These goals fundamentally offer purpose, business priorities and a call to action to business leaders, which in turn can enhance the vision, values, and the bottom line of any organisation.

The SDGs are the only keys that can unlock the incremental $12 trillion opportunity and create 380 million jobs by 2030. The Business & Sustainable Development Commission (BSDC) echoes that fact *'At the heart of the Commission's argument are the Sustainable Development Goals (or Global Goals)—17 objectives to eliminate poverty, improve education and health outcomes, create better jobs and tackle our key environmental challenges by 2030. The Commission believes the Global*

Goals provide the private sector with a new growth strategy that opens valuable market opportunities while creating a world that is both sustainable and inclusive. And the potential rewards for doing so are significant.'[15]

It is our shared responsibility to galvanise business industries, collaborate with governments and influential bodies that currently hold the keys to our future. They ensure that the SDGs are delivered on time and in full. Ultimately, they become part of a global mission to do good, deliver profit and harness the $12 trillion opportunity.

Armed with the SDGs, every organisation can make a once in a lifetime global IMPACT. They can be embedded at all levels of government, cities, and communities, so that every global citizen can commit to specific SDG targets, act and make the world a better place. They provide clear tangible goals that can be met through innovative business practices and solutions. When implemented, the SDGs identify growth opportunities, anticipate consumer behaviour, provide access to resources, strengthen supply chains, and mitigate risk. This is a new global blueprint that must be incorporated in every organisation for international trading, human existence, and a sustainable world.

'Our biggest challenge in this new century is to take an idea that seems abstract – sustainable development – and turn it into a reality for all the world's people.'
– Kofi Annan, Former Secretary-General of the United Nations

Think Global, Act Local

In the age of technology, business has become borderless. Yet today, to truly become a global organisation one needs to do more than coordinate sales, marketing, and customers in international markets. Today it is about placing the Sustainable Development Goals at the heart of the business to ignite the triple bottom line for People, Planet, and Profit.

The 17 Sustainable Development Goals (SDGs) are the blueprint that must be implemented at global, business sector and community levels to unleash monumental change. According to PwC when the *World*

Business Council for Sustainable Development (WBCSD) brought 200 CEOs[16] together to tackle and accelerate the progress towards the Sustainable Development Goals (SDGs), they found six areas of systematic transformations that are essential to achieving sustainable success:

6 AREAS OF SYSTEMATIC TRANSFORMATIONS

1 **CIRCULAR ECONOMY** HOW WE ARE RECYCLING AND REUSING SCARCE RESOURCES

2 **CITIES AND MOBILITY** TRANSFORMING URBAN ENVIRONMENT AND MASS TRANSPORT

3 **CLIMATE AND ENERGY** DECARBONISING OUR ENERGY SYSTEM TO TACKLE CLIMATE CHANGE

4 **FOOD AND NATURE** MAKING AGRICULTURE MORE SUSTAINABLE AND SAFEGUARDING THE BIODIVERSITY ON WHICH WE DEPEND

5 **PEOPLE** TACKLING INEQUALITY AND POVERTY

6 **REDEFINING VALUE** CONSIDERING BUSINESS VALUES IN THE CONTEXT OF ITS WIDER PURPOSE FOR MULTIPLE STAKEHOLDERS AND ITS SOCIAL AND ENVIRONMENTAL IMPACTS

Source: World Business Council for Sustainable Development (WBCSD)

At a global level these systematic transformations point to where the opportunities are and how industries can fast-track and influence the pace of delivering the SDGs. Identifying, translating, and measuring the SDGs from strategy to IMPACT is fundamental to achieving them over the next decade. Currently, no country is on track to achieving the Sustainable Development Goals by 2030. This is possibly because most organisations are neither set up with an SDG planning blueprint, nor do they have the capability to re-design their business models to achieve their environmental, social governance and commercial goals that make a positive lasting IMPACT.

Research by PwC found that despite 72%[17] of global organisations citing the SDGs in their annual reports, only 34%[18] included them in their strategic business planning. The picture gets a bit bleaker from there. Less than 14%[19] of companies included specific SDG targets and only 1%[20] actually measured their performance against the targets. Industry leaders must start by prioritising the SDGs that they believe are affiliated to their businesses. By aligning the corporate strategy, key performance indicators (KPIs) and SDG targets, organisations can start to connect the dots to achieve their business objectives and global goals.

WORLD OF ACTION

'To make the SDGs a reality, we need leaders across the world. You can't run a successful business in an economy that isn't thriving. Going forward, leaders must consider: 'How do you run your business in harmony with the world's needs and make these issues your own issues?'
– Lise Kingo, CEO and Executive Director, UN Global Compact

The Sustainable Development Goals (SDGs) and targets are set. Will they be delivered by 2030? Will they unlock $12 trillion and create 380 million jobs a year? Will they be a force for the socio-economic and environmental greater good? Or will we face the avoidable catastrophic consequences based on out-of-date economic systems?

Companies and business leaders must lead the change. According to Edelman's global *Trust Barometer*[21] survey, trust in business is higher (61%) than in NGOs (57%), government (53%) and the media (51%). Even more interestingly, people's trust in their own employers is at a staggering 76% and business is the only one seen as both competent and ethical. Business leaders are in a position to step up to the challenge and create a chain reaction that will have a resounding IMPACT for People, Planet, and Profit.

It's time to choose which side of the future you want to be on. You decide.

Cater to the Conscious Consumer

In a world of uncertainty, consumers are more mindful of where, what, and how much they consume and spend. Changing lifestyles, attitudes, and behaviours have been evolving for some time but the consumer wants a clearer conscience when making purchasing decisions. Conscious consumerism is not just about buying less or abstinence, but it is about making choices that actually have a positive social, economic, and environmental IMPACT.

The conscious consumer is highly intuitive and looks beyond price, packaging, and product. They are the ones who make informed purchasing decisions based on what a brand stands for and does to raise social or environmental consciousness. They are literally *putting money where their mouth is* by intentionally voting with their wallets as a form of brand activism to advocate a company's mission to do better for the world.

Purchasing decisions can be a minefield. At some point, without even realising, most of us have probably endorsed brands that are profiting from unethical archaic systems that promote slavery, poverty, exploit women and children, and contribute to the climate crisis and pollution. Every penny contributes to a cause, good or bad.

So today, whether it is a trip to the supermarket, browsing online, or even choosing our next employer or business partner, ethics and conscience have made us more aware than ever before. We have started to ask ourselves and other parties some crucial questions that are becoming part of our everyday decision-making:

- Does this product/service align with my core values?
- What is the carbon footprint?
- Who produced it?
- Do they have ethical practices?
- Is it good for the planet?

These questions are not meant to intimidate or alienate businesses, but rather inspire to create new economic solutions, sustainable models and respond to the consumer's call to action. Once there is a commitment to incorporate social or environmental practices within the organisation, it must be authentic, measurable and make a genuine lasting IMPACT. If not, clients, colleagues and the conscious consumer will hold organisations accountable.

Put Purpose into Practice

Over the last few years, *purpose* has become a major talking point in the business world. Leadership teams, global brands, non-profit groups are all asking themselves: Why does their organisation exist? What challenges can they resolve? How can they make a difference – beyond profit? What is their ultimate *raison d'être*?

Every company will have its own interpretation of what *purpose* means to them. Some believe it is a just a marketing tactic to drive sales. For others it is badge of honour that will enhance their corporate reputation. Then there are those who genuinely give back to their teams, customers, and society at large. All three options are valid, but it is authenticity that separates those that simply get on a buzzword bandwagon vs. those who take action and make an undisputable IMPACT in the world.

Purpose offers possibility. Purpose-led organisations grow six times faster[22] than their competitive set. They are the trailblazers that attract and retain top talent, stand out, accelerate growth, and form meaningful connections with consumers and business partners. They are the agents of change and magnets of success.

Even though 79%[23] of business leaders believe that purpose is pivotal to their strategy, most are unclear on how to identify, articulate and ignite a meaningful purpose. Business KPIs and growth are obviously the priority, but will not be able to garner loyalty or longevity without a genuine purpose. It is therefore essential to address some of the salient questions and challenges that are keeping leaders up at night:

- What are the sustainability challenges facing our industry?
- What are the critical sustainability issues that our business should focus on? How?
- What does sustainability mean to our customers and consumers?
- How can our business IMPACT the Sustainable Development Goals (SDGs)?
- How can we future-proof our business to remain resilient and relevant?

There is no one size fits all response to these questions and unfortunately most organisations are currently not structured to respond to them other than possibly theoretically. It is time to examine the values and outcomes of your organisation and how they align to the changing marketplace, conscious consumer, nature, and society as a whole. This is the launchpad that puts purpose into practice.

Make a Lasting IMPACT

As corporate leaders, entrepreneurs, and brand owners, it is our responsibility to deliver the SDG targets in a timely and innovative manner to maximise IMPACT. For some organisations, integrating the SDGs into existing business models may require strategic assessment and re-calibration. Understanding risks and opportunities is essential for stakeholders and shareholders alike. Incorporating the SDGs into business strategies and policies puts companies at the forefront of seizing the $12 trillion opportunity. More importantly, if not addressed, the risks posed by the socio-economic and sustainability challenges we face as humanity will increase substantially.

For years reputable organisations have made philanthropy part of their business culture and ethos, aligning 'giving' to their values and teams in a cohesive vision. Today, many are taking bolder steps to tackle the world's most critical issues. This new coalition of business leaders and brands are going beyond making a profit. They are on a mission to respond to the UN's 17 urgent SDG mandates, raising the bar as global citizens, and bringing their unique brand of social consciousness to the masses. They are IMPACT Game Changers™ paving the way for future generations to have a more sustainable society and planet.

THE TOP 5 WAYS TO COMMIT TO THE SUSTAINABLE DEVELOPMENT GOALS (SDGs) ™

1 BE PURPOSE-LED

2 BE TRANSPARENT

3 MAKE A QUANTIFIABLE IMPACT

4 DELIVER CIRCULAR STRATEGIES

5 COMMIT AND INTEGRATE THE SDGs INTO BRAND AND BUSINESS DNA

Commitment to the SDGs means that brands have a greater unique selling point, authenticity, purpose, and customer appeal. They are also less likely to get into the commercial margin entrapments, which often leave no room for manoeuvre. Forty-nine percent[24] of consumers believe brands can do more to cure social issues than the government. Still not convinced? Another 78%[25] are more likely to buy goods and services that have committed to the Sustainable Development Goals.

They are moving the dial from brand purpose to purpose-led to make the world a better place. They create circular economies of scale by taking responsibility in creating new solutions from alternative resources and waste. They offer full transparency to make us into more conscious consumers and ethical shoppers.

Welcome to the IMPACT Revolution™. These are the brands that are purchased in a split second and businesses that make a positive lasting IMPACT on People, Planet, and Profit. It's time to plan, persuade and profit with purpose for good.

'We're an IMPACT company that makes chocolate, we're not a chocolate company that wants to make an IMPACT.'
– Henk Jan Beltman, Chief Chocolate Officer,
Tony's Chocolonely

THE IMPACT ROADMAP™

*'Success is not measured by the amount of money you make,
but the number of lives you IMPACT.'*
– Anonymous

There has never been a better time to be an emerging or existing brand pushing the boundaries of innovation, agility, and consumer resonance. IMPACT Brands™ with attitude are purpose-led and shaking up all industry sectors. They win hearts, win purchases, and make a positive lasting IMPACT in the world.

For many brands, integrating sustainability and ethics into a value proposition that will captivate and convert consumers into customers can be a tall order. However, leading organisations can now turn to the Sustainable Development Goals (SDGs) as a time-bound global destination with clear targets ... but how do we get there?

Driving business growth and harnessing the SDGs requires a roadmap with a well-defined purpose, milestones, and momentum. The companies and SDGs may vary, but a strategic plan can open up endless possibilities and mitigate risk.

The IMPACT Roadmap™ Empowers Organisations:

- To go after untapped sustainable growth opportunities by understanding the market and targeting prospects to build the value proposition.
- To ensure that the SDGs are at the heart of their commercial, capability and cultural strategies to stand out in a crowded marketplace.
- To build industry partnerships – a unified vision to maximise resource and profit that will make a meaningful contribution to the world.

The IMPACT Roadmap™

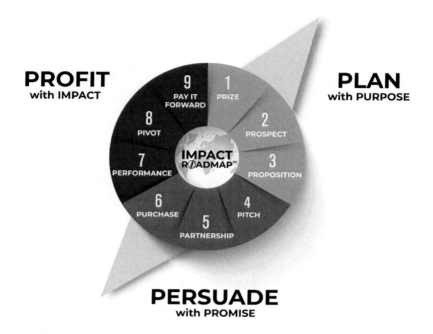

PROFIT
with IMPACT

PLAN
with PURPOSE

9 PAY IT FORWARD
1 PRIZE
8 PIVOT
2 PROSPECT
7 PERFORMANCE
3 PROPOSITION
6 PURCHASE
4 PITCH
5 PARTNERSHIP

IMPACT ROADMAP™

PERSUADE
with PROMISE

Plan, Persuade, Profit are the three steps that form *The IMPACT Roadmap™*. This approach allows business leaders to make informed fact-based decisions that deliver greater returns for investors, society, and the planet. It will begin to answer some fundamental questions:

- Can the organisation tap into the $12 trillion opportunity? If so, how?
- Does the business have the skills, portfolio, and infrastructure to achieve its commercial and SDGs targets?
- Will the value proposition deliver an ROI and be purchased in a split second?

Let's begin...

STEP 1 – PLAN with PURPOSE™:

In the race to drive commercial growth and make their mark, most businesses find themselves trying to navigate their way through a competitive landscape in search of a successful strategy, standout, and sales. Yet in order to make a flying start, one has to begin with a plan before making any large financial or resource investments.

The purpose of the plan is to clearly articulate the mission and translate it into actionable goals. Many brand owners are tempted to dive right into tactics and execution. However, planning out a sound strategic roadmap is a vital first step. It will test the viability of the desired outcome to start-up, scale-up or level-up.

This stage also sheds valuable light on the direction ahead, the necessary resources, and timeline to key milestones. Before you commence, use data and insight to fuel your objectives, strategy, and key performance indicators (KPIs). They will indicate the right course of action in a timely manner and sidestep any potential roadblocks. This insight will enable businesses to better manoeuvre the external landscape and weather any storms. *Warning: without an aligned plan grounded in fact, the business may go off course or remain at a standstill.*

PLAN Encompasses:

1. PRIZE: Map out the journey to the destination. Identify the size of the prize which will set the business direction. Discover your niche in the market, along with the commercial and Sustainable Development Goal (SDG) growth drivers and opportunities.

2. PROSPECT: Identify and nudge the conscious consumer who makes purchasing decisions with a socio-economic and environmental conscience.

3. PROPOSITION: Create a value proposition for good. Be a brand or business that seeks sustainable solutions which will improve the state of the world by 2030 and beyond.

STEP 2 – PERSUADE with PROMISE™:

Consumers don't buy products and services, they buy outcomes. They are looking for solutions that will solve a problem or fulfil a need. For a brand to truly succeed, looking through a wider customer lens can broaden the perspective. It is less about the unique selling point, and more about the IMPACT Unique *Solution* Point (USP)™.

The power of persuasion is the art of seduction. Getting people to make a purchase involves the ability to influence behaviours without them feeling like they are being sold to. By listening to and harnessing customer insight, one can successfully persuade anyone in their favour.

PERSUADE Encompasses:

4. PITCH: Create a meaningful connection from the conventional '*me, me, me*' brand pitch to a solution-based story in response to the customer's key question, '*What's in it for me?*'

5. PARTNERSHIP: Collaborate to multiply business outcomes. Attract more opportunities and investment, harness innovation and scale up as a tribe together.

6. PURCHASE: Influence buying behaviours by tapping into the barriers and triggers to purchase. Drive engagement and spend with the conscious consumer.

STEP 3 – PROFIT with IMPACT™:

One of the greatest ironies is that the most profitable companies are those that are not just focused on making a profit. Purpose-led companies grow six times[1] faster than their competitors. They win loyalty for their authenticity and tenacity to make the world a better place.

More and more consumers are making purchasing decisions based on how brands treat people and the planet. They question if the brand is taking bold steps to make a genuine and positive contribution to society and the environment. According to Deloitte '*Purpose is a core differentiator. Purpose-oriented companies have higher productivity growth rates, along with a more satisfied workforce who stay longer with them. These companies report 30% higher levels of innovation and 40% higher levels of workforce retention than their competitors.*[2]

In order to remain relevant with consumers and be profitable long-term, organisations must leverage their purpose for good. Profit is inevitable if the mission is connected to customers, innovation, and the Sustainable Development Goals (SDGs). Those that have the insight, agility, and boldness to act, stay on top of their game.

PROFIT Encompasses:

7. PERFORMANCE: Track and monitor progress towards the business objectives and the Sustainable Development Goals in an ever-changing marketplace. They will determine the return on investment and next steps.

8. PIVOT: Course-correct the plan to ensure that the business is fit for the future.

9. PAY IT FORWARD: Make a lasting IMPACT on customers, team, industry, and the world. Be human, be the change, and be a force for good.

Follow the Sequence:

The sequence of these steps is very important. One cannot launch a purpose-led proposition without aiming for the prize the business is going after. It is key to identify and understand who the target prospect is and how to create value for them.

Once the proposition is ready to go-to-market, make a meaningful connection with the target prospect. This requires a compelling pitch which delivers desired outcomes for them. Form lucrative business partnerships, drive purchase and loyalty.

Tracking and monitoring performance is essential to the process. Without it, there is no benchmark to gauge if steps 1 (PLAN) and 2 (PERSUADE) worked. This insight will inform key decision-makers whether the business is on track or needs to change course. Finally, remember to pay it forward to your team, society, and the planet to make a positive lasting IMPACT.

These steps will deliver groundbreaking results for companies of all shapes and sizes, whether they are global blue-chip or emerging brands. **The IMPACT Roadmap**™ provides greater opportunities, greater competitive edge, greater profits and greater business purpose.

Income Follows IMPACT:

> *'The brands that will thrive in the coming years are the ones that have a purpose beyond profit.'*
> – Sir Richard Branson

The IMPACT Revolution™ has arrived. Socio-economic and environmental IMPACT are attached to almost every single transaction we make today. If a business does not actively integrate the Sustainable Development Goals (SDGs) within their organisation, sooner or later the lack of IMPACT will catch up with them.

At the heart of the SDGs is a pledge made by the United Nations *'to leave no one behind'*[3]. It is about giving a voice and acting for those who are left behind in society, but also making sure that our planet is sustainable for future generations. Identifying which Sustainable Development Goals to focus on can be directly linked to a business solution or be part of a wider value chain.

Gone are the days when organisations can only survive by pursuing wealth for their shareholders. Now it is essential to provide full transparency that highlights a positive or negative IMPACT on people and planet. Customers are the judge and jury. They will either stay loyal, nudge, or leave the brand in question.

Can you imagine commodities such as soap, tea and petroleum jelly engaging consumers, making a positive lasting IMPACT and multiplying their turnover? That is exactly what global household giant Unilever® did in 2019 with their *Sustainable Living* range[4]. Over the last decade, their beacon brands such as Dove®, Lipton® and Vaseline®, along with their B Corp certified brands such as Ben & Jerry's®, Pukka® and Seventh Generation® and the rest of the sustainable portfolio, have delighted conscious consumers. In reducing their environmental footprint and making a social IMPACT at scale which have been felt worldwide, Unilever® have:

- Reached 1.3 billion people through their health and hygiene programmes
- Reduced their greenhouse gas emissions by 65%
- Achieved 100% renewable grid electricity across all of their sites
- Reduced their total waste footprint per consumer by 32%
- Achieved zero waste landfill across all their factories
- Reduced sugar by 23% in their tea-based beverages
- Improved 56% of their food portfolio which now meets high nutrition standards
- Enabled 2.34 million women to access safety initiatives and develop their skills
- Promoted women to hold 51% of management roles for gender-balanced workplaces[5]

Unilever's® *Sustainable Living* brands delivered 75% of the company's growth, 69% faster than the rest of the business.[6] This has been a game changer for the organisation. The company involved more than 40,000 of their employees[7] to capture insight into where the company could have the greatest IMPACT. Unilever hope that all of their brands will be purpose-led over the coming years, especially after their own market research found that two-thirds[7] of shoppers choose brands that act on social and environmental issues. The research also revealed that 90%[8] of millennials would switch brands to align with their values. This demographic will account for 75% of UK's working population by 2030.[9]

Purposeful IMPACT and profit are not restricted to large global organisations. They can lead by example to deliver change at scale to achieve their SDGs by 2030. However, businesses of all sizes are taking on the mission with *The IMPACT Roadmap™*. In fact, since Small and Medium Enterprises (SMEs) are more agile, they can drive change faster than their larger competitors. They can also benefit from lower costs, reduced risk, and gain new sustainable opportunities. SMEs are giving larger corporations a run for their money across many industry sectors.

Throughout this book and accompanying *The IMPACT Game Changers™* podcast series, you will acquire insight and expertise from some of the most dynamic leaders who bring the SDGs to life. These are businesses that push the IMPACT boundaries. They demonstrate an activist mindset and a brand attitude with a sincere desire to make a positive difference. They focus on solving real-world problems to deliver the SDGs, spearheading a new revolution of business known as the IMPACT Game Changers™.

Embracing and incorporating the SDGs into business models can achieve groundbreaking innovation and opportunities. They can unlock $12 trillion and create 380 million jobs[10] and make us better global citizens. Throughout this book and podcast, you will see and hear purpose-driven leaders making it their mission to take on some of the world's greatest challenges. The IMPACT Roadmap™ celebrates and enables leaders to become trailblazers, conscious consumers to become customers, and businesses to become forces for good.

The IMPACT Game Changers™ Podcast:

www.splitsecondltd.com

Score Your IMPACT:

If you haven't done so already, take The IMPACT Roadmap Scorecard™. What we are about to cover will allow you to focus in on the areas of the book that are most beneficial to you to Scale Profit with Purpose for People and Planet™.

The IMPACT Roadmap Scorecard™ is built on the 3 steps: PLAN with PURPOSE™ – PERSUADE with PROMISE™ – PROFIT with IMPACT™.

Be Part of the Solution. Start an IMPACT Revolution™.

www.splitsecondltd.com

STEP 1 – PLAN with PURPOSE™

'A goal without a plan is just a wish.'
– Antoine de Saint-Exupéry

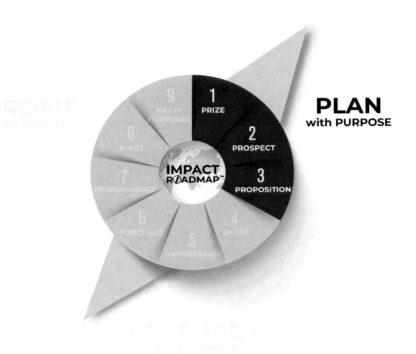

Putting pen to paper is often the most daunting part of writing a plan. Many business owners avoid translating their conceptual ideas into a commercial reality because it is a commitment to an unknown path. Yet would you ever consider building a house without a blueprint? A business without a plan is just as much of a risk and, unlike a house, a business is not static. It must constantly evolve in an ever-changing market.

According to the *Harvard Business Review*, 90%[1] of businesses fail to hit their strategic targets. They also found that 85%[2] of executive leadership teams spend less than an hour a month discussing strategy and 50%[3] do not discuss it at all. These are some astounding figures considering the amount of financial investment, human capital and operational infrastructure that go into setting up or scaling a business. Unfortunately, sometimes even when all the i's are dotted and t's are crossed, 95%[4] of company employees still do not understand the plan.

Strategic planning must take place to give your business the best chance of success. It ensures that the financial, operational, and strategic objectives are met to attract investors, win in the market and bring the purpose to life. It also means that there is a clear direction to go after new growth opportunities. The plan empowers you to map out the business journey which must be agile enough to pivot if necessary.

CHAPTER ONE: PRIZE

'It's good business to be a good business.'
– Juvencio Maeztu, Deputy CEO and CFO of Ingka Group, IKEA Retail

The first step of **The IMPACT Roadmap**™ plan is to determine the prize. What is the business going after and does it have what it takes to go after it? This will set the direction, identify growth opportunities, and determine the size of the prize. This critical stage will also define the short and long-term commercial and Sustainable Development Goals (SDGs), which will ultimately define how to make an IMPACT with purpose.

To start this journey, it is essential to assess the market universe in which the business operates. What is the proposition's market potential? Research the category, competitors, and prospects to provide valuable insight that will answer three fundamental questions:

- Where to compete?
- How to compete?
- How to succeed?

Plagued by shrinking markets, limited trading prospects and scarce resources, most companies are always on the lookout for new sources of growth. By harnessing their category trends and the SDGs, businesses can generate limitless financial and sustainable opportunities. Armed with this information, organisations can stay ahead of the competition with a formidable go-to-market plan and purposeful mission.

There is no time to delay in creating a better business, society, and planet. Companies now have the opportunity to reassess their business practices, set new Sustainable Development Goals (SDGs) and targets to unlock the possibilities. Integrating the Sustainable Development Goals (SDGs) to drive commercial objectives, stay ahead of the competition and make a lasting IMPACT requires vision and a clear process.

The SDG IMPACT Navigator™

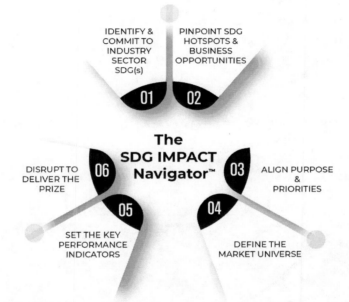

WHERE TO COMPETE?

IDENTIFY & COMMIT TO INDUSTRY SECTOR SDG(s)

PINPOINT SDG HOTSPOTS & BUSINESS OPPORTUNITIES

01 02

The SDG IMPACT Navigator™

DISRUPT TO DELIVER THE PRIZE

06

03 ALIGN PURPOSE & PRIORITIES

05 04

SET THE KEY PERFORMANCE INDICATORS

DEFINE THE MARKET UNIVERSE

HOW TO SUCCEED?

HOW TO COMPETE?

Organisations must re-examine their corporate, commercial, and operational strategies in order to ensure the overall balance between delivering a lucrative profit and delivering the SDGs. A meticulous audit of the business products and services must be undertaken in line with SDGs' policies and targets. **The SDG IMPACT Navigator™** is designed to determine which Sustainable Development Goal(s) to focus on and where opportunities can be found to establish the look of success.

1.1. WHERE TO COMPETE?

Identify and Commit to Sector Sustainable Development Goals

Even though the SDGs provide a clear global blueprint to drive sustainable change, selecting specific ones for established business models requires careful consideration. A study by PwC found that certain SDGs are prioritised by industry segments. The top five SDGs by industry, provide a strong indication of where the sector-specific opportunities are. By working together, they can generate a groundswell by sector. The SDGs also serve as a universal agenda and tracking system.

INDUSTRY SELECTION OF SUSTAINABLE DEVELOPMENT GOALS

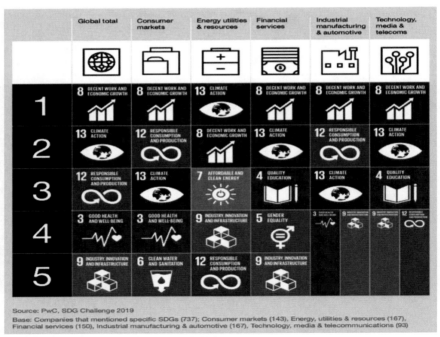

Source: PwC, SDG Challenge 2019
Base: Companies that mentioned specific SDGs (737); Consumer markets (143), Energy, utilities & resources (167), Financial services (150), Industrial manufacturing & automotive (167), Technology, media & telecommunications (93)

Source: PwC Creating a Strategy for a Better World report

Identifying and committing to an SDG enables strong accountability and alignment to the business strategy, vision, and values. If the goals are not adhered to at a local level, the targets will not be achieved. Isolating, educating, and ensuring that the SDGs are executed at a municipal level completes the IMPACT cycle. This will bring the SDGs to life at a grassroots level, thereby creating a more conscious culture in the workplace, local community and beyond.

Pinpoint SDG Hot Spots and Business Opportunities

According to the *Business & Sustainable Development Commission*, the SDGs open up 60 of the biggest market hot spots. By 2030, they will be valued at just over $12 trillion a year in four economic areas:

- Food and Agriculture = $2.3 trillion
- Cities and urban mobility = $3.7 trillion
- Energy and material = $4.3 trillion
- Health and wellbeing = $1.8 trillion[1]

60 BIGGEST MARKET OPPORTUNITIES RELATED TO DELIVERING THE GLOBAL GOALS

	Food and Agriculture	Cities	Energy and Materials	Health and Well-Being
1	Reducing food waste in value chain	Affordable housing	Circular models - automotive	Risk pooling
2	Forest ecosystem services	Energy efficiency - buildings	Expansion of renewables	Remote patient monitoring
3	Low-income food markets	Electric and hybrid vehicles	Circular models - appliances	Telehealth
4	Reducing consumer food waste	Public transport in urban areas	Circular models - electronics	Advanced genomics
5	Product reformulation	Car sharing	Energy efficiency - non-energy intensive industries	Activity services
6	Technology in large-scale farms	Road safety equipment	Energy storage systems	Detection of counterfeit drugs
7	Dietary switch	Autonomous vehicles	Resource recovery	Tobacco control
8	Sustainable aquaculture	ICE vehicle fuel efficiency	End-use steel efficiency	Weight management programs
9	Technology in smallholder farms	Building resilient cities	Energy efficiency - energy intensive industries	Better disease management
10	Micro-irrigation	Municipal water leakage	Carbon capture and storage	Electronic medical records
11	Restoring degraded land	Cultural tourism	Energy access	Better maternal and child health
12	Reducing packaging waste	Smart metering	Green chemicals	Healthcare training
13	Cattle intensification	Water and sanitation infrastructure	Additive manufacturing	Low-cost surgery
14	Urban agriculture	Office sharing	Local content in extractives	
15		Timber buildings	Shared infrastructure	
16		Durable and modular buildings	Mine rehabilitation	
17			Grid interconnection	

Source: Business & Sustainable Development Commission 'Better Business Better World Report

Organisations can begin to tap into the hot spots across their value chain. In fact, the economic SDG prize could potentially be two to three times larger than $12 trillion. This assumes that the entire economy will be operating in tandem with greater labour and resource productivity.

For instance, the Commission suggests a single SDG such as gender equality could contribute up to $28 trillion to the global GDP by 2025.[2] The overall prize could be staggering, whilst making a tremendous IMPACT in the world. The Commission stresses, *'to capture these opportunities in full, businesses need to pursue social and environmental sustainability as avidly as they pursue market share and shareholder value.'[3]* It therefore pays to integrate the Sustainable Development Goals (SDGs) into a commercial planning process.

1.2. HOW TO COMPETE?

Align Purpose and Priorities

This stage defines the short and long-term objectives. To ensure the objectives are achievable, they must be realistic and align to:

- The customer problem(s) being solved
- The core business purpose and strategic priorities
- The relevant Sustainable Development Goals (SDGs)

If the objectives are not clear, then attracting customers and making an IMPACT will be near to impossible. This process will begin to zero in on the target market and potential value the business can generate. Companies often get excited about their brand without stepping into the target customer's shoes to understand their unmet needs. The brand exists to serve the customer, society, and the planet – without all three, there is no business.

Define the Market Universe

Market analysis is a quantitative and qualitative assessment of the overall business landscape. It looks at the size of market, both in terms of volume and value, as well as the various customer segments and buying patterns, the competition, economic environment, and any barriers to entry. Valuable insight can be ascertained by means of a detailed analysis of the:

- Market Size and Profitability
- Competitors
- Category Dynamics
- Consumer Demographics
- Customer Segmentation
- Cost Infrastructure
- Distribution Channels
- Long-Term Trends

This step provides a clear picture of the threats and opportunities out there and indicates how prospects may respond to a value proposition. The analysis can range from in-depth tailored research to an adaptation of simpler techniques using readily-available data.

1.3.   HOW TO SUCCEED?

Set the Key Performance Indicators

The 17 Sustainable Development Goals (SDGs) are tied to 169 specific targets. These make the SDGs tangible and achievable by 2030. They seek to address the economic, social, and environmental challenges by each individual Goal, so delivering them within any organisation is straightforward and transparent.

Let's say your business is in Fast-Moving Consumer Goods (FMCG) and you have decided to aim for *SDG#12 Responsible Consumption and Production*. You can refer to the United Nations SDG site and download all the targets. For example, the first three targets for *SDG#12*[4] are:

- *SDG12.1* Implement the 10-year framework of programmes on sustainable consumption and production, all countries taking action, with developed countries taking the lead, taking into account the development and capabilities of developing countries.
- *SDG12.2* By 2030, achieve the sustainable management and efficient use of natural resources.

- *SDG12.3* By 2030, halve per capita global food waste at the retail and consumer levels and reduce food losses along production and supply chains, including post-harvest losses.

The relevant targets pertinent to an organisation can be incorporated to the strategic and commercial objectives. Obviously, one business can deliver only a proportion of these targets, but if every company was to adopt their appropriate targets, then the SDGs can be achieved by 2030.

All goals and targets can be found at:
https://www.un.org/sustainabledevelopment/sustainable-development-goals/

Ingka Group, owner of IKEA stores, have also made a commitment to sustainability initiatives. They have invested 600 million Euros[5] on top of their original 3.2 billion Euros[6] over the past decade. Their aspiration is to become climate positive across their value chain by 2030. The organisation is focussed on three key areas: renewable energy, innovative start-ups, and making its stores and warehouses more sustainable.

IKEA have ambitious targets to reduce their greenhouse gas emissions by 2030. From raw materials, manufacturing, to customer usage and disposal, the retailer plans to implement *Circular Economy* principles such as:

- All IKEA products in 10 years will be made from renewable or recycled materials, and designed to be reused, resold, or recycled. In 2020, they gave 47 million[7] products a new lease of life to reduce waste.
- They aimed to remove all non-rechargeable alkaline batteries from their global home furnishings range by October 2021. IKEA calculates that '*if all its customers switched to its rechargeable batteries and charged them 50 times, its global waste could be reduced by as much as 5,000 tons on an annual basis[8].*' They have recently said: '*At IKEA we are committed to enabling and inspiring the many people to live more sustainable lives at home. As a step on this journey, we announced that non-rechargeable alkaline batteries would be phased out from the global IKEA range by October 2021. Phasing out certain products is always a gradual process that requires advanced*

planning to ensure commitments towards suppliers are fulfilled, and that wasting large volumes of products is avoided. In markets where the Covid-19 pandemic has had a severe impact on retail operations, the amount of stock still in stores may prolong the phase-out period beyond the initial projection of October 2021.[9]

- IKEA are testing the first second-hand store in a recycling mall in Sweden and gaining customer insight. According to ReTuna Shopping Centre, the initiative *'will help IKEA understand why some IKEA products are turned into waste, what condition they are in when thrown away, why do people choose to donate or recycle products, and if there's an interest in buying the products that have been repaired.'*[10]
- IKEA have installed 750 000 solar panels on their buildings and invested in 416 wind turbines around the world to reduce carbon emissions.[11]
- Ingka Group owns and manages 935 000 solar panels and 547 wind turbines (FY21) for further details please see: https://www.ingka.com/static/annual-summary-fy-21.pdf.[12]
- IKEA have a strategic partnership with the Ellen MacArthur Foundation to ensure that the company becomes fully circular by 2030.

As part of their *climate positive* sustainability initiatives, IKEA have launched the 'circular hub' buy-back scheme offering vouchers for second-hand furniture to reduce landfill waste. Customers will receive spend-in-store vouchers for items that are returned in good condition. The roll-out of this scheme is set to be implemented in 26 countries[13] around the globe after successful trials in various cities. IKEA have also formed a partnership with Gumtree, the second-hand online marketplace, which will broaden their reach.

IKEA's *Sustainable Life at Home* range of 500 products has grown to 1.7 billion Euros.[14] They have around 170 million customers worldwide, the equivalent of 83 million households which have led them to declare that *'even a small percentage of our customers could have an IMPACT on the environment if they tried to live a more sustainable life at home. What if all 170 million of us made small changes in the way we live? Together, we really could make a difference to the planet.*[15]

Disrupt to Deliver the Prize

Integrating the Sustainable Development Goals (SDGs) can open up a world of opportunities and transform all aspects of a business:

- Business models
- Products and services
- Customer segments
- Supply chains
- Raw material options
- Transport and distribution
- Innovation pipelines
- Product life cycles
- Strategic planning, sales, and marketing

The conventional approach forces businesses to go after the same opportunities as the competition, deliver copycat innovation and get lost in a sea of lookalike propositions. Yet armed with the SDGs, businesses can discover a niche in the market, commercial opportunities, and collaborative partnerships. The new generation of IMPACT Brands™ are solving the world's biggest challenges: from food waste to climate action, to reduced inequalities, to building sustainable cities and communities. The Sustainable Development Goals are all within reach, so let's make them happen.

'Sustainability is no longer about doing less harm.
It's about doing more good.'
– Jochen Zeitz, CEO and Chairman of Harley Davidson Inc.

Chapter One – PRIZE Exercise:

Get to know your market to define where the growth opportunities are:

1. Which Sustainable Development Goal (SDG) best corresponds to your industry sector?
2. How will you align your business purpose and priorities to make the biggest IMPACT?
3. What is the size of the market prize?

CHAPTER TWO: PROSPECT

'People care about brands that care about the world.'
– Anonymous

We live in a world where consumers are bombarded with at least 5000 marketing messages[1] a day vs 500 messages[2] in the 1970s, and 99% make almost no impression. We are inundated with communication and overwhelmed by choice. With purchasing decisions made within 20 seconds,[3] either in person (13 seconds) or online (10-19 seconds), it is clear that competition is rife, differentiation is key, and the pressure is on. So how does one cut through the noise?

Today's most successful brands are the ones that have recognised the difference between the consumer mindset and the shopper mindset. Although a consumer may be inspired and even desire a brand, it is the shopper who ultimately decides which brand is purchased. The distinction between the consumer and shopper is vital. It places the spotlight on the brand and shopper interaction, rather than the brand and end-user, that may or may not be the same. It focusses on the purchasing decision as opposed to the purchasing intention. Start with the split second moment at the point of purchase, and work back from there to win hearts, minds, and wallets.

2.1. TARGET CUSTOMER

David Ogilvy, known as the '*Father of Advertising*' once said, '*Study the product you are going to advertise. The more you know about it, the more likely you are to come up with a big idea for selling it.*'[4] That may have worked back in the day, but in our competitive world it simply won't do. Today, one must also study the target prospect that may be intending to purchase the product. The more you know about them, the more likely it is you will create value for them and ultimately drive purchase.

For most businesses the conventional start point is the brand. Passion, energy, and resources are put into building a brand strategy, followed by marketing campaigns and activities to generate sales. It can be a bit of a Russian roulette: sometimes you win and at other times the competitor wins. Yet without the customer, there is no brand. The two are inextricably linked. Businesses must find every possible occasion to get close to the would-be customer, capture the insight and fuel the brand.

Zero-In on the Target

When trying to identify the prospect, the objective is to find them, get close to them, and understand them by means of behaviours, preferences, and lifestyles so that the brand provides solutions for them. Otherwise, there is a risk of trying to be all things to everyone and probably master of none.

Market segmentation is fundamental to understanding who the most likely consumers are to buy a brand or service. A segmentation is a cluster of people who share or demonstrate similar behaviours, patterns, goals, and other key characteristics. This process distils the data to specifically identify who to engage and what motivates them. Segmentation does not mean that you are excluding consumers that do not meet the criteria. Instead, it enables you to zero-in on a specific segment of the population to focus time, resources and valuable marketing spend on those who are more likely to purchase.

Target with Technology

Technology and advanced analytics have enabled a two-way mirror between prospects and suppliers with greater transparency of the behaviours and interaction before a sale is made. Many prospects are willing to share their personal data in exchange for something they deem of value (promotions, memberships, access to freebies, etc.). Rich insight keeps the segmentation up to date and provides an understanding of the types of customers your business is interacting with.

Other factors that may affect the segmentation are emerging social, economic, and technological trends which may alter purchasing and usage patterns. If a market segmentation is not conducted or is ignored, then the business may end up in no man's land without a target. It also offers greater competitive advantage, customer retention and a stronger marketing mix. The strategic direction and insight into the target prospect enable the development of a tailored proposition.

A segmentation study will clarify the number of segments to pursue and the percentage of the overall target market it represents. This research is key to a business strategy, but it does not delve into the prospect's motivations and personal stories that would provide insight into their pain points and the outcomes they seek.

It's time to get personal...

Target Personas

For decades, many organisations have had a very successful track record of turning commodities into lucrative brands. They have grown their brand share by having a strategic foundation based on the 5Ws: who to target, what to say, where to say it, why say it, when to say it – as well as how to say it. The 5Ws start to build a demographic and psychographic pen portrait of the prospect.

Demographics identify 'who' the prospect is through: age, location, gender, income level, education, family or marital status, occupation, and ethnic background, etc. Psychographics explore: lifestyle, spending habits, hobbies, personality, attitudes, values, and behaviours. The two streams determine how products or services can align to the prospect's hierarchy of needs and wants. How and when will they use these products? Which features will be most appealing? What will influence the purchase?

The benefit of this type of pen portrait profiling is that it engages consumers on a more personal level to deliver the right message, products, and promotions at the right time. This intelligence is captured through various tools and techniques such as interviews, surveys, observations, focus groups and analysis that enable one to get into the hearts and minds of the target prospect. It is accurate, because it is based on real people, behaviours, motivations, and lifestyles within a category context.

Buyer Personas

Personas take a deeper look into the prospect by being present online wherever they are. They generate inbound leads by sharing relevant content at the right time and place for the ideal prospect to interact with, consume, and ultimately buy. The traditional pen portrait may consider the basics, such as what type of magazine the prospect reads, but studying the buyer persona will provide more 'live' detail about their online behaviour. One will begin to understand what they interact with and get social proof through key word searches, barriers, and triggers to purchase, types of content, customer journeys, touch points, advertising, and anything else digitally available.

The objective is to get deeper insight into the prospect by connecting the online and offline behaviour, their motivation, how they can be influenced, and what prompts them to act. Why would they consider a brand? What experiences have they had in the past with a similar brand, and how have competitors influenced them? What platforms do they trust? What do they use the most, search engines or other digital touch points?

Create Personas

If we think of personas like key characters in a feature production, they start to bring potential customers to life. They can represent actual target groups with similar characteristics and values that would potentially buy your products or services. These personas offer insight into the buying potential, rather than being nameless and faceless numbers in a statistical spreadsheet.

Building personas has many business benefits as nearly 9 out of 10 companies[5] say that they:

- Improve customer engagement
- Generate more leads
- Build more trust
- Increase web traffic
- Deliver greater sales revenue

Whether the focus is on offline pen portraits or online personas, attracting prospects begins with research. Start by analysing the existing customer base or prospects that may be interested in your proposition through their perspective. Imagine and trace a day in the life of the target prospect: What are their needs? Challenges? How can they be addressed?

Consumer and Shopper Personas

Understanding a target prospect's behaviour, usage, and consumption habits have always been part of a successful marketing equation. Yet what happens if the shopper is not the consumer? How do we tap into the purchasing decisions? What about the barriers and triggers to purchase? What makes the prospect choose one proposition over another?

Every category has consumers and shoppers. They may or may not be the same. The end consumer is the person who consumes or uses a product or service. They use the computer, eat the food, drive the car, feed the dog – but may not have made the purchasing decisions themselves.

The shopper on the other hand is the one that may research the product or service, compare prices, and make the purchase. Sometimes the consumer and shopper are the same, but sometimes not. A pet owner purchasing treats, a friend buying a round of drinks or a parent purchasing baby clothes, are all examples of where the lines can get blurred.

The distinction between the consumer and shopper is more than semantics. Without it, one may be force-fitting a superfluous proposition into the market that is destined to fail. Why? Prospects will only purchase something if it is of added value to them. The richest insight will come from understanding why they do not purchase, which is what most organisations are afraid to face. It also enables organisations to develop their marketing mix, channel mix, and proposition based on insight and market gaps. Being clear on who is doing the purchasing and who is influencing the decision to purchase is the key to making or breaking customer relationships, generating sales and winning the market.

'Brand IMPACT is no longer just about instant gratification, short-term sales and marketing. The most successful brands are attracting conscious consumers and shoppers by being relevant, being where they are and being sustainable. It is about the IMPACT on People, Planet and the World we live in.'
—Simon Reberga, Category and Shopper Expert

2.2. TARGET PAIN POINTS

Why do you believe that your product or service will appeal to the target prospect? Is it a hunch? Or have you asked them? If you take the time to engage and step into the prospect's shoes, one can begin to experience the specific problem which they may be experiencing that your product or service can resolve. These pain points result in opportunities.

Whether we realise it or not, pain points are used to appeal to our natural instinct to 'fix a problem' or 'do the right thing'. They are often part of a sales technique or identify where other forms of support are required. From political campaigns, to charity donations, to just supporting a good cause – pain points are the backbone of many successful organisations' strategy.

Look for the Pain

How does the prospect solve a problem? What are they complaining about? Is there a current solution? Is it acceptable? Will it alleviate the pain? What are the consequences and results of the current pain points? These are all valid questions that need a diagnosis and solution.

Identify the Pain

Pain points are as diverse as the target prospects themselves. Prospects are not always aware that they are experiencing any specific 'pain', so engaging them can be a challenge. Making them aware and convincing them to drive purchase requires a targeted approach towards one of the many pain points. Here are a few different types:

6 TYPES OF PROSPECT PAIN POINTS™

- **Financial Pain Points:** Spend reduction, earn more money, credit management
- **Business Pain Points:** Sales, delivering profit, distribution, market stand-out
- **Productivity Pain Points:** Time management, efficiency, processes
- **Health Pain Points:** Physical, mental, emotional health and wellness
- **Service Pain Points:** Customer experience, competence, delivery
- **ESG Pain Points:** Environmental, social governance for consumer conscience and positive IMPACT on people and planet

The way to resolve pain points is to focus on them one at a time. For instance, take ESG pain points. As consumers become more and more conscious about their purchasing decisions, tapping into their pain points not only benefits the planet and people, but a company's profit as well. So how does one resonate with target prospects?

- **Drive Change:** Ensure and share with your prospect how every purchase made has a positive IMPACT on the Sustainable Development Goals (SDGs).
- **Less is More:** Offer tips on how to reduce their ecological footprint.
- **Sustainable Resources and Recycling:** Create circular economies to benefit business, society, and the environment.
- **Inspire Communities:** Support communities and supply chains with sustainable practices.
- **Elect Democracy with Co-operatives:** Co-ops empower the majority vs the few.

Commercial opportunities begin to open up as companies re-evaluate their purpose and re-invent themselves.

Fix the Pain

Now that the diagnosis is in, one can begin to treat the pain points. Harness this insight to identify the solutions. This will build long-term trust, credibility, and potential loyalty as the 'go to' brand.

So how do you know if you are able to fix a prospect's pain? When there is an increase in:

- Sales and distribution
- Customer satisfaction and loyalty
- Innovation and business expansion

In some cases, fixing the pain can be a question of supply and demand. The solution depends on the pain point in question. If the customer journey becomes too confusing or difficult to navigate, there is a greater chance that the prospect may abandon the actual or virtual shopping cart before making a purchase.

Overall, the prospect must feel reassured that they can interact and communicate with a brand at multiple touch points such as: live chats, calls, email, chatbots, WhatsApp, etc. The objective is to win their trust, resolve their 'pain' and become their go-to trusted brand. Resolving after-sales pain points can make all the difference to a brand's customer loyalty.

No Pain, No Gain

There is no one-size-fits-all solution for different prospects' pain. So, understanding the pain points is not only essential to converting them into customers, but vital to long-term commercial growth. Fortunately, in today's digital era there are so many research tools available at our fingertips to anticipate the prospect's next move. Identifying customer pain points and resolving them offer a range of opportunities for any business. They can attract new customers away from competitors, harness customer loyalty and set higher sustainable and ethical standards of excellence by industry sector.

2.3. TARGET CONSCIENCE

Prior to the pandemic, conscious consumers were a perceived threat to brands and retailers. They were seen as groups discouraging spend and showcasing an inconvenient reality. Fifty-five percent[6] of conscious consumers wanted to take greater action in the name of people and planet but were not always sure how.

Ethics, authenticity, trust, and transparency are the values consumers are seeking most. Despite 63%[7] of businesses stating that their approach to sustainability is customer-driven, 69%[8] of consumers struggle to identify with it. Now, with the rise of electric cars, plant-based diets, re-purposing clothes and a reduction of household consumption, brands have the opportunity to lead by example and address the consumer's social and environmental conscience.

In recent years, some markets have experienced a 20%[9] increase in sustainable product sales. The Sustainable Development Goals (SDGs) represent the key societal and environmental drivers that can lead to groundbreaking innovation, education, and a positive lasting IMPACT. According to *Edelman's Brand Trust Barometer*, 74%[10] of consumers or purchasers say a brand's IMPACT on society is the reason why brand trust has become more important. This trend is only set to grow over the next few years as a new brand democracy, where consumers vote with their wallets.

The LEGO Group is the world's largest toy manufacturer with an entire value proposition that hinges on the abbreviation of two Danish words '*leg godt*' meaning '*play well*'. Founded by Ole Kirk Kristiansen in 1932[11], after he found himself a widower with four boys to raise, he began carving wooden toys to entertain his children. Then in 1958[12], the plastic bricks we know today were launched. The company has been passed down from father to son, currently in the hands of Kristiansen's grandson. Family and trust have been at the heart of the organisation since the start, building rapport with parents and children of all ages. As part of that earned trust, comes responsibility: responsibility to the shoppers most often being the parents, and responsibility to the consumers generally being the children. Appealing to both parties is critical to driving purchase, creating brand love, and aligning on values.

Today, parents are becoming increasingly more concerned with the state of the planet that their children will inherit. Finding alternative raw materials to plastic has been integral to The LEGO Group's sustainable commercial strategy to do right by kids, parents, and the planet. The company has pledged to make all of their products from sustainable materials by 2030 and they have invested $400 million[13] USD towards sustainable solutions. The LEGO Group's sustainability strategy will *'focus on a range of social and environmentally-friendly actions to inspire children through learning and play, making the business more circular, and achieving carbon neutral operations. The activity will drive meaningful, long-term change aligned to two United Nations Sustainable Development Goals: #4 Quality Education and #12 Responsible Consumption and Production.'*[14]

The LEGO Group have also expanded their range of Bio-based (Bio-PE) elements to produce their colourful bricks made from 98%[15] sugarcane (which is 100% sustainably sourced) versus oil-based plastic. Currently, there are approximately 150 components made from Bio-PE (such as the LEGO® plant elements and LEGO® Minifigure accessories) and nearly half of their sets are designed to contain at least one of these elements. The LEGO Group's Bio-PE bricks are completely interchangeable with the original LEGO® bricks. So as consumers, parents, can rest assured that the toys they are purchasing are climate conscious.

During the 2020 pandemic, The LEGO Group made a $50 million[16] USD donation through its foundation to support children most in need and ensure they continue to have access to learning through play which helps develop life-long skills. The donation was split between three groups of charity partners. One of them being *Education Cannot Wait*, which provides education for children caught in emergencies and crises. Other donations were also made to provide children and families with essential supplies and support during the crisis.

Build the Change has also become a strategic focal point for The LEGO Group to give all children the opportunity to learn about sustainability through play. The programme aims to give children a voice on climate challenges that matter most to them. In October 2021, they launched the first free educator course on biodiversity and climate change, reaching more than 50,000 children[17] in its first two months. The *Build the Change* initiative adds to existing family-based activities.

In November of that year, at COP26, the *Build the Change* team, with the help of employee volunteers, delivered more than 25 workshops to nearly 1,000 children[18] from Glasgow and beyond. Working with partners such as The Ellen MacArthur Foundation and Daydream Believers, children were asked to share their thoughts and ideas on circular economy and climate change solutions. *Learning through Play* programmes and activities with the support of the LEGO Foundation have also reached over 3.5+ million children[19] so far. As they celebrate their 90th anniversary, The LEGO Group will progress *'to have a positive IMPACT on the world the children will inherit – and inspire and develop the builders of tomorrow'.*[20]

> *'I think there will be a push for companies to be good citizens and delivering on purpose and not just optimising the financial bottom line.'*
> – Jørgen Vig Knudstorp, Executive Chairman of The LEGO Group

Chapter Two – PROSPECT Exercise:

ID the Target

Build your target prospect profile by mapping out the following:

- Select a specific target population segment based on socio-economic demographics
- Select a designated geography and location
- Identify the external and local circumstances that may IMPACT buying decisions

Ensure that potential prospects align to your business or brand, based on a strict criterion. Then figure out where to find these prospects and how to engage them.

CHAPTER THREE: PROPOSITION

'People don't know what they want, until you show it to them.'
– Steve Jobs

Doing good is fast becoming the cornerstone of 21st century society. As consumers make conscious decisions, they begin to echo their values in their purchasing behaviours. They take a stand, want their voices heard and their ideals met for this new form of brand activism.

As a result, to win the conscious consumer, today's winning value propositions must be purpose-led. They should take genuine social and environmental action to create and nurture trustworthy customer relationships. Activating and sharing an authentic purpose are key to creating value, creating a market, and creating IMPACT Brands™ that will make the world a better place.

3.1. CREATE VALUE

'If you build it, they will come'[1] is a vision that many ambitious brand owners hold. Yet unlike in the film *Field of Dreams*, in reality, this principle only works if the brand is in great demand, has a unique selling point and a queue of customers ready to purchase. However, most businesses are constantly striving to attract more customers, often without a deep understanding of who they are *building* for and why *they* will buy – leaving it up to chance.

People only pay for what they perceive to be valuable, which is a matter of personal opinion. In a fiercely competitive environment, creating value for a prospect is an opportunity to convert them into brand champions. Value creation sells more products and services, generates returns for shareholders, and puts the brand on a positive growth trajectory.

Value perception for the consumer has to deliver on at least one of the three key principles:

- It must resolve a pain point, an unmet or unsatisfied need vs. the competition;
- Deliver quality product/service that connects with the prospect's personal values;

- Have a clear purpose that makes a positive IMPACT on people and the planet.

The sum of these principles will determine how valuable a prospect deems the proposition to be before becoming and remaining a loyal customer. According to McKinsey, the top three brands in consideration of a particular category secure at least 70%[2] of sales. The brands placed fourth or below, face diminished sales opportunities of 40%[3] or less. Winning early consumer consideration goes well beyond driving brand awareness through expensive marketing campaigns. In today's competitive world, it is essential to proactively increase the odds that will tip the scales and, more importantly, the sales in your favour.

Product or Solution?

With the advent of technology, brands can now pinpoint and engage their target in real time. The 'hard sell' approach is dead. If you don't grab the prospect's attention within seconds, the sales window is closed forever. And given that the prospect may already have explored a brand's digital platforms, they are likely to be familiar with its benefits. So, by the time you do get their attention, what will you say? Will you list the proposition's features like every other brand? Or will you take the time to listen and alleviate their pain?

Products come and go, but a unique selling point (USP) commands higher brand value. In 2001, when all other brands were listing the many features of an MP3 player, Steve Jobs simply said, '*Look, the iPod is 1000 songs in your pocket.*'[4] This USP delivered a practical solution of accessing a wide variety of music anywhere at any time without the physical hassle of carrying other accessories. He rarely ever talked about the technical features of Apple's many devices. He looked at everything through the customer's perspective. He understood that consumers didn't care about or want to hear IT jargon; they just wanted to enjoy their music. His focus on one Unique *Solution* Point – the IMPACT USP™ surpassed sales of all other MP3 products in the market.

Functional or Emotional?

Value means different things to different people. Price, product, place, and promotion form the basic mantra of a marketing strategy. However, there are other factors that influence someone's purchasing decision such as time, experience, quality, trust, etc. The final verdict often boils down to whether it is a functional or an emotional purchase.

Picture an hourglass. Imagine the bottom of the hourglass represents functional purchases for practical use: cleaning products, weekly grocery staples, car insurance, gym membership (although this could arguably be classed as an emotional purchase as well). These are the basics that keep our day-to-day lives going by satisfying our need for sustenance, security, convenience, utility, and health.

Now envisage that the top of the hourglass represents emotionally-driven purchases – such as the pair of designer shoes, the romantic holiday, the personally inscribed watch. Do you need them or simply want them? These purchasing decisions are usually triggered by emotions of love, pride, nostalgia, rejuvenation, envy, or status.

What role does your proposition play in a consumer's life? Choose a side of the hourglass, otherwise you run the risk of being squeezed out of the market without a clear *Unique Solution Point*™ and a lack of differentiation. Sometimes the line between functional and emotional is blurred depending on the category. For instance, during the 2020 pandemic, many commodities were in high demand, such as flour. A functional product that also served as family 'feel good' baked treats, thus playing a dual role on the hourglass. External circumstances can sometimes influence value perception.

Planet-Passive or Planet-Positive?

Over the years, we have all seen the stark images of children stitching clothing in overcrowded sweatshops, rainforests being destroyed in search of palm oil, single-use plastic pollution and oil spills in our oceans. Sadly, the list goes on. Greenpeace and other NGOs have been on a mission to combat these issues by starting social IMPACT movements and challenging some of the world's biggest planet-passive companies.

Our oceans are already filled with 165 million tons of plastic, 25 times heavier than the Great Pyramid of Giza.[5] One of Greenpeace's recent crusades asked the public to pick up plastic from beaches and waters. It then went on to ask people to name and shame the brand culprits on social media with #IsThisYours campaign. These brands are not only polluting our planet with their single-use plastic packaging, but many are working hand in hand with the fossil fuel industry, since it is responsible for 99% of plastic production.[6] If they carry on promoting disposable plastics, then plastic production could double in the next 10 to 15 years and triple by 2050.[7] This is what makes people sit up and question a brand's ethics, the value it adds to their lives and how it affects the planet.

By 2050, the oceans could have more plastic than fish[8] – a frightening prediction made by the Ellen McArthur Foundation, an international charity that develops and promotes the circular economy. Driven by design, the circular economy is built on three principles, to eliminate waste and pollution, circulate products and materials (at their highest value), and regenerate nature.[9] Circular economy is not just a popular buzzword. It is imperative to our long-term survival. Approximately 92%[10] of the world's resources are only used once. Metals, plastics, wood, chemicals, concrete, and other materials are developed into a single product before becoming waste. These resources must be re-used, recycled, recovered, and reduced to protect the environment and can tap into the $12 trillion opportunity.

Over 69%[11] of consumers have growing concerns about brands' IMPACT on society. They want greater transparency from businesses that align to their values. Almost 53%[12] want brands to make greater social IMPACT and take a more active role in saving the planet. However, there is still some convincing to do. Currently, only 21%[13] believe that their brands do right by society and the planet, so the opportunities are endless.

On average, there are 46,000 pieces of plastic[14] in every square mile of ocean. More than 89%[15] of it is single-use plastic which sits at the bottom of the ocean floor. Luxury swimwear designers Hannah Daykin and Annabel Humphrey, founders of Pursuit the Label are committed to ethical fashion. Their brand is where 'purpose meets swimsuits.' They use ECONYL® fabric regenerated from man-made waste such as plastic bottles, discarded fish nets and other matters that don't belong in the ocean and turn them into high-end statement swimsuits produced in small batches. These designers are acutely aware that companies and people's actions can alter the current trajectory and have a positive IMPACT on the ocean and all its organisms.

Sir Richard Branson has named Pursuit the Label Swimwear as *'One of five environmentally friendly Virgin start-ups that you need to know about...'*[16] in a recent article he wrote. The brand has also been featured in Sports Illustrated with supermodel Haley Kalil wearing their Viper Sculpt suit. Co-Founders Hannah and Annabel believe *'Fashion brands are under constant pressure to step up their game and it's only getting faster and faster ... and becoming more wasteful. We want to be responsible towards fashion, our customers, and the planet by designing curated lines – sustainable fashion rather than fast fashion.'*[17] With a strong Gen Z following, their approach is centred around 'The 3Ss', style, social status, and sustainability. They turn waste into wear, bringing social consciousness to the fashion world and its clientele.

'From the ocean back to the ocean': www.pursuitthelabel.com
Hear Pursuit the Label's Story on
The IMPACT Game Changers™ Podcast:

www.splitsecondltd.com

3.2. CREATE A MARKET

'If you separate from the market and build your own market, you can generate as much money as your market will allow.'
– Daniel Priestley, Author and Founder of Dent Global

Which came first, the market or the brand? Most companies develop a brand, then take it to trade with marketing campaigns in the hopes that it will sell. A standard formula in a crowded market which often feels like a *do-or-die* situation. Even if you have the greatest brand in the world, it is utterly worthless without anyone buying it.

Whether the proposition enters an existing market or is first to market, one must prove how it will deliver value to make the prospect's life better. By first creating a market, one has the opportunity to test the customer's appetite before investing time, money, and energy into product development. Many crowdfunding business models adopt this approach. This way one can find out what the target prospect wants, and the proposition can be amended for greater success at launch.

What if you received signals that people are willing to pay cold hard cash for your proposition before launch? Or better still, it is sold out before it hits the market? Many brands successfully create a hype, a demand for their brand to drive profit. Where there is hype, there are customers. Ever notice the more a product, service or event is in demand, the more people want access to it? From the latest technology, exclusive experiences, or personalised items – everything is up for grabs when you create intrigue and excitement.

Focus on Prospect First, Product Second

It pays to put the customer at the heart of the proposition strategy. Customer-centric companies are 60% more profitable[18] than their competitors. By understanding the prospect's behaviours through customer insight, businesses can thrive by providing a positive experience and build long-term relationships. This approach can also uncover innovation opportunities to drive purchase.

The shift from focusing on the prospect ahead of the product can take time and effort. Many organisations believe that they are customer-centric, but the truth is that they are mostly brand-centric. The distinction between the two is vital to the long-term profitability and loyalty to the brand. Is your business irrefutably customer-centric?

Focus on Category First, Brand Second

What is the real objective of a marketing campaign? More Customers? Sales? Loyalty? Profitability? Yes, to all of the above. There is a way to meet all of these objectives, not by building a brand alone, but by winning the entire category.

Start by spotting a gap in the market, addressing the consumer pain points, and innovating to fill the gap to grow the category. Take the electric vehicle (EV) category for instance. It responds to consumer concerns around greater energy efficiency, rising petrol costs and carbon emissions. This category is able to get more miles for money spent, more discretionary income back into the consumer's pocket without any more trips to the petrol station and is drastically reducing pollution.

Today, with almost every nation signed up to the Paris Agreement on climate change, the race to zero emissions has begun. The world must work together to bring the global temperature down and not go beyond 1.5°C by reducing greenhouse gas emissions and to net zero by 2050.[19] According to the United Nations, technology enables the net zero goal to be affordable and achievable. Renewable energy sources, such as wind and solar power, are cleaner and cheaper alternatives to fossil fuels. Electric vehicles powered by renewable energy play a significant role in realising the net zero ambition as more and more countries pledge to phase out fossil fuel transport. Yet the EV category has struggled for years, even though it has everything going for it. There was no innovative proposition to fill the gap, no sustainable battery source to power-up the vehicle and no scale for *a clean energy* drive.

Since 2008, Tesla, the luxury brand has stepped up to address the challenges by developing a portfolio that has made the category viable. Although Tesla were not the first-to-market with electric cars, Elon Musk certainly put the category on the map with his brand promise, *'To accelerate the advent of sustainable transport'*.[20] Unlike most conventional car manufacturers, Tesla do not advertise in mainstream newspapers or radio. Instead, the company simplifies the purchasing process by putting the would-be customer in the driver's seat via their inbound sales model. They are confident that target prospects will find them online with full transparency of the price, product, and overall customer experience. They provide an interface that allows prospective buyers to select, customise and order their vehicle of choice at the touch of a few buttons.

Named after Nikola Tesla, a major pioneer of the AC electric motor used in Tesla cars, the brand and polarising Elon Musk, have a loyal cult-like following. They have not only conquered the EV category but have designed their vehicles as software giants would, vastly different to conventional car manufacturers. Tesla are able to update their software remotely whenever necessary with little use of parts and labour. Musk is constantly defying category conventions, following in the footsteps of Henry Ford, who a century ago offered an affordable car to replace the horse and carriage. Visionary category leaders are the innovative pioneers that drive change and progression. As Ford said, '*If I had asked people what they wanted, they would have said faster horses.*'[21]

Many customers have become brand evangelists and want to be part of the Tesla tribe. They buy into Musk's innovative vision, which has disrupted the industry whilst other manufacturers are playing catch-up. With 79%[22] of the American EV market share, Tesla dwarf any and all competitors. In fact, this category leader is expected to grow almost five-fold and reach an estimated global market size of $803 billion U.S. dollars by 2027 (+20% CAGR).[23] Although Tesla are enabling conscious consumers to have a greener drive, ensuring that the entire supply chain is ethically and sustainably compliant still requires some work. The brand is not without its controversies and an end-to-end self-audit to track IMPACT on people and planet is just as critical as profit to ensure that the Sustainable Development Goals are delivered on time and in full.

Many describe a brand as the tip of the iceberg and the category as the iceberg itself. This analogy is quite powerful because a brand ceases to exist without the category. Instant *Polaroid* cameras, cd players, videotapes – where are they now? So many defunct categories that have taken the brands down with them. If we are drawn to the category, we are drawn to purchase the brands within them. So, one must always evolve and innovate to push the category boundaries that will ultimately drive commercial and more importantly, purpose-led sustainable growth with a positive IMPACT.

Focus on Long-Term Scalability First, Short-Term Tactics Second

Renowned start-up CEO, entrepreneur, mentor, and investor Giles Brook has had a phenomenal track record in backing and creating categories from inception. He is one of the most successful British food and drink entrepreneurs who has been behind challenger brands such as Pip & Nut, Vita Coco, NEAT and BEAR – the latest sold for £70m a few years ago. As former Commercial Director of Innocent Drinks Ltd. and as part of the leadership team that took the business from £17m to £120m[24] in four years, he is an expert at spotting long-term category potential, driving commercial growth and scaling businesses.

Over the years, Giles, along with other angel investors, has injected over £1.5bn into budding start-ups.[25] His decision to develop or invest in a business is based on one or more of his five criteria:

1. Invest in the founder, ahead of the business
2. On-trend scalable category
3. Healthier and better for you
4. Strong ethics and values
5. Cause-led business that does good for the world

'A business has to be based on strong ethics and sustainable values. If I see an amazing opportunity but it isn't underpinned in those, I just won't invest'[26] says Giles. When he first came across the coconut water category, Giles was not an 'instant believer'. He knew that it was number one in the soft drinks' category in its native Brazil. He also knew that it had taken off in the U.S., but he needed some convincing. He is a firm believer that, *'There is no formula that throws categories and brands into a washing machine to see what comes out. Some categories simply won't make it out.'*[27]

He started to investigate the opportunity. He looked at various category and market data points, the health credentials, consumer insight and he spoke to some of the biggest UK retailers about their potential interest. Once all those boxes were ticked, Giles found that unlike so many other 'try hard' products out there, people had a real emotional connection to the reminiscent experience of having healthy, low-calorie, low-sugar coconut water while laying on a sunny beach. His mission was clear. He had to establish a healthy category with an authentic tropical brand for consumers to get excited about, which he did in the form of Vita Coco. Today, Vita Coco crack open 3 million coconuts a day, generate £40m[28] in sales in Europe, and have been one of the biggest global success stories in soft drinks.

Some of the other success factors that accelerated the category and business growth were:

- Consumer insight to create a USP
- Creative marketing and PR that consumers could relate to
- Key Investors and celebrity endorsements

Marketing tactics are also critical to winning the market. Giles' advice to start-ups is to *'keep the message very simple and communicate it over and over again.'*[29] Great brands with tiny budgets must have crystal clear communication on:

- What is your category and product about?
- What does your business stand for?
- Why is your proposition better?

Despite developing new markets and being the leader within them, Giles welcomes competitors. It means that the strategy is working and that the business is onto a good thing. He does, however, offer a word of caution to the 'me too' brands that try to hop on the coat tails of the category leaders through gimmicks and copycat manoeuvres. Ultimately, strong players can establish the category credentials, grow the market, and attract loyal customers.

As part of his long-term scalable sustainable vision, Giles and the team have committed to raising one million people out of poverty in coconut farming communities through their *Vita Coco Project*. Their focus is on Sri Lanka and the Philippines, two of the largest coconut producing countries in the world. As outlined in the organisation's IMPACT report,[30] the team is on a mission *'to protect natural resources, build thriving communities with their grower network and champion health and wellness in society'* with tangible and inspiring results:

- 30 classrooms built in their growing communities

- 69,000 seedlings planted promoting biodiversity and replacing aging trees
- 7,000 farmers trained in regenerative and agronomic best practices
- 6.5+ million meals donated to communities experiencing food insecurity
- $2.1 million through in-kind product donations
- 30,000+ community members positively impacted in growing networks

According to the brand's IMPACT report 'Coconut farming communities in remote parts of the world face many challenges, including weak infrastructure, outdated farming practices, and a shortage of schools. Through our give, grow, guide philosophy, we work to help our coconut farmers increase their annual yield, diversify their crops, and grow their coconuts sustainably. We also provide educational programs in order to invest in the future generations of these communities.'[31] The ambition is to positively IMPACT 1,000,000 people[32] in coconut farming communities around the world.

'Give, Grow, Guide': www.vitacoco.com
Hear Vita Coco's Story on The IMPACT Game Changers™ Podcast:

www.splitsecondltd.com

3.3. CREATE AN IMPACT BRAND™

Launching a brand in a competitive marketplace can feel like 'judgement day'. The time, energy and investment are all riding on other people's preferences, competitors, and market dynamics. Yet more often than not, the rewards are greater than the pitfalls. Today, however, there is one pivotal question that all brand owners must ask themselves: '*Do I want to create brand impact or create an IMPACT Brand™?*'

Despite the subtle word play, there is a world of difference between the two. Creating brand impact has its roots firmly grounded in making money, its sole purpose of existence. However, an IMPACT Brand™ goes beyond generating cash. It delivers a triple bottom line: the economic, social, and environmental equilibrium. It also challenges the status quo and drives action as a force for good towards the 2030 Sustainable Development Goals (SDGs).

This new generation of IMPACT Brands™ is committed to a higher purpose, which is also what the consumer is looking for. Over 62%[33] say that they want brands to stand up and take a position on social, cultural, environmental, and political issues. A further 63%[34] prefer to advocate brands that align to their values through the power of purchase. They support and hold brands accountable to the causes that they champion. These are not just challenger brands stealing share away from the mainstream brands. These brands are going the extra mile to do good and so, ultimately beat the competition.

Finding that competitive edge lies in building genuine and rewarding customer relationships. Create brands that tap into a target prospect's personal values. Organisations that take this approach, demonstrate their insight, authenticity, and commitment to the Sustainable Development Goals (SDGs) resulting in loyal and enlightened customers who will make more conscious choices.

Whilst many companies highlight their positions on socio-economic and environmental challenges in their annual reports and Corporate Social Responsibility (CSR) statements, these pledges must become the cornerstone of their brand strategy and greener core values. Organisations need to demonstrate their ethical and sustainability credentials in order to build trust, collaborative partnerships, and category leadership. The time has come to proactively commit, connect, and build communities that will create IMPACT Brands™ to deliver the 2030 SDGs.

Commit

Now more than ever, consumers want to engage and purchase brands that stand for more than just profit. According to Accenture, 53%[35] of consumers who are disappointed with a brand's words or actions on a social issue will complain about it ... 47%[36] will walk away in frustration and 17 %[37] will never return. Today's consumer wants full transparency, interaction, experiences, and above all alignment to their values. If a brand shies away from declaring its position or getting involved in global or local issues for fear of losing revenue, then the consumer will likely turn to those who do. They want to support and champion brands that will make an IMPACT, not just money. Ironically, the brands that put purpose ahead of profit, make more money.

Historically, most brands have remained tight-lipped and neutral on socio-economic political subjects to protect their brand image. This is no longer an option. Consumer research tells us that inaction or complacency can risk alienating them, as well as potentially losing billions in revenue. Not taking a stance makes consumers question a business's practice and ethics. They want a sense of reassurance that the brand is human, has its finger on the pulse and is aligned to their values. Sharing a brand's point of view builds rapport and trust.

Even though 193 world leaders signed up and committed to tackling the 17 Sustainable Development Goals (SDGs), they cannot do it on their own. This is a call to action for all businesses, brands, and global citizens to step up and collectively own the SDGs. It is both a massive responsibility and a $12 trillion opportunity.

Some organisations may find that they are connected to more than one SDG in their strategic planning. One way to strike the balance is to identify which one is for People, Planet, and Profit – *The Triple Bottom Line* for any business. Align the value proposition to the relevant SDG(s) based on organisational priority and capability. This can then be further embedded into the brand strategy and linked to the business and SDG prize.

There is however a clear distinction to be made between an IMPACT Brand™ and a social movement. Most successful companies embrace both. Yet in order for an IMPACT Brand™ to instil confidence with the conscious consumer, they must deliver on the core purpose and commitment to the SDG in question. A social movement on the other hand, represents an incremental change that may or may not be directly linked to the business's mission.

For instance, an IMPACT Brand™ such as Pursuit the Label swimwear are clearly aligned to *SDG#14 Life Under Water*. Yet when millions took to the streets and onto social media following the murder of George Floyd and in support of #BlackLivesMatter, they also felt compelled to respond. They endorsed this social movement, which falls under *SDG#10 Reduced Inequalities*, by sharing part of their profits with the #BlackLivesMatter platform. This act of solidarity against racial injustice and discrimination is part of a bigger global movement to beat the *other* global pandemic: racism.

pursuitswimwear As we have all been witnessing devastating events in the USA and across the globe, we have made it our mission to educate, listen & support.
To our customers & community we want you to know that we stand by you, we stand with you and we support you & the #blacklivesmatter movement as we believe in inclusivity and equality!
We will be donating a % of our profits to @blklivesmatter to help those who have been effected by injustice in anyway that we can!
This is a GLOBAL movement for our future generation! #TogetherWeStand 🖤
Source: Pursuit the Label Instagram

Social movements tend to be led by millennials who are known as the *crusader generation*, 94%[38] of whom want to use their skills to benefit a cause. Why is that important? They currently make up 35%[39] of the UK workforce and an astounding 50%[40] of the global workforce. They put brands under greater scrutiny and share their perspective on matters that mean the most. The actions must be authentic and not just an excuse to jump on an opportunistic bandwagon, which most consumers can sense a mile away. Many brands and people have got that wrong in the past, so they must tread carefully. The aim is to listen, act and raise social consciousness from a place of sincerity.

The United Nations has been championing the fight against racism for decades as they recognise that *'Racism and racial discrimination take many forms and IMPACT key aspects of life. IMPACTS could include the ability to find a job, get an education, have equal access to healthcare, or get fair treatment in a court of law. Racism, xenophobia and related discrimination and intolerance exist in all societies, everywhere. They affect us all – directly or indirectly. We all lose in a society characterised by discrimination, division, distrust, intolerance and hate.'*[41] Unconscious bias occurs when people think better of someone because they believe they are alike and think less of someone because of a difference in race, religion, culture, age, gender, or other factors.

Diversity and inclusion go beyond 'accepting' someone for the colour of their skin, marching in a protest or talking about it on social media. They also mean genuinely welcoming diverse points of views and perspectives without judgement. How a person thinks and feels are based on their life experiences, which may or may not align with others. This does not mean it is negative, confrontational, or wrong - just different. Even though most people feel that they have progressive outlook on the world, look around your own professional and personal circles, how much diversity do you actually have around you? How do you react when the topic of racism is brought up? Do you take it as a an afront, become indignant or defensive? Your colleagues and friends of colour maybe feeling isolated, frustrated, and misunderstood. Take the time to seek out, understand, and even celebrate new perspectives, rather than judge, negate or alienate. A little empathy goes a long way. Diversity brings rich cultural insight and a wealth of opportunities ... literally.

In business terms, diversity drives financial performance. EBIT margins for companies with diverse management teams are nearly 10% higher[42] than for companies with *'below-average management diversity'* according to Harvard Business Review (HBR). After surveying 1700 companies of varying sizes from across the world, using innovation as the indicator of products and services launched within the last three years, Boston Consulting Group (BCG) also found organisations with above-average diversity delivered more revenue. In fact, those diverse companies produced a greater proportion of income from innovation, delivered 45% of total revenue[43], compared to companies with below average diversity at 26%.[44] Thus, innovation-related advantage equals +19%[45] overall better financial performance.

Every person and every employee should feel that their views are valued. Gender is also another area where businesses can benefit. Women control 40%[46] of global wealth and make or influence up to 80%[47] of all purchases, which means gender-balanced teams have a higher return on equity. Credit Suisse Research Institute found that *'companies with one or more women board members had higher average ROI and better average growth than companies with male-only boards. With such benefits from gender diversity, one wonders why 77% of The Standard & Poors 500 (S & P 500 stock market index tracking top 500 performers) company boards are more than two-thirds male, and only 2% have more than 50% of female members.'*[48] Why indeed?

A diverse culture requires commitment from the top leadership team for best in-class performance and company culture. Start by appointing diversity in the head of diversity roles, an obvious but often missed opportunity. Many leaders and entrepreneurs deprioritise diversity and believe they will circle back to it once the organisation has grown, which can then appear as an insincere quota filling exercise. Yet integrating diversity is far easier and more authentic from the ground up in order to create a cohesive, authentic, rich culture and proposition.

> *'Our ability to reach unity in diversity will be the beauty and the test of our civilisation.'*
> – Mahatma Gandhi

Connect

It is clear that a brand's contribution to solving socio-economic challenges acts as point of difference. Yet how do you take the target prospect on the journey with you? In order to truly connect with them, start with the IMPACT the brand is on a mission to make with the values, cultural spirit and ethos that are unique to the business for People, Planet, and Profit. Lead with those, and the target prospects who share a similar vision and values will lean in.

The concept of how an idea or a product gains momentum and diffuses through a population or social system over time, was first made popular by E.M. Rogers in 1962. His model *Diffusion of Innovations*[49] explains that in order for someone to adopt a new behaviour, purchase a new product or embrace a new idea, it must be perceived as different or innovative, an objective not easily achieved.

There are varying psychological characteristics behind people who adopt innovation early and those who adopt it over time. Rogers' model has five key 'adopter' categories[50] with assigned percentages to each group. Although most of the population falls into the central sets, it is useful to understand where specific target groups sit, to appeal to them.

1. **The Innovators (2.5%)** – First to adopt new concepts and ideas, risk takers and pioneers.
2. **The Early Adopters (13.5%)** – Embrace change and seek to adopt new ideas.
3. **The Early Majority (34%)** – Adopt new evidence-based ideas before the average person with the help of success stories and proof of concept.
4. **The Late Majority (34%)** – Sceptics of change; only adopt innovation after it has been tried by the majority.
5. **The Laggards (16%)** – Highly conservative and resistant to change.

Source: E.M. Rogers Diffusion of Innovations

The objective is to creatively engage and influence people at every stage of adoption. It will drive purchasing decisions, champion the cause, and make a positive lasting IMPACT.

Community

Traditional marketing has two clear objectives to drive sales and build brand equity. It is a top-down approach with an emphasis on brand engagement. This conventional style often assumes that the target prospect is indifferent and isolated, just waiting to be enticed by gimmicks and tactics.

Consumers are you and I, part of a tribe searching for identity, a voice, and a sense of belonging. It is a tribe with a primal instinct for sustenance, security, and survival. Today, we live in an era of social marketing, which takes us back to our roots where the aim is to achieve communal social good.

Building communities is not new in the world of business, but IMPACT Brands™ do have a distinct advantage. With so many platforms available to us, it is easy to unite people together. Active communities with open invitations to other like-minded enthusiasts with shared values are connecting hearts and minds. They intentionally consider their role in society as a start point that aligns to a target prospect's personal values. One of the best ways to build and harness customer relationships is to invite them into a curated community. The intention is to focus on a cause with a committed tribe. By waking the consumer's conscience, IMPACT Brands™ are becoming social tribes that deliver socio-economic SDG and business goals, like never before. Whether they are championing animal rights, human rights, anti-racism, or sustainability, every voice and purchase become a vote to make the world a better place.

Social Tribes often find one another and create even larger communities. These communities can be formed at an organisational, industry sector, national or international level – all connected by a common purpose. The B Corporation is a global non-profit certification that promotes companies to meet social sustainability and environmental performance standards. It brings thousands of businesses together that share a collective vision and values. In turn, they themselves also have their own active social tribes.

One such B Corp certified business is the Impact Hub, one of the world's largest networks focused on *'building entrepreneurial communities for impact at scale that create tangible solutions to the world's most pressing issues'.*[51] Co-Founder and Executive Director of Impact Hub Network, Tatiana Glad believes in the power of community. Since the 2020 global pandemic she has seen *'a real shift and a sense of greater urgency for collective decision-making and action. It has been a big challenge in sustainability work since the beginning.'*[52]

During her time at Impact Hub Amsterdam, she went through different stages before formalising the community. As a team, they started off by developing and sharing groundbreaking ideas with a clear vision of wanting to make their city a better place by taking locally rooted action. They found that peer-to-peer support and learning was very important. It stimulated a growing community dedicated to societal innovation and entrepreneurial action. Tatiana says, *'Impact Hub Amsterdam was born out of a community that came together quite informally as social entrepreneurs trying to create a better world.'*[53]

Today, this social tribe is driving systemic change by tackling some of the biggest challenges towards the Sustainable Development Goals (SDGs) across different industry sectors. Tatiana says '*Early on, we realised that the SDGs form one of the biggest global agreements we have, so we couldn't really ignore it. Despite the agreement not being perfect, the key question for us was 'what's our role in that global agreement?'. When we had someone from the United Nations visit us, they were surprised how well we had embraced the SDGs, because when they thought of the private sector, they automatically thought of large corporates not entrepreneurs and SMEs. We incorporated the SDGs by looking at what every entrepreneur in our community does and how they connect to them. You can look at the SDGs at a superficial level or you can start to make very specific links to the 169 SDG targets. Most of our entrepreneurs don't define themselves by the SDGs but can align to the ones that they are serving through what they are doing.*'[54] This community promotes sustainability and drives innovation to activate change. They collaborate with some of the most dynamic companies to start, grow and scale IMPACT.

The shift from talking at a prospect vs actively listening and responding to a prospect, is the value intersection. Whether it is the prospect's pain point, society's pain point or the planet's pain point – it is time to address them. Invite prospects to be part of the solution. Engage, educate, and empower them to build meaningful relationships that will make a positive lasting IMPACT together. The brand's socio-economic contribution in delivering the Sustainable Development Goals (SDGs) will ensure it stands out in the eyes of the conscious consumer. The proposition will then offer a *Unique Solution Point (USP)*™ that will leave competitors behind, generate a healthier profit, and become a change agent towards a higher purpose.

'We engineer serendipity to enable transformational impact':
www.impacthub.net

Hear Impact Hub's Story on The IMPACT Game Changers™ Podcast:

www.splitsecondltd.com

Chapter Three – PROPOSITION Exercise:

In order to get critical mass behind an idea, concept, or innovation, go through this checklist to see if your business is on The IMPACT RoadMap™:

- Map out goals, milestones, and the looks of success
- Get support and endorsements from key people of influence and respected groups for initial adoption of your concept
- Provide incentives for early adoption until critical mass is achieved
- Introduce and share concepts with supporters first before taking them mainstream

Some factors to consider which may affect the process:

- The degree to which the concept is regarded as innovative and the gap it fulfils
- Alignment to the target prospect's values, experiences and needs
- The level of complexity in adopting and using the innovation
- The option to test or try the concept before committing to it
- Tangible benefits from adopting the concept

Score Your IMPACT:

Take the next action step to Scale Profit with Purpose for People and Planet by completing The IMPACT Roadmap Scorecard™.

The IMPACT Roadmap Scorecard™ is built on the 3 steps: PLAN with PURPOSE™ – PERSUADE with PROMISE™ – PROFIT with IMPACT™.

Be Part of the Solution. Start an IMPACT Revolution™.

www.splitsecondltd.com

STEP 2 – PERSUADE with PROMISE™

'The people crazy enough to think they can change the world are the ones who do.'
– Steve Jobs

PERSUADE
with PROMISE

The world has changed for good. 2020 accelerated many of the trends that were already in motion, which has made us reflect on our behaviours, lifestyles, and actions. As people, we want to live in a safer, more inclusive, and greener society. Most of us are more conscious of our consumption habits and are looking for sustainable solutions to make the world a better place.

Now, there are greater consumer expectations for businesses and brands to step up and protect people, planet, and communities. Social responsibility, wellbeing, compassion, and action are not only expected, but imperative for organisations to deliver if they want to stay in the game.

Consumers and customers are seeking purpose-driven persuasion that promises a better tomorrow.

People don't buy products and services, they buy outcomes. As human beings, our decision-making is not always rational. It is led by our beliefs, backgrounds, emotions, and behaviours. The power of persuasion is the ability to influence attitudes and actions. When mastered, it can deliver objection-free pitches, collaborative partnerships, and customer conversion to purchase that will make a greater and positive IMPACT.

CHAPTER FOUR: PITCH

'Do what others don't, and you'll get what others won't.'
– Anonymous

Some entrepreneurs, executives and brand-owners relish the exhilarating idea of it, others find it the most daunting experience on earth. Love it or loathe it, the pitch is a rite of passage that must be embraced. Coming up with creative ideas can be easy but selling them can be the *make or break* for companies big and small.

Whether we realise it or not, pitching is part of our daily lives. From ascertaining business funding, inviting friends over for dinner or even asking your kids to tidy up their rooms – all start with a pitch. Obviously, selling a product or service is not the objective in every case, but we do need to engage the other party and put our most persuasive rationale forward if we hope to convince someone of a specific outcome.

Once a plan is ready to leave its head office nest for the big bold business world, it's time to put a compelling pitch together. According to Harvard, 95%[1] of our purchasing decisions take place in the subconscious. So, despite being able to reach someone on a functional level, telling is not selling.

As a brand owner it may feel natural to walk into a client meeting and share the passion and enthusiasm for a proposition. However, that is only a small part of the process. Most brand-only pitches fail. Time and time again, people lose their audience's attention within seconds because they pitch the brand *'me, me, me'* when the prospect's key question is *'what's in it for me?'*

4.1.   IMPACT PITCH™ PREP

Every pitch is an audition. With attention spans getting shorter and shorter, cutting to the chase is vital in a successful pitch. Everyone is under pressure to deliver commercial results, build collaborative partnerships and stay ahead of the ever-changing market landscape, so time is of the essence.

Get to Know the Audience

The best way to ensure a positive outcome in a timely manner is to step into the prospect's shoes. Whether the audience includes investors, retailers, or any other type of commercial buyer, preparing a pitch through their lens mitigates any possible challenges. There is only one chance to make a first impression.

The first step to audience engagement is to understand their strategic objectives, market performance, marketing, and long-term vision. By aligning the pitch to their strategy, the key synergies, and lucrative opportunities for both parties will become clear, and one is able to accelerate a constructive dialogue.

Customer insight always supercharges any pitch, drives standout, and provides a competitive edge. The insight may vary by audience, objective, distribution channel and overall barriers and triggers to purchase. It will however reassure the audience and give them the confidence that the strategic pitch is tailored to their needs – the ultimate sales weapon.

Get to Know the Challenges

We live in a competitive market and a proposition is not going to sell itself. Landing the perfect pitch means that one has to get to know the audience inside out so that the proposition is *the* solution to the customer's pain points. The proposition must be so attractive that it is impossible to refuse.

Connecting the dots between their pain points and your proposition is key to winning the pitch:

- Evaluate their business model and how to achieve their IMPACT strategic goals
- Identify their competitive threats and advantages in the market
- Explore how collaboration can be a catalyst for growth

The assessment will in no doubt keep the audience engaged and on side. Integrate the challenges within the pitch to ensure alignment. This will provide an opening to deliver an authentic Unique *Solution* Point – the IMPACT USP™.

> *'Know everything about the people that you're pitching in front of. What does their company do? What does their company stand for? Who are the competitors? Preparation is the single biggest piece of advice I'd give to brand-owners. Yet don't boil the ocean and spend time thinking about things that don't necessarily matter to the buyer, get to the jugular really quickly.'*
> – Tom Elliott, Former Senior Buyer, Sainsbury's Future Brands Team

'Live Well for Less': www.sainsburys.co.uk
Hear Sainsbury's Story on The IMPACT Game Changers™ Podcast:

www.splitsecondltd.com

Get to Know the Look of Success

What does success look like? Is it realistic? Is it measurable? Is it meaningful? Identifying the audience's look of success can provide some integral clues into what will make a winning pitch. Businesses cannot grow in a meaningful way without an obsessive focus on Key Performance Indicators (KPIs).

KPIs provide an analytical snapshot of the state of a company, strategy, or aspiration. By understanding the other party's KPIs, one can tailor the dialogue and pitch accordingly, which is likely to get greater alignment and traction. The focus must be on the meaning behind the KPIs to truly understand the look of success. Are they concerned about profit margin? Conversion rates? Customer retention? By asking the right questions, the target audience will share what is driving the KPIs and what success looks like for them.

Most reputable businesses now have a sustainable strategy that they publish online, but how are they measuring this plan? Are they actually tracking success towards their objectives? How can your proposition help them achieve their vision?

As sustainability becomes an increasingly critical part of global consciousness, it is an area to be explored with your prospect. This will not only demonstrate the organisation's values and purpose beyond profit but offer a competitive edge. The key is to identify their commercial, organisational and Sustainable Development Goals to align on common strategic growth drivers that will be a win-win for all.

4.2. IMPACT PITCH™ PERSUASION

Understand Buyer Expectations

No matter the industry, the buyer in the audience is likely to be responsible for developing and engaging a supplier base, purchasing goods and services, and setting the transaction terms. In other words, the buyer determines what to buy, whom to buy it from and how it will drive business growth.

Put yourself in the buyer's shoes for a moment, faced with hundreds if not thousands of commercial decisions a year. Every week starts with numbers, reviewing the challenging commercial targets and potential issues that may get in the way of their objectives. And in any given week, in walk a dozen very passionate brand owners pitching their plans and hoping for their proposition to be adopted. The decision is not always an easy one.

The buyer has to consider which brands will drive business growth, have customer appeal, and deliver commercial returns to remain competitive in the market – a tough balancing act with massive implications. By recognising the position and pressure the buyer is under, the buyer's

KPIs and taking the appropriate steps, one can begin to mitigate potential obstacles and hopefully prevail with persuasion.

Manage Buyer Expectations

Give your brand the chance to shine in the best possible light by pre-empting the likely pitch challenges that will come up. Anticipate and rehearse potential questions that may come up based on the buyer's expectations. Incorporate their challenges and the look of success into the pitch, then just listen.

Think about it: the words 'listen' and 'silent' contain the same letters. The power of silence can unlock pivotal answers towards a deal. It allows time for prospects to contemplate what's on offer, possibly in your favour. It enables the prospect to lead the dialogue and share information that could be very valuable to your pitch. It highlights mutual opportunities and purpose.

If the buyer's expectations are not considered, then there is a risk that it may work against the proposed pitch:

- Negotiations may be more difficult due to a lack of preparation and insight
- Building trust and credibility may be more of a challenge
- Experienced competitors may seem more attractive to work with

Anticipating and examining buyer expectations will lay a solid foundation for an impending collaborative partnership.

Help the buyer help you ...

Exceed Buyer Expectations

According to Gartner research, B2B buyers spend 27%[2] of their time researching independently online and only 17%[3] meeting potential suppliers. With more and more people working from home, sales leaders believe that digital channels are twice as important today compared to pre-pandemic environments. Therefore, buyer engagement is more crucial and more complex than ever. Go the extra mile to design a comprehensive, articulate, and compelling pitch with a buyer-first approach.

5-STEP BUYER-FIRST APPROACH™:

1. Conduct a full evaluation of the potential client (strategy, performance, etc.)
2. Step into the client's world (website, outlets, etc.)
3. Identify the client's Strengths, Weaknesses, Opportunities, and Threats (SWOT)
4. Align your Unique *Solution* Point – The IMPACT USP™
5. Find examples to demonstrate purpose-led proof of concept to create consensus

All the content building blocks should be well researched, grounded in insight, and tested before they make their way into the pitch storyboard. Remember you are selling a lucrative opportunity aligned to the buyer's commercial strategy and objectives that will drive purchase with purpose.

4.3. IMPACT PITCH PERFECT™

Great pitches start with a big shift. The shift that separates those who thrive from those who simply survive. Identify what has changed from the old world to the new world. Navigate them through this new, unknown world with the one thing that makes your brand different and compelling to prospects.

Show them the size of the prize – an opportunity they will not want to miss. Above all, don't pitch. Share a compelling authentic story. A purpose-led story that creates an emotional connection and provides solutions to the 17 specific Sustainable Development Goals which will make a positive lasting IMPACT.

Pitch SPARK

Asking anyone to take a bet on your pitch involves a certain level of risk. The audience is not just a potential source of revenue, but it is made up of people. No one wants to see a 50-page presentation full of dry facts and figures. Create pitch content that connects with people's values to inspire and action with IMPACT. Don't bury your IMPACT proposition on slide 25 of the presentation as an afterthought. Make it the heart of your pitch and your proposition. No greenwashing please - Authenticity and IMPACT go hand in hand.

7-STEP IMPACT PITCH ™

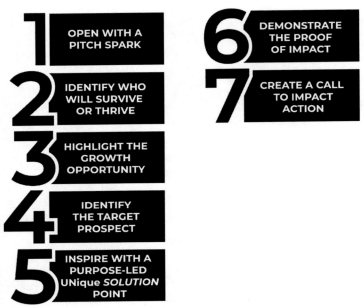

1.   **Pitch Spark**: Rather than opening the pitch with awkward pleasantries about the weather, the traffic, apologies for any technical glitches or a cringe-worthy thank you, just jump straight into the big shift with a killer insight, a thought-provoking question, or stimulating story. Start with a statement that will make the audience sit up and take notice of the big shift in a split second. This will set the tone for the entire pitch. Here are some examples:

     'More than 1.5 million pounds of waste is dumped in oceans every hour. Plastic makes up 90% of it ...'

     'Can you imagine a world where ...?'

     'By the year 2050, our lives will be very different ...'

2. **Identify Who will Survive or Thrive:** Who are the ones that failed to embrace change, sustainability, agility vs the innovators, change-makers in the industry? What side of the big shift do they want to be on?

3. **Highlight the Growth Opportunity:** Don't talk about your brand (yet)... highlight the current unsolved problem in the market, society, or the world. The white space that is theirs for the taking. Size the prize and seize the opportunity.

4. **Identify the Target Prospect:** Describe the segment of the population who have certain pain points that need to be addressed.

5. **Inspire with a Purpose-Led UNique *Solution* Point – IMPACT USP™:** Does your brand or business exist beyond profit? Are you working towards the UN Sustainable Development Goals? How can the buyer make the world a better place in partnership with you and your business? How will your purpose-led brand solve the problem? Share the purpose-led principles. What is your mission? Vision? Values? Why do they matter? Are there any points of strategic alignment?

6. **Demonstrate the Proof of IMPACT**: Why will the concept work? Has it worked in other markets, distribution channels, retailers? Can you demonstrate key successes by means of awards, customer feedback, recognition and performance, endorsements, etc.? Can you share how it will make an IMPACT on People, Planet, and Profit?

7. **Call to IMPACT Action:** Don't end the pitch with a predictable and awkward *thank you* but rather ask them to join you on your mission. Agree the next steps and timeline. Inspire the audience with a clear call to action to make a positive lasting IMPACT in the world.

If you could ask the buyer anything (aside from purchasing from you) what would it be?

Getting time with a buyer is priceless, so prepare some key questions that would open up a valuable dialogue. This is part of the engagement process so don't make the questions all about your brand. Ask them questions about their business which will give you clues on what is driving their strategic, commercial and sustainability agenda. If the buyer is showing signs of interest in your proposition, then don't derail the line of questioning as it will likely lead to more fruitful next steps. Create a pitch spark and things will be off to a flying start.

Pitch HERO™

Once the Pitch SPARK has been mastered from a content perspective, focus on the delivery of the pitch. One must not underestimate audience engagement in winning a pitch. Even with the best content, if the delivery is poor, then the message is lost.

A pitch should not even feel like a pitch. It should be a visceral experience – an extremely powerful detail that some presenters overlook. Take the audience on an emotional journey that enables them to connect with the speaker.

From Storytelling to Story Selling

Mankind has been sharing stories since the dawn of time. From heroic myths and legends, to religious scripts and fairy tales, stories are woven into the fabric of our history. These stories are passed down from generation to generation, connecting the past, present and future. A story speaks to us emotionally and compels us to think, feel and act.

Whether it's in a good book, Oscar-worthy film, or a Netflix boxset, a good story lets the storyteller take the reader or audience on a journey. Every story has a clear structure and flow:

- An introduction that establishes the key characters, setting and context
- A challenge, obstacle, or a villain
- A climax or pivotal moment when the protagonist faces a difficult encounter
- A turning point when the conflict needs a solution

- A resolution or an outcome

Story selling combines the art of telling a story with specific outcomes where the success lies in having:

- The ability to persuade
- The ability to connect
- The ability to act

When it comes to social and sustainability communication, many companies develop IMPACT reports and share them online. Facts and figures provide data and insight, but strong narratives give them meaning. Commitment, transparency, progress, and action build trust. Share the company's commitment to the Sustainable Development Goals (SDGs) and how the business strategy and activities link back to the broader global targets. Today, pledges to people, planet and community are the most relevant and vital stories your business can share. Business stakeholders and investors alike realise that these persuasive narratives are the ones that will determine our fate and make a positive lasting IMPACT.

Pitch GAME CHANGER™:

Master storytellers go beyond selling. They take the audience on an emotional journey into a world where despite certain challenges, they convert spectators into change makers. This is how IMPACT Game Changers™ pitch as they empower everyone to take action that will make the world a better place.

Meet Rob Wilson, Chief Toaster at Toast Ale, a British planet-saving craft beer company whose mission is *to lead a brewing movement to eliminate bread waste and fix the food system*. According to the United Nations, people waste over a billion tonnes of food a year.[4] This is the equivalent to 74kgs per person a year[5] around the world. In the UK, this equates to around eight meals per household per week.[6] The UN also reported that over 17%[7] of food waste is generated in restaurants and shops, some of it lost on farms and in supply chains. This wastage, along with intensive farming produces over 10%[8] of the emissions fuelling the climate crisis, the main cause of the biodiversity crisis and global pollution.

The food industry has a massive IMPACT on climate change through deforestation, transport, and carbon footprint with one-third of all food produced equivalent to a billion tonnes that is never even consumed. Across Europe, consumers throw out around £143[9] billion of food a year with bread being one of the worst culprits; 44%[10] goes directly into the bin. So, food waste activist and author Tristram Stuart decided to tackle the issue by reviving a thousand-year-old beer recipe which replaces a third of barley with yesterday's bread. He teamed up with Rob, and together they have rescued over +1million slices[11] of surplus bread, reclaimed land and water that has helped mitigate climate change and produced a delicious award-winning, planet-saving beer. They also open-source the recipe for home-brewers and collaborate with breweries to inspire the entire beer industry to follow suit. Rob says, '*As a B Corp, every business decision that we make, we consider People, Planet and Profit.*'[12]

Rob and his team stand firmly behind *SDG#12 Responsible Production and Consumption*, through their circular economy business model, and in 2018 won the SDG award for it. Specifically, they champion *SDG#12's 12.3* target to '*halve per capita global food waste at the retail and consumer levels and reduce food losses along production and supply chains, including post-harvest losses.*'[13] Their beer is made with fresh surplus bread from bakeries that would otherwise go to waste. 100% of their profits go back to charities fighting food waste, which is the best thing since sliced bread!

They have created a circular economy based on 4 founding principles[14] to inspire consumers to '*get wasted on waste*':

1. Brew great beers that engage drinkers
2. Use surplus fresh bread to prevent waste
3. Raise awareness of the issue of, and solutions to, food waste
4. Maximise profits to reinvest in charities fixing the food system

By using surplus bread as part of their grain bill, they are able to truly measure their IMPACT. They use less water = 108 m3 and less land = 7.5 hectares and avoid carbon emissions = 11 tCO2e.[15] Rob says '*I think we are* all acutely aware that climate change is an almost insurmountable challenge to try and comprehend, but when you break it down you realise that the food system has the biggest IMPACT on the planet. We are wasting one-third of the food we produce, that for me, feels like such an obvious place that you would start to try and chip away at this problem. The food industry uses a huge amount of transportation, energy, and causes a huge amount of deforestation. With Toast, there is a wonderful circularity to it. The beer industry has always been a natural solution to the food waste problem. The first ever beer recipe which was discovered nearly 4000 years ago was brewed with surplus bread. Local bakeries would partner up with local breweries to use the surplus, the carbohydrates, the nutritional value. Turning bread into beer was the norm for millennia. It wasn't until the industrial revolution that we completely ceased doing this. So, what we're trying to do through this kind of circular economy solution is actually bring beer production back to its origins, reminding people to make that normal again!"[16] Rob and his team at Toast Ale also donate time, money and product to charitable organisations that deliver systemic change to fix the food system.

'Raise a Toast. Save the World. Cheers!': www.toastale.com
Hear Toast Ale's Story on The IMPACT Game Changers™ Podcast:

www.splitsecondltd.com

IMPACT Game Changers™ have the ability to make a positive IMPACT. They go against conventional pitching by shining a spotlight on issues that jolt consumer consciousness with brands as means to a mission. They live and breathe a set of values that resonate with their customers and consumers alike by harnessing values-based principles grounded in making a social and sustainable IMPACT.

IMPACT PITCH TOP 10 GAME CHANGER PRINCIPLES ™

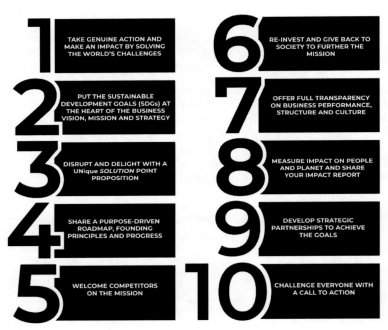

1 TAKE GENUINE ACTION AND MAKE AN IMPACT BY SOLVING THE WORLD'S CHALLENGES

2 PUT THE SUSTAINABLE DEVELOPMENT GOALS (SDGs) AT THE HEART OF THE BUSINESS VISION, MISSION AND STRATEGY

3 DISRUPT AND DELIGHT WITH A UNique *SOLUTION* POINT PROPOSITION

4 SHARE A PURPOSE-DRIVEN ROADMAP, FOUNDING PRINCIPLES AND PROGRESS

5 WELCOME COMPETITORS ON THE MISSION

6 RE-INVEST AND GIVE BACK TO SOCIETY TO FURTHER THE MISSION

7 OFFER FULL TRANSPARENCY ON BUSINESS PERFORMANCE, STRUCTURE AND CULTURE

8 MEASURE IMPACT ON PEOPLE AND PLANET AND SHARE YOUR IMPACT REPORT

9 DEVELOP STRATEGIC PARTNERSHIPS TO ACHIEVE THE GOALS

10 CHALLENGE EVERYONE WITH A CALL TO ACTION

When applied, these principles win pitches, build partnerships and drive purchase. Tom Elliott, former senior buyer at Sainsbury's Future Brands Team says, '*There are three things I always think about when evaluating brand pitches: Does the brand look good? Does the brand taste good? Does the brand do good? Customers want brands that are sustainable, have values and purpose. They don't want something that will make someone rich and in five years' time they sell it to a global blue-chip organisation. The idea of it actually being about doing good for the world is increasingly more important.*'[17]

'Helping Everyone Eat Better': www.sainsburys.co.uk
Hear Sainsbury's Story on The IMPACT Game Changers™ Podcast:

www.splitsecondltd.com

Chapter Four - PITCH Exercise:

Using the 7-STEP IMPACT PITCH™ develop your own IMPACT Pitch™:

CHAPTER FIVE: PARTNERSHIP

'Business is a vital partner in achieving the Sustainable Development Goals. Companies can contribute through their core activities, and we ask companies everywhere to assess their IMPACT, set ambitious goals and communicate transparently about the results.'
– Ban Ki-Moon, Former United Nations Secretary-General

The mission is clear. The goals are set. Time is running out for a world in which people can prosper, the planet can flourish and profit can make a positive IMPACT. We must act now as business leaders, groundbreaking innovators, and global citizens to attain the Sustainable Development Goals (SDGs) by 2030.

Purpose-led partnerships are at the core of this big shift. When working in tandem, the collective effort propels businesses to not only find their common ground, but together they can cover more ground. Knowledge exchange, mapping out mutual opportunities and sharing responsibilities build a strong foundation. They enable both parties to accelerate the progress towards achieving the SDGs with a shared vision of change.

The partnership goals must be aligned and valued across both organisations from leadership top down in order to build trust and success. Setting and achieving the targets requires cohesive teamwork and a unified approach. Joint performance metrics underpinned in purpose enable businesses to collaborate, communicate and co-create. The strength of the relationship determines how to successfully realise the vision and its overall IMPACT.

5.1. COLLABORATE

'It makes no sense to pit purpose against profit. There is plenty of evidence to show that sustainable companies enjoy better performances and sustainability is a business opportunity.'
– Francois-Henri Pinault, CEO of the Kering Group

Businesses that consistently collaborate with their suppliers, customers and peers are in a much stronger position to develop partnerships. By adopting creative solutions and dynamic innovation they become category trailblazers. They serve their customers, employees, shareholders, and society, bringing *SDG#17 Partnerships for the Goals* to life.

Drive Purpose-led Action

Scaling action on the Sustainable Development Goals requires industry-wide collaboration across the entire value-chain. Whatever the type of co-operation, it all starts with an aligned purpose. Ensure that the partnership is grounded in shared values because systemic change is only possible through unified action. Purpose-driven partnerships gain trust and business. Since the 2020 pandemic, 75%[1] of consumers prioritise purchase from organisations that give back to society. After all, actions speak louder than words.

Develop a Collaborative Strategy

No matter what the company size, it all boils down to how much is invested in cultivating the relationship – a priceless currency. There are varying shades of collaboration which determine the depth of the relationship, the level of influence and in some cases the 'power' dynamics. It is a broad spectrum classed in three levels: transactional, tactical and the trusted go-to partner. An aligned collaborative partnership can deliver a lucrative profit and create a powerful groundswell.

5 STEPS TO AN IMPACT COLLABORATIVE STRATEGY™:

1. Identify mutual growth opportunities
2. Co-create a long-term purpose-led vision
3. Set up an agile process
4. Collaborate across the full value chain
5. Measure the triple bottom line – People/Planet/Profit

This approach will ensure a cohesive outcome based on a shared vision, values, and purpose.

Deliver Sustainable Solutions and Socio-Economic IMPACT

In September 2009, Merijn Everaarts was enjoying a lovely day of sunshine at the beach in the Netherlands, when suddenly he saw waves of plastic being washed up all around him. He thought a coastal clean-up team would show up and pick up the trash, but that was not to be. Instead, the tide took all the plastic back into the ocean and then some.

Eight million tons of plastic are swallowed by the oceans every year, a truckload every minute.[2] This is the equivalent weight of a fleet of 150 Titanic ships or four million cars. Scientists in Spain have found that the negative effect of bottled water on natural resources is 3500 times higher than that of tap water.[3] In fact, if the entire city of Barcelona was to drink bottled water, the cost of resource extraction would exceed £60.3 million a year[4], not to mention the 17 million barrels of oil required to produce the plastic bottles. Plastic never decomposes as it enters the food chain, a real threat to fishes in the water, birds in the sky and all living species.

Merijn wondered why consumers were purchasing (and polluting) single-use plastic bottles when they could drink straight out of the tap? Yet for the last 25 years, most of the big drinks' brands and health authorities have been telling consumers that hydration is essential to our wellbeing. So how do you persuade consumers to change their habits?

Frustrated by what he had witnessed, Merijn decided to act. He launched a design competition to find a sustainable alternative to single-use water bottles and the ocean-saving bottle Dopper was born. With a dual mission to reduce plastic waste and provide clean drinking water, this social enterprise is changing consumers day-to-day habits away from single-use plastics. Merijn and his team encourage consumers to fill up Dopper bottles with tap water to reduce ocean plastic pollution.

Dopper is now a global brand, shipping bottles all over the world. Although shipping by boat is eco-friendlier per product than air freight, this mode of transportation is far from clean (90%[5] of everything we purchase is shipped by boat). If we do nothing, then the shipping carbon footprint will be the size of the United States by 2050.[6] Is there a solution? Dopper decided to partner up with GoodShipping, container ships using

100% renewable biofuel. They are the world's first shipping company that actually decarbonise supply chains, by replacing fossil fuels with sustainable alternatives rather than offsetting them. Other biofuels use palm oil waste or generate deforestation during the production process, whereas 'good fuels' biofuels are made from cooking oil waste or from crude oil from the pulp and paper sector. Shipping via renewable biofuel has now reduced their CO2 by 85%.[7]

Dopper have also teamed up with key partners to kickstart global water projects. According to the World Health Organisation, 2.1 billion (3 out of 10)[8] people do not have access to safe drinking water. So Dopper have ensured that a percentage of their sales are allocated to safe drinking water projects in rural communities and urban areas of Nepal, in partnership with Sebac and the WASH (water, sanitation and hygiene) programmes. Together, they install water points and toilets, and tens of thousands of Nepalese now have better access to drinking water and sanitary facilities. UNICEF Executive Director Anthony Lake says, 'As we improve these services in the most disadvantaged communities and for the most disadvantaged children today, we give them a fairer chance at a better tomorrow.'[9]

A key objective of *SDG#6 Clean Water and Sanitation* is to ensure availability and sustainable management of water and sanitation for all by 2030. Dopper's joint business model with key partners is designed to make an IMPACT on the wider community, reaching hundreds of thousands of global citizens. Merijn says, '*The message is the bottle. A commitment to P-E-T free world for clean oceans and clean water for everyone.*'[10]

www.splitsecondltd.com

5.2. COMMUNICATE

Communication is fundamental in any partnership, but more so in purpose-led alliances. They need to be forged on common values and aligned to the Sustainable Development Goals. In the past, brands owned the consumer world. Their primary focus was to deliver unique quality products and services at competitive prices and customers were happy to purchase.

Today, brands are having to work much harder in order to win conscious consumer loyalty. They now have to go head-to-head with charities, sustainability influencers and politicians to define their purpose and values to openly declare their IMPACT on socio-economic and environmental issues. Younger consumers especially demand it, as they are more informed and more concerned about people and the planet. They are not afraid to communicate, question and even challenge a brand's purpose and actions. Navigating this new world is not as straightforward as a putting a sustainability corporate statement out or invoking a recycling programme. Winning this new generation of conscious consumers requires an interactive dialogue, taking charge, taking accountability, and taking everyone along on the journey.

Take Charge

The fashion industry generates 2% of global GDP and employs 400 million people.[11] Sadly, less than 2% globally earn a fair wage, often trapped in poverty.[12] The industry produces and sells around 80 to 150 billion[13] garments a year globally. Yet unfortunately, nearly three-fifths[14] of all manufactured clothing ends up in incinerators or landfills within a few years of being produced. The United Nations reports that '*20%[15] of global wastewater and the clothes in our closets are doomed to pollute the earth.*' This is fast fashion. It produces 8 to 10%[16] of global greenhouse gas emissions – astonishingly, more than the aviation and maritime shipping industries combined. So, will we ever be able to shift from fast to sustainable forever fashion?

Tackling such immense challenge requires action and pace. So, partnerships that can take charge and confront these issues head-on are a welcomed by the fashion industry. Francois-Henri Pinault, CEO of The Kering Group, believes that one way to create sustainable change is to innovate in partnerships with start-ups and academia to find new sourcing solutions. His luxury conglomerate includes the renowned fashion houses of: Gucci, Saint Laurent, Bottega Veneta, Balenciaga, Alexander McQueen, Brioni, Boucheron and many more.

The Kering group founded a sustainability division back in 2003 that brought Pinault's vision '*Crafting tomorrow's luxury*' to life as he believes that '*Luxury and sustainability are one and the same*'.[17] The group began to publish and communicate their Environmental Profit & Loss account (EP&L) – an innovative tool that measures the IMPACT of business activities on the environment in monetary terms. Their ambition is to reduce their EP&L by 40% and carbon emissions by 50% by 2025.[18] The Kering group also founded its Materials Innovation Lab (MIL) to produce sustainable fabrics for its many brands across multiple categories in fashion, leather goods, watches, and jewellery.

According to Sustainable Fashion Expert Chetna Patel founder of Chillies and Clothes, '*The luxury fashion industry, like every other industry is having to wake up and take account of the IMPACT, positive or negative, its business is having on the planet and people in the chase for profits. The industry is becoming increasingly conscious of the role it plays on the global stage. With stakeholders, investors and consumers demanding more transparency and holding businesses accountable for their actions, there seems to be a greater drive and momentum for organisations to clearly state their purpose and place in society.'*[19]

The Kering group has many strategic partnerships focused on sustainability, including the London College of Fashion's Centre for Sustainable Fashion which aims to instil the principles and understanding of ethics among its students. Kering have also partnered up with Worn Again whose mission is to *'Replace the use of virgin resources by recapturing raw materials from non-reusable products. We exist to propel the shift to a circular economy.'*[20]

As a sustainable fashion expert Chetna believes that *'the fast fashion industry has much work to do – not only does it need to balance people and planet whilst making a profit, but it also needs to make sustainable and ethical fashion financially accessible to the masses. Traditional ways to buy and wear clothes will change over the next decade with new business models emerging with resale and rental taking the lead. There will be less focus on ownership and more focus on experience. The 'sharing community' is set to continue to grow.'* Once the luxury fashion industry acts, the high street retailers follow.[21]

'Sustainable Fashion, Shopping more Consciously':
Instagram@chilliesandclothes
Hear Chillies and Clothes' Story on The IMPACT Game Changers™ Podcast:

www.splitsecondltd.com

Take Accountability

Despite the conscious consumers' passion for brands to take on social and political platforms, one must proceed with caution. Consumers expect total honesty, authenticity, and accountability with the brand's values as well as their own. Otherwise, backlash may ensue, as Swedish plant-based Oatly found out when they sold a stake of their business to private equity firm Blackstone.

The oat milk giant came under fire for signing a $200 million[22] investment deal because it is headed up by a rich campaign donor who also served as a chairman in Trump's strategy and policy forum. The oat milk category has been in 347% year-on-year growth[23] and Blackstone's 10% stake[24] of the business amounts to $2 billion[25] after the sale. Blackstone is said to be the driving force behind the deforestation of the Amazon. The Amazon's dense vegetation produces one-fifth[26] of the world's oxygen supply. Protecting the Amazon is critical to our civilization as we know it.

Oatly defended the controversial partnership and acknowledged that Blackstone was an *'unexpected choice, which would expand our sustainable mission and create more plant-based products.'*[27] Yet this did not appease some consumers and activists who took to social media to express their disdain for the investor. As per the brand's Instagram account, some consumers felt betrayed: *'You're ignoring everything you led us to believe you stood for...'.*[28] However, Oatly took it on the chin and responded to every single comment that came their way.

UK General Manager Ishen Paran told Plant Based News magazine, a mission led, multi-award-winning resource creating awareness about ethical consumerism, sustainability and the plant-based lifestyle *'As long as people have those conversations, and listen to both sides of the story, that's all we can ask for, and then people can make their minds up ... I'm confident that over time, more information, and data will show that the choice we've made is the right one. You can't judge us on the decision today, but in the coming years. Change happens by raising the conversations and moving forward. It doesn't happen by closing the door on things. So, for us, that's how we've always done things and that's how we will continue.'*[29] Time will tell...

Oatly is one of the most popular alternative milk brands, regularly praised by vegans and non-dairy drinkers. It is well-known for its sustainable approach. The greenhouse gas emissions from Oatly's products are around 73%[30] less than those from cow's milk. So, when consumers begin to question a brand's authenticity and purpose, it is vital to have an open and honest dialogue about every aspect of their business, including partnerships. Brands owe it to their consumers in the spirit of trust and transparency.

Take Everyone on the Journey

The transition from existing business models to sustainable models can take time. It requires businesses to re-evaluate their current infrastructures, supply chains and raw materials in order to find people and planet-friendly solutions. Along with this internal audit, brands must be able to take stakeholders, shareholders, and consumers on the social and sustainability journey to drive lasting change.

H&M are the world's second-largest clothing retailer. Despite some of the challenges they have faced, this fast fashion organisation has started taking steps to become more ethical and sustainable. They have set a science-based target to reduce its greenhouse gas emissions by 2030 and pledged to use 100% recycled or sustainable materials also by 2030. Like many other retailers, H&M have various factors to consider, such as their: environmental IMPACT, supply chain transparency, labour conditions, wages, animal welfare, sustainability, and ethical standards. Juggling these factors whilst generating a profit and appealing to consumers requires insight, innovation, and collaboration.

The Swedish retailer operates in 74 countries worldwide and has a sustainable ethos with its *Conscious Collection* and recycling programme, allowing customers to return a bag of any-brand clothing for a £5 voucher.[31] They are also using sustainable materials such as melted recycled glass with no added colour pigments and chunky-soled sandals made from Bloom™ (a flexible foam partly produced with algae biomass).[32] According to market research, two out of three consumers[33] think brands that make a public promise to be sustainable are more trustworthy. So how can brands honour and take their promise to the masses?

H&M have recently partnered up with actor Maisie Williams as their Global Sustainability Ambassador to lead the world towards a more sustainable fashion future. Williams has joined H&M in an effort to meet their *'goal of only using recycled or other sustainably sourced materials by 2030.'*[34] She will join them *'throughout the year to drive change in fashion in the virtual world and in real life. Encouraging the reuse, remaking, and recycling of unwanted garments in a united effort to close the loop in fashion.'*[35] This partnership between H&M and the actor focusses on key initiatives based on circular economy principles. They have created a digital avatar of the actor to engage target consumers, inspire action, drive empowerment, diversity, and environmentalism.

The company have also launched H&M Looop Island in partnership with Nintendo's popular game Animal Crossing: New Horizons. This game is named after H&M's garment recycling machine which takes pre-loved clothes and turns them into new ones. According to their website where Global Head of Sustainability Pascal Brun says, *'The future of fashion needs to look different, and we want to be part of the solution.'*[36] There is still a long way to go, but these are some steps in the right direction that will make conscious consumers think twice before they are tempted to purchase more disposable and trendy fashions.

Finding creative solutions in partnership with key players, can jump-start the social and sustainable awareness to make a more effective IMPACT. Strategic partnerships can be in the same or complimentary category with a joint vision and communication. Above all, they must be grounded in customer insight and the Sustainable Development Goals in order to be purpose-led, have traction, and generate a profit that will make a lasting positive IMPACT.

5.3.   CO-CREATE

'Our world has limited resources – whether financial, natural or human – and as a society we must optimize their use. The fundamental core of good partnerships is their ability to bring together diverse resources in ways that can together achieve more: more IMPACT, greater sustainability, increased value to all.'
– The United Nations Partnering Initiative

For many organisations, partnerships are still not part of the core strategy. They are often seen as too complex, potential competitive threats and challenging to implement. Yet with the right approach, partnerships can unlock greater profit, systemic change, and the delivery of the Sustainable Development Goals.

Co-creation is a key approach to meeting a challenge head-on, a collaboration between innovators, stakeholders, and customers. It is a way to design and solve a problem that can offer a mutually beneficial outcome. It often involves multiple parties that bring their unique and dynamic resources together to offer innovation, education, and transformation.

Offer Innovation

In order to navigate through a constantly shifting market with volatile consumer expectations, brands must embed purpose in their innovation pipeline. At the heart of this purpose-led innovation is a mission to do good: innovation partnerships that genuinely create a lasting socio-economic and environmental lasting positive IMPACT.

Commitment to the Sustainable Development Goals can be a significant profit driver when assessing the long-term growth opportunities of the business. Consumers can see through disingenuous propositions that are not true to their purpose as they are looking for a connection, experience, and a clear conscience. So, purpose-led innovation offers a point of difference for shoppers and a competitive edge for brands in a saturated market.

The Isle of Wight's sustainable Mermaid gin and vodka, *'Strive to live in harmony with the natural world … are passionate about connecting with their community and driven to consider the wellbeing of the whole planet. Inspired by the ocean, they're especially determined to treat this hidden kingdom well – starting with practices at their distillery door.*[37] Mermaid's innovation pipeline is inspired by the local landscape as they ethically source local and natural ingredients for their range: *'Rock Samphire is foraged from our shoreline, Boadicea hops are harvested from Ventnor Botanic Gardens and elderflower is handpicked from local fields, while our strawberries are grown in the lush and sun-soaked Arreton Valley.*[38] Shoppers can also rest easy as the Mermaid range is in plastic-free bottles that are 100% recyclable with plant-based and biodegradable packaging.

Using 10 ethically sourced botanicals, the distillery has been recognised as a Net Zero business, which means that their activities have no net IMPACT on the climate from greenhouse emissions. They have achieved this in partnership with a specialist consultancy that assessed every part of their organisation to remove carbon across their supply chain, distilling process, raw materials, and packaging. As a result, they found that their carbon footprint was lower than that of their competitive set. Yet they even went beyond these standards to proactively invest in environmental projects that offset greenhouse emissions by similar amounts.

However, it is the organisation's environmental partnerships that really stand out and make an IMPACT toward the SDGs. According to Mermaid, *'It's estimated that 92% of these meadows have been lost over the last 100 years, damaged by pollution, human activity, reduced water quality, disease, and the effects of climate change. So, we're working with the Hampshire & Isle of Wight Wildlife Trust to monitor and restore seagrass meadows in the waters surrounding our island home.'*[39] In addition to the preservation projects, Mermaid are working with the Ocean Foundation[40] to promote seagrass rejuvenation. They protect the delicate marine ecosystems for coral reefs, turtles, and other endangered species. These ocean-based projects are critical in our fight against climate change. Mermaid also have a partnership With One Seed, a forestry programme that replants forests with a mission to end poverty and hunger.

The complexity of global challenges to achieve the SDGs is far too great for any business to take on independently. Partnership and collaboration can drive real momentum towards 2030, but such efforts require innovative leadership, creativity, and responsibility. Co-creation with industry disruptors, charities, start-ups, government bodies, competitors and social environmental groups is not out of the realm of endless possibilities.

In our quest to protect the planet and drive sustainability, business partnerships can unlock new opportunities and innovation that can transform a brand and wider industry with meaningful IMPACT. Over the last decade, The Collective Dairy have had phenomenal global success with their range of fun and tasty dairy products such as yoghurts, Kefir, and The Collective Kids' range. As a challenger brand, they have disrupted a £1.5 billion[41] commodity category of established brands and engaged shoppers who are often *sleep-walking* through the store aisles. Their cheeky tone of voice, innovative flavours and unique packaging have attracted consumer attention and loyal customers. They are known as the '*dairy shaker uppers.*' So why change?

The Collective Dairy are on a mission to become the most sustainable dairy company in the world. They strive to be a fully carbon neutral business by 2025 with their '*Eat better, do better*' mantra. UK & Europe CEO Sarah Smart says that they can '*lead on how we can change and make change better. Being a challenger brand, we've kind of almost got the permission to do that bit more and that really excites us, to be able to influence and have a net positive IMPACT on the dairy industry and other brands out there. The founders who started the business decided that we kept People, Planet and Profit well balanced in our business... it was part of our business DNA when we were set up and still is.*'[42]

The Collective Dairy launched the world's first carbon neutral yoghurt which has been achieved through carbon offsetting via a partnership with sustainability experts ClimatePartner. From '*Riding on a climate neutral bus, using a climate neutral face cream, taking climate neutral ice cream home with you, or reading a climate neutral book or magazine*' over 4000 companies[43] have collaborated with ClimatePartner. They calculate carbon footprints, rigorously reduce CO2 emissions, and engage in carbon offset projects to compensate for any unavoidable emissions. The result is a climate neutral product that stands for climate action. All clearly labelled and traceable. Sarah says, '*We're working on it with our suppliers, our farmers and communities, and we're actually going to put our money where our mouth is.*'[44]

Today it is essential to stay ahead in the race to net zero. Many business partners in the supply chain are now setting their own targets and expecting the same of their trading partners. Grocery retailer Tesco have pledged to be net zero across their entire supply chain by 2050 and in their own operations by 2035. They have asked suppliers to align to their four key principles to: disclose their current greenhouse gas emissions, establish their own net zero ambitions by the end of 2022, set science-based targets to support the delivery of these ambitions by the end of 2023, and switch to renewable energy now '*as a simple initial win*'.

Tesco's Chief Commercial Officer Ashwin Prasad says *'If we are to avoid the most severe consequences of climate change, urgent, collective action is required to meet the UK's climate goals and shift our economies onto a zero-carbon pathway. We have no time to waste.'*[45]

In 2022, Tesco launched a campaign called *Better Baskets*, which addressed the barriers that conscious consumers face when looking when trying to fill their baskets with healthier choices for people and better options for the planet. Research found that 86% of Tesco shoppers[46] wanted to eat more healthily, with 77%[47] saying that they wanted the supermarket to help them achieve this goal. The *Better Baskets* campaign focussed on foods high in fibre, plant-based options, low and no alcohol drinks, snacks and treats under 100 calories, and products that have reusable, reduced and recyclable packaging.[48] Fifty billion calories have already been removed since 2019 from the Tesco range and they plan to remove 50 billion more by 2025.[49] They have also improved the packaging for more than 1,500 different products and removed 1.6 billion pieces of unnecessary plastic, including multipacks, additional lids, films, and bags.[50] Tesco have partnered up with Jamie Oliver to educate and promote veg-packed recipes. They have also joined forces with WWF as part of their commitment *'to halve the environmental IMPACT of the average UK shopping basket.'*[51]

'Eat better, do better': www.thecollectivedairy.com
Hear The Collective Dairy's Story on
The IMPACT Game Changers™ Podcast:

www.splitsecondltd.com

Partnerships are key for the social and environmental challenges ahead. The Dairy Collective's new range is a great example of a business that has taken a proactive approach to meeting the sustainability challenge. The product is packaged in 100% recyclable pots, made from 100% recycled material. It contains 11% less sugar and is 12.2% below the current category average.[52] *'Giving back has always been a part of our DNA at The Collective,'* says Sarah. *'From creating more sustainable and nutritious products, to giving back to causes we are passionate about – people, the planet and our communities are at the heart of everything we do.'*[53]

Offer Education

Most children have used wax crayons at some point as toddlers, offering hours of fun and creativity for kids and a respite for parents. It is no secret that little ones often have their likes and dislikes, enjoy exploring and may start munching on their crayons now and then. Crayons are generally not considered dangerous. However, many contain ingredients that if ingested in large quantities, could cause illness and issues for children. Pigments, paraffin wax and petroleum could be harmful to kids and the environment as they are not bio-degradable.

Japanese company Mizuiro decided to team up with designer Naoko Kimura[54] to develop a sustainable alternative to everyday crayons. Oyasai Crayons are made from discarded food waste. Leaves, husks and pigments from apples, carrots, yams, onions, corn, cassis, and purple potatoes combined with rice oil and wax make up some of the 10 colours in the pack. Tackling the global food waste epidemic is an urgent call to action as:

- Nearly one-third of the world's food is wasted equalling 1.3 billion tons per year[55]
- 1,000 tons of food is wasted every minute[56]
- Up to 50% of food is lost at the production stage alone[57]
- 1.6 billion tons of raw food is never turned to consumable food to feed the hungry[58]
- 8 million people worldwide suffer from hunger and malnutrition[59]
- Saving just one-fourth of the total global food waste can feed all the world's hungry[60]

Oyasai Crayons teaches lessons on natural sustainable alternatives to existing products, lessons on food waste and purpose-led innovation. This is a brand on a mission do its part to deliver the SDGs, providing a worry-free, eco-friendly triple win for kids, parents, and the planet. How will you educate your consumers and shoppers?

Offer Transformation

'If you want to go quickly, go alone.
If you want to go far, go together.'
– African Proverb

Certain purpose-led partnerships can be the catalysts to transformational change. They accelerate the pace towards the SDGs. They innovate, disrupt, and set common goals to solve some of the world's complex global problems. They action insight, leverage investments and create economies of scale to find sustainable solutions.

When L'Oréal, the world leader in hair and beauty announced its venture with Swiss start-up Gjosa, specialists in unique water-saving solutions, they launched a partnership that could revolutionise the salon industry. How? Together they developed the Water Saver micronisation technology with a showerhead cartridge containing haircare products that could save billions of litres of water annually.

Today the average salons use nearly 700 litres[61] of water every day literally going down the drain. The innovative showerhead from this partnership splits the flow of water to create droplets 10 times[62] smaller which are then accelerated for quicker and more effective rinsing. The technology uses two litres of water per minute compared to eight litres used by standard showerheads, reducing water consumption by 80%.[63] The UN says that *'the costs of wastewater management are greatly outweighed by the benefits to human health, economic development and environmental sustainability – providing new business opportunities and creating more 'green' jobs.'*[64] With a global rollout from 2021–2023 across 10,000 salons, this venture promises universal water and energy savings.[65]

Purpose-led partnerships represent substantial financial growth opportunities for brands and businesses. Finding the right strategic partner can create transformational change by turning a global mission into grassroots, local, social, and environmental action. More importantly, these collaborations are doing good that can deliver the Sustainable Development Goals by 2030.

Chapter Five - PARTNERSHIP Exercise:

Design your IMPACT Partnership™ using the 5 Steps to a Collaborative Strategy:

1. Identify mutual growth opportunities
2. Co-create a long-term purpose-led vision
3. Set up an agile process
4. Collaborate across the full value chain
5. Measure the triple bottom line - People/Planet/Profit

CHAPTER SIX: PURCHASE

'Price is only an issue in the absence of value.'
– Anonymous

Post 2020, consumers are being offered endless choice with up to 82%[1] of them purchasing online, even now that in-person shopping is available. These shoppers with promiscuous spending habits are much harder to track as they navigate their way through the physical and virtual worlds indiscriminately. That's why everyday goods need to fight harder to have a share of voice, consumer resonance and lucrative sales in a crowded marketplace. Some are no longer the 'It' brands they once were and others are simply trying to enter, stay relevant or survive the trading battleground.

The art of brand seduction requires some finesse and a certain level of insight to really understand the would-be customer. Many answers can be found in market data and research but connecting the dots in an ever-changing customer landscape is also critical. Decisions at the point of purchase are made in a matter of seconds. So does your business start with the brand, customer, or purpose?

It is vital to work back from the split-second moment when the shopper is about to choose between one brand over another. This moment provides clues into the barriers and triggers to purchase that offer a wealth of insight for planning, persuasion and ultimately profit. This is a fundamental step that can alter the course of any business.

With the clock ticking towards the 2030 UN global goals, consumer consciousness is being raised in People, Planet, and Profit – not always in that order. Today's customer is looking to make more ethical and sustainable choices when making purchasing decisions. Many are rethinking how they live, shop and act as good global citizens. This conscience is deeply rooted in the health of all people, society, economy, and the planet.

The world has been hearing about the human and environmental challenges for quite some time, but now consumers want to act. According to Edelman's *Trust Barometer* report 68%[2] of consumers believe that they have the power to force corporations to change. In fact, another study by Accenture reports that 62%[3] want companies to take a stand on the social, cultural, environmental, and political issues that they care about the most. Two-thirds[4] of consumers feel that boycotting brands and calling them out on social media will drive change.

Consumers want to make informed purchasing decisions based on brands that align to their values and provide calls to action. Steps can be taken to influence the path to purchase as many of those decisions are made between two and 20 seconds.[5] This is a critical moment when the power of purchase can make a vital IMPACT to your brand. Make every second count.

6.1. PATH TO PURCHASE

In an ideal world, a consumer becomes aware of a brand, sees it, buys it, loves it, buys it again and advocates it. However, when it comes to catching someone's attention on the path-to-purchase, it can be quite a minefield. Despite a compelling brand proposition, there are so many other brands vying for the prospect's attention and spend, it may get lost in the crowd. Therefore, making a clear distinction between consumer behaviour and shopper behaviour is quite critical. Pinpoint the exact moment a decision has been made.

The conventional start point for many companies is to focus on the brand and wait for a consumer response. Yet for the more profitable businesses, understanding the consumer to shopper behaviour on their path-to-purchase is at the heart of their marketing strategy. They ensure that the brand is at the right place at the right time to drive sales conversion and build a lasting loyalty.

Moments of Truth

For years, marketeers have relied on Procter & Gamble's First and Second Moments of Truths (FMOT & SMOT) when shoppers encounter a product, select it, interact with it, and hopefully purchase it. This was the most opportune moment to appeal to them in that split-second moment when they convert a browser into a buyer. Today, in the age of the internet, things are a bit different. Before there is any thought of purchase, there is some sort of a stimulus to get online and research the product for an occasion, replenishment, a need, or a desire.

Google has identified this pre-cursor to the FMOT & SMOT models as the Zero Moment of Truth (ZMOT).[6] It captures the consumer's online research, a stage prior to interacting with a brand and making a buying decision. This is naturally dependant on the category, but a ZMOT goes beyond what the brand chooses to share. It enables shoppers to assess anything and everything that is available on the brand online – from instructional YouTube videos, reviews, promotions, brand experiences, digital ads, social media; the list is endless. They all make an impression on the prospect before a purchasing decision. ZMOT plays a critical role on the path to purchase.

THINK WITH GOOGLE: WINNING THE ZERO MOMENT OF TRUTH:

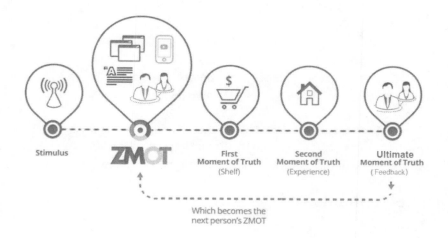

Source: Think with Google

On average, people conduct +100 billion[7] searches a month on Google. From perfume to puppies, to cars and anything one's heart desires, every search is an opportunity to influence a purchasing decision. ZMOT has the power to influence decision-making across a wide spectrum of categories and channels. This is the moment when brands can actively reach out via social media, email marketing, ads and more before the customer even approaches them for more information. A proactive strategy increases the chance of purchase.

ZMOT is followed by the First Moment of Truth (FMOT) when shoppers interact with brands and then actually purchase it. That is the Second Moment of Truth (SMOT). Then the path to purchase leads to an Ultimate Moment of Truth (UMOT), which is feedback based on customer experience. Positive or negative feedback is shared about how a customer feels about the product, brand, or company. They can choose to post it as online reviews, send their thoughts to the brand-owner or simply share it with friends and family. The rich insight that comes out of the Ultimate Moment of Truth (UMOT) stage is the gold dust that can steer a brand in the right direction (when properly implemented) to drive commercial success.

So how to implement this model in practical terms?

- Engage prospects via digital touch points and social media
- Harness E-Commerce, Mobile-Commerce, and Social-Commerce capabilities
- Inspire and educate with content to facilitate purchasing decisions and experiences
- Capture, act and respond to customer feedback
- Be transparent to build long-term loyalty

Businesses must explore their own unique moments of truth within their customer journeys and seek to improve these moments in meaningful ways through their marketing and customer experience campaigns.

Micro-Moments

Despite appearances, the path to purchase is no longer linear. Consumers are faced with a myriad of messages, channel options and decisions before they even get into the shopper mindset. An individual's customer journey is defined by all the interactions he/she has with a brand before making any purchase. Every brand interaction with apps, ads, emails, social media, etc., that engages the would-be customer on their journey through a series of channels is defined as *micro-moments*[8] a term coined by Google. These *micro-moments* provide brands with the opportunities to proactively engage and build relationships with potential shoppers, passengers, patients, guests, employees, etc. depending on the business's target prospect and channel.

Although an individual's perception is that it is one journey with one brand, there may be various departments within an organisation that they interact with such as sales, marketing, customer service, loyalty teams, etc. To demonstrate this, go back to when you bought your last smartphone through your mobile phone provider. You may have rung them up knowing that you were due for an upgrade and after some negotiations with the sales team, anticipated a next-day delivery of the new device. Twenty-four hours later, you find that there is no text update, no email and above all no phone. The aggravation leads you to ring the provider and investigate the delivery status. You are then tossed around from department to department whilst being put on hold for hours and having to repeat your case over and over, with no follow-up and no phone. Frustrating right?

The customer experience on that particular journey is nothing short of unacceptable. Every micro-moment on that journey has led to brand dissatisfaction. Mapping out the micro-moments is vital before engaging prospects in order to maximise the brand's opportunities. Now how would you harness the micro-moments for your potential customer?

Moments They Will Remember

You may think that only larger organisations have the capability to tailor the micro-moments on the customer journey. However big or small, companies that put customer experience first in all the micro-moments, always win.

One such example is The English Cream Team Company, where founder Jane Malyon anchors her business values on '*do what you say you are going to do*'. Simple but effective. Jane's thriving e-commerce company delivers and welcomes guests to have a quintessential English cream tea experience wherever they are in the country. Jane and her team believe that attention to detail in exceeding the customer's expectations at every stage of the journey will bring them back time and again.

When mapping out the customer journey, Jane found that she had an added layer of complexity. The shopper making the purchase was not always the end consumer, because they were gifting her products and experiences to others. So, capturing the insight from both parties was essential in being able to deliver service excellence at every micro-moment.

From her YouTube channel, to personalised handwritten notes, to sending orders in four-hour taxi rides, to made-to-order cream teas at her *Sconery*, to bespoke corporate hospitality ... tapping into the micro-moments on the customer's journey has been key to Jane's commercial success. She has pushed the boundaries of customer engagement by catering to her prospects through multiple touch points so that they can immerse themselves in an authentic cream tea experience that they will treasure.

Yet Jane is on a bigger mission. In her TEDx talk '*How afternoon tea could save the world*'[9], she says that her business is aligned to *SDG #16 Peace, Justice and Strong Institutions*. She believes that this ritual brings people together, creates a sense of camaraderie and an opportunity for rapport building. Jane states that sharing and getting to know each other's experiences actually reduces prejudices. '*These customs literally melt away age, race, socio-economic status.*'[10] She says building relationships is vital in any environment, especially in business. So, it's best to create memorable moments with customers that they will come back for again and again.

'Delivering a Fresh Take on Tradition': www.englishcreamtea.com
Hear ECT's Story on The IMPACT Game Changers™ Podcast:

www.splitsecondltd.com

6.2. POINT OF PURCHASE

The point of purchase is the moment where all the planning meets the powers of persuasion to tip the scales and sales in your favour. Traditionally, brands have used various tools and tactics to entice the would-be customer. However, today's savvy conscious shopper is not easily swayed by short-lived gratification. They want genuine experiences and build trust with the brands that make a positive, lasting IMPACT.

If we want to live in a world where businesses are a force for good to attain the Sustainable Development Goals (SDGs), then we have to act fast and act now. In the past, potential prospects on the path to purchase were targeted with two key questions: *'did they have an intention to purchase?'* and *'did they actually purchase?'* So, what may have held them back?

Studies from across the globe highlight some revealing insight from conscious consumers:

- 62% want companies to reduce plastic and improve the state of the planet[11]
- 62% believe that a company's ethics and authenticity influence purchasing decisions[12]
- 65% want to see employees treated well[13]
- 71% want to do more to be sustainable at home[14]
- 74% want more transparency on product sourcing, and elimination of animal-testing[15]
- 76% want brands that are committed to using good-quality ingredients[16]
- 90% would switch to sustainable brands if price and quality were equal[17]

Today's conscious consumers want to interact, experience and purchase brands that align to their principles, but more importantly action them. Brands and businesses can lead the way with purpose, responding to what consumers are asking for and delivering on the SDGs. It's time to give consumers a choice by guiding them seamlessly on how and where and what to shop for.

How We Shop

Imagine your target customer at the point of a purchase about to select a competitor's brand within a matter of seconds. You have a great brand that people desire, yet somehow that desire is not converting into sales. With smart phones as the new shopping accessory, 82%[18] turn to their device for web advice. One in four shoppers[19] change their minds while still in the queue. This is the reality facing most brands today.

Creating Google's '*I-want-to-buy moments*' for prospects in a 24/7 world has its challenges. Purchasing decisions have become complex. Is price, branding and complexity preventing the purchase? Or is it something else? Understanding and influencing the barriers and triggers behind those decisions can unlock a wealth of insight and commercial growth.

In order to truly tap into the Zero Moment of Truth (ZMOT) when someone begins to interact with a particular category and the brands within it, one has to be able to influence their purchasing decision. ZMOT is the stage where someone begins to research, read reviews, evaluate competitors, and educate themselves on something they are considering buying. This is a pivotal moment in how we shop.

7-11-4

The secret is in three little numbers: 7-11-4[20]. According to Google, these are the most important numbers to win customers. People need seven hours of interaction at eleven touch points in four different locations before they make a purchase. It sounds challenging but having a website or brochure is simply no longer enough.

Seven hours of interaction could be on social media platforms such as Instagram Lives, Facebook workshops, YouTube channels, blogs, podcasts, and other digital content that will let the prospect get to know you and your business. Eleven touch points could include listening to a podcast once, visiting the website three times, reading a blog and a testimonial, visiting a Facebook page three times, reading a published article then calling for a chat or quotation, depending on the category. Spreading the digital content across a minimum of four locations – a website, social media accounts, online store, YouTube demos, networking events, interviews, physical office, or shop, etc. – will enhance the brand's credibility and customer experience.

Understanding how we shop is key to engaging prospects. Developing and re-purposing hours of content for the customer journey will expand a business's footprint. The 7-11-4 approach can influence purchasing decisions in the ZMOT to create the ultimate customer magnet.

Where We Shop

We don't shop the way our grandparents used to. They typically went to one or two merchants for a product or service as that was all they had. Today, we have endless choice in the number of distribution channels, business models and touch points that are constantly evolving. The dot.com boom changed the way we shopped forever. Compared to pre-pandemic levels, 2020 accelerated the growth of e-commerce with UK sales volumes up by 46%[21] vs 2019.

Mobile first shopping has been in play for several years now, with Google prioritising mobile websites in response to their popularity. However, just when we think we have seen it all, along comes a new technology to surpass the last. Voice shopping was set to explode to £3.5 billion[22] in the UK by the end of 2022. With 10%[23] of households already in possession of smart speakers, this figure is set to increase to 50%[24], with 44%[25] using the devices to shop. Yet technology is just one of the elements that is changing 'where' we shop.

Retailers are always looking for new ways to attract shoppers: price, packaging, and products. Today, many of them are making a commitment to sustainability and being more purpose-led. Luxury department store Selfridges are on a mission to re-invent retail. They believe that they 'can create a profitable business that respects our world, builds trust and embodies creativity and innovation.' They have launched Project Earth, which in their words 'is an exploration into how we can change the way we shop by 2025. We believe that by driving a transition to more sustainable materials, exploring new business models, and challenging the mindsets of our partners and customers as well as our own teams, we can offer an alternative perspective on retail and create a sustainable future.'[26]

Most companies have a Corporate Social Responsibility (CSR), Sustainability or Environmental, Social Governance (ESG) plan in place these days. However, those who make a public declaration of their commitment are the ones who grow in popularity and profit. UK department store and owner of Waitrose supermarket, The John Lewis Partnership, have mapped out a purpose-led strategy that highlights 'The themes of tackling inequality, of wellbeing and sustainable living will be at its core.'[27] According to the Guardian newspaper, this mission is supported by their Chairman Sharon White who believes that these themes are extremely relevant, in post-pandemic times of economic uncertainty and social inequality. In their quest to reduce plastic waste, they had over 100 specialist start-ups[28] pitching ideas on alternative packaging, sustainable materials, recycling, and plastic-free products. To date, they have reduced 65% of black plastic food packaging[29], removed all disposable takeaway coffee cups – saving 52 million cups a year[30] – and have alternatively introduced new, durable carrier bags made from 70% recycled material.[31]

Others exhibit purpose at the point of purchase to entice shoppers. UK grocery retailer Waitrose and Boots pharmacy have created virtual shelves to stock and sell B Corporation certified goods. B Corp brands balance purpose and profit. They are legally required to consider the IMPACT of their decisions on their workers, customers, suppliers, community, and the environment. Retailers that carry these products demonstrate their commitment, values, and partnerships as a positive force for good to their existing and prospective customers. They also enable conscious consumers to find purpose-led brands more easily, making these retailers a purchase destination. In other words, giving shoppers a meaningful reason to go in and spend.

A research study by the Capgemini Research Institute (Consumer Products and Retail: How sustainability is fundamentally changing consumer preferences) highlighted that businesses are lagging behind the conscious consumers' perspective of what 'good' sustainability looks like. They surveyed 7,500 consumers and 750 large organisations and spoke with sustainability leads from large organisations 'to understand how sustainability influences consumers' purchasing patterns and how organisations are responding.'[32] The research found that eight out of ten consumers[33] are making sustainability-based purchase choices. Organisations are unaware how quickly consumer preferences and loyalty are evolving towards sustainability. They can maximise key opportunities on scaling sustainability to drive loyalty, employee churn, commercial growth and ESG performance metrics. According to the study *'A significant majority of consumers (79%) are changing their purchase preferences based on sustainability. This contrasts sharply with 36% of organisations who believe consumers are willing to make this change in their choices/preferences based on social or environmental IMPACT. Such a gap represents a risk of ~6% of brands and retailers' revenue if unaddressed.'*[34] The report also found:

SUSTAINABILITY IMPACTS CONSUMERS' PURCHASE PREFERENCES AND MAKES THEM HAPPY:

- 64% of consumers say buying sustainable products makes them feel happy when shopping
- 52% of consumers feel an emotional connection with a product or organization which is sustainable
- 79% of consumers are changing purchase preference based on the social or environmental impact of their purchases[35]

Source: Capgemini Research Institute, "Consumer Products and Retail: How sustainability is fundamentally changing consumer preferences" July 2020

Paul Hargreaves, CEO of Cotswold Fayre & Flourish, and author of *Forces for Good* and *The Fourth Bottom Line*, has responded to these consumer needs by bringing them to life. As leader of a B Corp food wholesale and retailing business, Paul says that *'customers really do want to deal with good companies that are doing their utmost for positive IMPACT. As a company we have secured two large chunks of business within the last year worth several million pounds where our position and action on environment issues was a significant factor for those making the buying decisions.'*[36] As part of Paul's aim to become net zero by 2030 (20 years earlier than the UK government), his business has already become carbon neutral.

They have reduced their carbon emissions by 46% and are offsetting the rest. He says, *'As a distribution company delivering 1.5 million cases of product a year, this was a large offset bill which will reduce as we completely eliminate carbon from our supply chain. Yes, it is true that being better for the environment does cost money. With consumers making better choices, this extra money spent will be recouped in many cases. It certainly has for us; in those two years our revenues increased by more than 50% and our profits more than doubled.*[37] Paul attributes his success to his people, the cornerstone of his book *The Fourth Bottom Line* in which he describes how to be a more compassionate leader that can make a meaningful difference. This inspiring style of leadership opposes injustice and strives to make the world a better place.

'We are a speciality and fine food wholesaler, delivering ambient and chilled products to the retail sector. A certified B Corporation, using our business as a force for good to benefit both People and Planet.': www.cotswold-fayre.co.uk
Hear Cotswold Fayre's Story on
The IMPACT Game Changers™ Podcast:

www.splitsecondltd.com

What We Shop

Purchasing behaviour keeps changing as consumer confidence ebbs and flows. Since the pandemic, the economy (88%) and personal health (82%)[38] have been the two main concerns for the UK general public. Some have felt fearful and anxious, whilst others have taken a more nonchalant business-as-usual approach. Yet one thing is certain, consumers have become more conscious of the economy, health, family and friends, society, and the planet. These conscious consumers have re-evaluated their purchasing behaviours and often seek to make a positive

IMPACT in their lives and beyond, by choosing brands and businesses that best align to their personal values. According to Capgemini, there is a *'significant gap between the perception and practice of sustainability'* as consumers are not always aware of their purchase IMPACT on the planet:

- 78% of consumers who purchase a bar of chocolate are unaware that it takes one thousand litres of water to produce one chocolate bar.
- 68% of consumers who purchased a burger are unaware that the average burger patty results in more carbon emissions than driving 15 km in a large car.
- 60% of consumers who order online delivery are unaware that nearly one-third of solid waste in the US comes from e-commerce packaging.[39]

ORGANISATIONS MUST ALIGN TO NEW CONSUMER SUSTAINABLE PREFERENCES

- 24% of organisations say their consumers are willing to switch from well-known brand(s) to lesser known brand(s) which they perceive as sustainable.
- 53% of consumers say they have switched to lesser known brands and organisations whose products/services they perceive as sustainable.[40]

Source: Capgemini Research Institute, "Consumer Products and Retail: How sustainability is fundamentally changing consumer preferences" July 2020

Whether we are shopping habitually, seeking variety, looking for instant or delayed gratification, price and quality are constant factors that determine what we shop for. However, as conscious consumers we are more mindful and strive to be more sustainable, buy less, reduce waste, and make a purposeful contribution through our purchases. Brands and businesses must appeal to this new consciousness by integrating some of the key attributes in their offer.

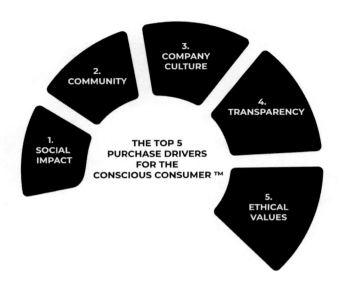

1. **Social IMPACT:** Acknowledge the effect on people and society as a result of action or inaction, positive or negative. Studies have found that 51%[41] of global consumers will pay extra for products and services committed to positive social and environmental IMPACT.

2. **Community:** Find genuine ways to connect and build communities. About 80%[42] of consumers feel more connected to their communities than ever before.

3. **Company Culture:** Give people a behind-the-scenes peek into brands and businesses they currently or plan to purchase. More specifically, 66% want to see a positive company culture and 65%[43] expect them to deliver on promises made to their employees.

4. **Transparency:** Share the company's strategy and operations openly. Sixty-six percent of consumers are more likely to be attracted to a brand that shares details on raw materials, supply chains, business partners, customer satisfaction and the IMPACT made on society and the planet.

5. **Ethical Values:** Describe the company's values. Conscious consumers (62%)[44] want businesses to share their values in everything they do, to win hearts and minds.

Consumers reward authenticity, leadership, and integrity. When companies demonstrate these qualities, they earn trust, purchase, and loyalty. One such brand that has had phenomenal success with consumers is Pip & Nut. Chief 'Squirrel' Pippa Murray says, *'As a business, we want to take responsibility for our IMPACT on the world around us. This means looking at the people within our business, the communities we interact with, and the environment.'*[45]

The seed of the Pip & Nut concept was first planted back in 2013, when Pippa was making her own nut butters as a healthy fuel for her marathon training. In less than a decade, she has built one of UK's leading FMCG brands. Pippa attributes her success to seven strategic drivers that have accelerated commercial growth for her value IMPACT proposition:

- Put purpose alongside profit
- Be distinctive to disrupt
- More attitude over experience
- Focus on building a community
- Innovate to keep your brand fresh
- Surround yourself with the best business partners
- Celebrate the big and small moments

Pippa always had a clear vision for her brand to become a national and eventually an international success. The company's values reflect the business's key attributes: playful, honest, ambitious and accessible. Business highlights include:

- They have never nor will they ever use palm oil in their products
- They have a happy team of 'squirrels' (that's employees to you and I)
- Every 'squirrel' volunteers in local communities[46]

Pippa's journey from kitchen to retail has made Pip & Nut a household brand, winner of many industry awards and become a force for good.

'Help people love the food that loves them and the planet':
www.pipandnut.com
Hear Pip & Nut's Story on The IMPACT Game Changers™ Podcast:

www.splitsecondltd.com

6.3.   PATH TO PURPOSE

Purpose starts with values. It is an opportunity to create value for internal stakeholders, customers, society, and the planet. Companies that successfully activate their purpose reap financial and purposeful rewards. Every decision companies take, centres on their core purpose to deliver the Sustainable Development Goals (SDGs).

In today's competitive landscape, prospects make more informed purchasing decisions and welcome transparency and authenticity. They seek out brands that can deliver tangible results that truly make a positive lasting IMPACT. A purpose-led approach allows companies to clearly activate, articulate and accelerate how the product or service can entice the conscious consumer and do good in the world.

Activate Purpose

The purpose of business is changing. In the past, the main objective was to solely deliver profit, but today businesses must have more meaning. The leadership team puts the strategy, mission, and actions in motion to bring their organisation's values to life.

Activating purpose, internally and externally, is essential to influence the business culture, shareholders, industry bodies, existing and would-be customers by:

- Sharing the business's authentic purpose and values
- The IMPACT the brand or business can make towards the SDGs
- Taking purpose-driven action to deliver on the promise

Businesses must identify the challenges of today to build the IMPACT Brands™ of tomorrow.

Articulate Purpose

'Nothing is lost, nothing is created, everything is transformed.'
– Antoine Lavoisier

Having a purpose on its own is not enough. One has to articulate it to inspire employees, customers and communities that together will drive a positive change. Purpose can be expressed in many ways, but actions always speak louder than words. The intersection of what a business says and does towards people and the planet is where a positive lasting IMPACT can be made.

IMPACT Brands™ generate business and socio-economic value. These brands and businesses not only articulate, execute, and engage prospects with creative campaigns, but they also create IMPACT Experiences™. By designing a 360° environment, prospects are able to immerse themselves in purpose-led brands and ideally become advocates for them.

Fashion retailer The United Colours of Benetton have 'articulated' their purpose in the form of a sustainable concept store in Florence, Italy. Conscious consumers can purchase upcycled natural materials whilst walking around this state-of-the-art store on gravel flooring from the river Piave with waste beech wood from the 2018 storm that hit the Veneto region. The walls are covered in mineral paints that *'reduce pollutants in the environment'*.[47] The interiors are stitched from textile scraps, display units are made from used buttons' compound, and energy-saving technologies reduce consumption by 20%. Mannequins and shelving are constructed from Rossino, a material created from upcycled mixed textile fibres. This store is a culmination of their mission '*to become a model for sustainable fashion – not only in Italy but throughout the entire world.*'[48]

The SDGs are a mandate that call on everyone to progress the sustainability and socio-economic agenda through innovation, investment, and ethical practices. By articulating them, consumer consciousness is raised through purpose-led marketing and business models to build customer relationships, drive purchase and loyalty. Thus, the SDGs can be ultimately manifested.

Accelerate Purpose

Cutting through the noise in a busy marketplace, battling for mind share, wallet share, and market share is an enormous challenge. However, translating purpose into IMPACT can uncover opportunities that will accelerate growth, deliver the SDGs, and celebrate brands with compassion and shared values. The focus for IMPACT Game Changers™ is on value creation for customers – blue-sky thinking that sets new precedents to do the right thing.

What sets IMPACT Game Changers™ apart is:

- They respond to the needs of the conscious consumer
- They collaborate and invest in ethical and sustainable innovation
- They take risks and break with convention as part of their DNA

Founded in 1954, American fast-food chain Burger King has almost 18,000 outlets in 100 countries and is the world's second largest-burger chain. Known for its signature grilled Whopper® and sense of humour in advertising campaigns, the brand has always had its finger on the pop culture pulse. With 64%[49] of consumers saying that brands have a responsibility to listen to customers' concerns and complaints, Burger King have been no exception. They have accelerated their vegan strategy and innovation pipeline by opening their first entirely plant-based restaurant for a limited time in Cologne, Germany. The chain partnered up with Dutch brand The Vegetarian Butcher® to serve a vegan-only menu.

Burger King's plant-based trial has resulted in the launch of the Whopper® Vegetal in Mexico, the plant-based Whopper® in China, and a variety of vegan options at Burger King's United Kingdom locations. UK CEO Alasdair Murdoch told Veg News that the chain's UK menu *'is expected to become 50% plant-based by 2031 as the chain continues to replace meat with fully vegan options.'*[50] Global sales skyrocketed by an additional +30% when the plant-based range was introduced. It drove customer spend and traffic, and their sales were up +26% ahead of their key rival McDonald's.[51] The Impossible Whopper® requires half the land of an animal-based beef burger, one-quarter of the water and generates one-eighth of the greenhouse gas emissions.[52]

In truth, many brands will likely have to rip up their marketing playbook and radically evolve their customer and sustainability strategies to respond to the ever-changing landscape. The good news is that now, more than ever, successful brands no longer need to be only conceived in giant conglomerates. They can flourish by tapping into the target prospect's behaviours, accelerate their purpose and innovate accordingly. To win in this marketplace, one has to understand the new rules and to be steps ahead of target prospects by anticipating their needs. Businesses can leverage the power of purchase with a path-to-purpose.

'Earth provides enough to satisfy every man's need,
but not every man's greed.'
– Mahatma Gandhi

Chapter Six - PURCHASE Exercise:

Map out the purchase drivers for your brand and business:

Score Your IMPACT:

Take the next action step on your own IMPACT Roadmap and complete **The IMPACT Roadmap Scorecard™**.

Be Part of the Solution. Start an IMPACT Revolution™.

www.splitsecondltd.com

STEP 3 – PROFIT with IMPACT™

'When you are led by values, it doesn't cost your business, it helps your business.'
—Jerry Greenfield, Ben & Jerry's

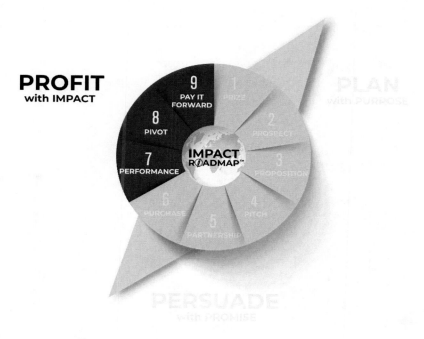

According to authors Jim Collins and Jerry Porras, who wrote *Built to Last* which analysed *visionary* companies over a 70-year period, purpose-led organisations deliver six times[1] more returns than those solely focussed on profit. These companies win business through their authenticity and tenacity to make the world a better place – a distinct competitive advantage. As we look to harness the Sustainable Development Goals' $12 trillion a year opportunity, it's time to redefine the bottom line.

The conventional view of business is only to generate a profit – the more the better, driven strictly by financial performance. Capitalism has created corporate titans, global conglomerates, and billionaires like never before. With the arrival of digital transformation and disruptive practices, businesses have had to balance keeping up with change and delivering a profit. Yet this equation fails to capture a more meaningful purpose for people and the planet.

A Harvard Business Review study revealed that although 90%[2] of executives say they understand the importance of purpose, only 46%[3] put it into practice. However, integrating employee, customer, ethical, environmental and SDG benchmarks into a company strategy can transform organisational capability, purpose, and profit. To do this, companies must stay on top of their performance, pivot if necessary, and pay it forward as forces for good.

CHAPTER SEVEN: PERFORMANCE

'In sport, progress is only ever made when performance is measured, whether it be against others or oneself. Without an indicator of performance to challenge yourself with, as a human being you will find a way to not fully commit. With a performance indicator there are no hiding places. Our performances take place on a global stage: the world is watching and judging. The pressure is immense, but the rewards are astronomical. When the pressure to perform is on, you find a way. With the mindset of an elite sportsman looking for any performance gains, one can always find an advantage, even a small advantage, over your rivals. The world of business is no different.'
– Neil Fachie MBE, Paralympic Gold Medal Cyclist and Author

Whether your business is a start-up, looking to scale-up or level-up, tracking and evaluating performance are imperative to success. Business performance metrics, KPIs, and customer feedback guide progress towards the intended goals. They pinpoint whether the business is on or off-track in an ever-changing marketplace and it is people and purpose that truly determine the endgame.

No one can deny that the world is changing and is more connected than ever before. Purpose beyond profit is not just for charities anymore. It is being endorsed by consumers, brands, and business leaders. Studies prove that purpose-driven brands focussed on improving the quality of life outperform the stock market by 120%.[1] They have also seen their valuation surge by 175% over the past 12 years, versus a 70% growth rate[2] for lethargic brands without a mission. These purposeful organisations also surpass the market by 42%[3] in their financial performance. In fact, certified B Corp businesses in the UK are growing at a staggering 28 times faster than the national economic growth of 0.5%.[4] Leading B Corp Fast-Moving Consumer Goods brands grew on average 21% in 2017, compared to a national average of 3% across their respective sectors.[5]

Performance metrics tell a very clear story. Today, consumers seek out purpose-led IMPACT brands™ and are more loyal to them. Purpose-led IMPACT workforces increase productivity, wellbeing, and allegiance. Purpose-led IMPACT businesses outperform the market. With the

Sustainable Development Goals' (SDGs) looming 2030 deadline, this trend is only going to grow. Strategic and operational performance measures of success enable organisations to monitor the metrics that matter.

7.1.   MEASURES OF SUCCESS

Growing businesses need to be closely and carefully managed to ensure success, investment, and scale. While some small businesses can run themselves without formal metrics and targets, others will cease to exist without them. Many brand owners find that as their businesses grow, the gap between the strategic and operational functions can sometimes widen due to a lack of performance metrics in place.

Tracking and evaluation provide vital information about business performance and the actions required towards achieving strategic goals. They serve as navigation tools that can alert the organisation if it is headed in the right or wrong direction vs. the projected forecast. Internal and external alignment on key performance indicators (KPIs) are vital to success.

Performance Priorities

Collecting, analysing, and reporting performance metrics are integral to an organisation's success. These analytics must be accessible, interactive, and insightful in order to drive change. Yet before setting up any reports, the organisation must determine its business priorities.

7 BUSINESS PERFORMANCE PRIORITY PRINCIPLES™

01 DEFINE THE PERFORMANCE PRIORITY LOOK OF SUCCESS

REVIEW KEY PERFORMANCE INDICATORS (KPIs) **02**

03 ALIGN THE METRICS / UNITS TO THE INDUSTRY

DEVELOP SCORECARDS AND DASHBOARDS **04**

05 TRACK & MEASURE PROGRESS

GATHER MARKET INTELLIGENCE **06**

07 CONDUCT BUSINESS HEALTH CHECKS

7 BUSINESS PERFORMANCE PRIORITY PRINCIPLES™:

1. **Define the Performance Priority Look of Success:**
   - Financial – Sales, spend, profit margins, etc.
   - Customer Acquisition – Attracting prospects or improving satisfaction/loyalty
   - Products and Services – Brand extensions, New Product Development (NPD), etc.
   - Quality – Achieving quality standards accreditations
   - Technology – Introducing new technology to drive efficiency
   - Operations – Processes, production, upgrading premises, etc.
   - Talent – Recruitment and capability development
   - ESG – Deliver Environmental, Social Corporate Governance.

2. **Review Key Performance Indicators (KPIs)** that were set at the *Plan* stage as results will be directly linked to current business performance. A clear one-page strategy is a good start point for defining and designing KPIs. Identify the questions your business needs answered and the data requirements to interpret the performance.

3. **Align the Metrics/Units to the Industry** as they will vary by sector (value, volume, etc.).

4. **Develop Scorecards and Dashboards** for consistent evaluation.

5. **Track & Measure Progress** between the business goals and day-to-day operations by collecting the relevant data to provide an accurate picture of business performance.

6. **Gather Market Trend Intelligence** to evaluate competitors, new product development (NPD), customers, shoppers and wider marketplace that will provide vital clues of the direction the wider marketplace is headed in. The insight will ultimately enable the business to pivot growth strategies and best practice.

7. **Conduct Business Health Checks** for internal and external stakeholders on a regular basis to answer the key 'so what?' with

tangible actions aligned to business KPIs and SDG IMPACT that will deliver sustainable growth.

Despite how critical it is to track and evaluate business performance, many companies simply do not do it. From large global blue-chips, SMEs to start-ups, people often shy away from a task that may shatter the illusion of success. They are either intimidated or uninterested and, in some cases deny the facts, but numbers don't lie. Performance assessments are powerful tools that inform, educate, and drive a clear call to action. If acted upon, they ensure long-term profitable performances.

S.M.A.R.T. Priorities

Once the priorities have been identified, they can be turned into S.M.A.R.T. (Specific, Measurable, Attainable, Relevant, Time-based) objectives. Vague ambitions result in poor performance. These priorities must be achievable, realistic and timebound.

Some S.M.A.R.T. examples are:

- *'To achieve a 35% net profit by November 30th from online sales ...'*
- *'To recruit three new people in marketing by January ...'*
- *'To reduce our plastic consumption by 28% by 2024 ...'*

The objectives can also be based directly on the UN's Sustainable Development Goals, specific targets and indicators as listed on: https://sustainabledevelopment.un.org/content/documents/11803Official-List-of-Proposed-SDG-Indicators.pdf[6]

For instance, *SDG#8 Decent Work and Economic Growth*[7] promotes sustained, inclusive and sustainable economic growth, full and productive employment, and decent work for all:

'8.8 To protect labour rights and promote safe and secure working environments for all workers, including migrant workers, in particular women migrants, and those in precarious employment by 2025.'[8]

People must be able to articulate, action and measure S.M.A.R.T. goals to assess the progress towards the desired outcome.

Assign Priorities

In order for the priorities to be brought to life, they must be assigned to key stakeholders and functions within the organisation. There must be regular proactive updates to understand the pace and progress towards business priorities and objectives. Assigning the priorities will ensure accountability and action to deliver the goals.

7.2.   MONITOR FOR MOMENTUM

'A recommitment by governments, cities, businesses, and industries to ensure that the recovery reduces carbon emissions, conserves natural resources, creates better jobs, advances gender equality and tackles growing poverty and inequalities is a further imperative ... A brighter future is possible. We must use the crisis to transform our world, deliver on the 2030 agenda, and keep our promise to current and future generations.'
– António Guterres Secretary-General of the United Nations

By understanding performance metrics, one can start to communicate in a common language internally and externally. The metrics should include category and brand performance to pricing, promotions, availability, distribution, KPIs, targets and the business IMPACT on people, community, and planet. This rich insight can inform and navigate every strategic decision in the organisation to deliver an effective performance.

THE 3 BURNING PERFORMANCE QUESTIONS EVERY BUSINESS MUST ASK:

The 'What?' Analyse the performance data sets in question.

The 'Why?' Understand the key drivers behind the performance in a given period.

... And the 'So What?' Act on the insight implications to stay ahead of the market.

Whether it is market research, product research, market positioning, customer reviews, or any other data, organisations will be empowered to give themselves a competitive edge. Collecting and organising data leads to stronger and strategic decision-making. Be under no illusion that your company is the exception to the rule where performance analysis is not required.

The 'What?'

Business performance can be assessed in many ways: sales, market share, repeat business, recruitment, production costs, staff turnover, ROI on marketing spend, brand awareness, social media engagement, etc. However, long-term profitability is the goal for most businesses. Even though there are a number of financial metrics as businesses expand, cash flow still plays a fundamental role during the growth phase. So, one must ensure a balance between spend and profits.

No matter the market sector, category or brand, the priority is to focus on quantifiable data that can be measured over time. Quantifiable data answers questions such as '*what is the current performance*?' with answers such as '*sales are down by 2%*'. It is a descriptive analysis that looks at past data and tells us what happened. It is often used to track Key Performance Indicators (KPIs), revenue, sales, and more. While sales and financial data are the most widely used, some non-financial measures can be just as illuminating such as customer experience scorecards which may have an effect on the overall performance.

The 'Why?'

When you find out that the '*sales performance is down by 2%*', does it tell you why? Once data analysis shows that something negative or positive has happened, diagnostic analysis provides clues as to why it happened. Understanding the number of customers that have purchased in a given period, how often they purchased, amount they purchased, amount they spent and whether they purchased again, all provide critical clues on business performance.

Since customer acquisition and retention are key for any business, it is worth stepping into their shoes and getting to know them. Customer satisfaction feedback and loyalty are essential factors that determine a company's financial performance. They can be directly linked to various business KPIs such as an innovation pipeline, customer experience, increased market share, pricing, marketing, and overall business strategy.

The 'So What?'

Imagine reviewing the sales figures and finding that on average, the business is selling £50,000 worth of products and services a week. On the surface it may look like a good performance, surpassing expectations. However, on closer inspection, the numbers tell a different story.

The overall category is down. If the category is down, then it is just a matter of time till the brand will suffer the same fate. Since data can be cut in many ways, upon investigation there are several underlying potential possibilities. Perhaps people are buying less often, spending less, or switching to other categories? Whatever the reason, the implications are critical. Context is key and it is up to every business to investigate their performance to answer the 'so what?' and make informed choices.

Predictive data analysis enables organisations to future-proof themselves against potential threats. This type of research is derived from past data used to forecast long-term scenarios for a plan of action. It enables organisations to make strategic decisions for long-term sustainable growth, have a greater competitive edge and customer loyalty. If a business can demonstrate all three, then a prosperous future is in sight.

7.3. METRICS THAT MATTER

External conditions can affect internal performance – especially if one is out of touch with the industry climate and cannot change course if required. Comparing and contrasting data and insight from different sources provide an accurate view of an ever-changing landscape. It is the ultimate business barometer that measures the Return on Investment (ROI).

The ROI is fundamental to any business and is not always a given, because data alone will not get you there. The journey requires patience and big-picture strategic thinking as well as getting into the minutia of detail. Many companies equate data reports with valuable insight. This can be misleading. Insight can only be extracted by connecting the dots, testing hypotheses, using intuition and experience.

Sadly, the organisations that rely solely on data rarely seem to make a dent in the marketplace or win against competitors. Market leaders not only interrogate the data and extract the insight but set themselves on a performance trajectory that gives them the foresight on how to stay ahead, become centres of excellence, and deliver a sustainable ROI. Yet in order to truly secure customer loyalty in a precarious climate, brands must demonstrate their purpose-led IMPACT to win hearts, minds, and wallets.

IMPACT REPORTING

Companies perform better when they align themselves to their industry sector SDGs. This is corroborated by a study of 74%[9] of citizens who say that they are more likely to use goods and services from organisations engaged with the SDGs. By aligning their corporate strategy, KPIs and SDG targets, organisations can start to connect the dots to achieve their business and global goals.

IMPACT reporting clearly shows the positive change a business's intervention has on its profit by going beyond to people and planet. This report is equivalent to a financial report that makes the organisation accountable for their social and environmental actions. First and foremost, the key is to have a clear IMPACT measurement model.

John Elkington's Triple Bottom Line (TBL) model captures and measures progress on People, Planet, and Profit.[10] The IMPACT report should be transparent and accountable. Yet measuring sustainability can be a challenge as there is no universal performance metric. In many ways, this is an advantage, as it allows organisations to adapt the model to their own business, processes, projects, geographies, and infrastructure. Data and insight are at the heart of measuring the SDGs through three key lenses: People, Planet, and Profit.

People IMPACT

The first lens of the triple bottom line highlights a business's societal IMPACT and its commitment to people. For decades, conventional organisations have focussed on company shareholder value as the key measure of success. Yet over time, forward-looking businesses have begun to embrace and integrate a wider set of stakeholders into their strategic planning such as: employees, customers, supply chain, charities, and broader society with common purpose-led goals.

A business's IMPACT on the people of a specific community or region requires certain metrics in place depending on the nature of the project, campaign, or initiative such as:

- Embedding ethical business practices
- Forming purpose-led partnerships
- Leading action on diversity and equality
- Being a pillar in the community
- Taking corporate social responsibility

Over recent years, there has been a rise in people's expressed importance to living life with a sense of purpose: 80% in 2016, 89% in 2017, 91% in 2018,[11] so organisations must step up and exceed those expectations. Another study conducted by *Great Place to Work* reports that *'employees who feel that their job has a special meaning: this is not 'just a job' are 4 times more likely to give extra, 11 times more committed to staying with their organisations and are 14 times more likely to look forward to coming to work than employees at peer companies.'*[12] Implementing and measuring progress on people initiatives means that organisations must audit their social programs, review their policies and survey internal and external stakeholders to benchmark their IMPACT.

Planet IMPACT

'The earth has music for those who listen.'
– William Shakespeare

Since the industrial revolution, giant corporations have generated an unprecedented amount of pollution that has been a major contributor to the climate crisis. Over 200 of the largest global companies report more than $1 trillion[13] in climate risk, much of which is likely to come into effect within the next five years – but how will this risk be mitigated? Over a hundred companies in the energy sector alone are responsible for 71% of industrial carbon emissions.[14] According to 2020 research by Harvard Business School, there is a direct correlation between environmental footprint and an organisation's sales (2%)[15] and operating income (20%) with values that exceed 10% and 100% respectively in 11 of 67 industries.[16]

Now as the world becomes more eco-conscious, businesses have an opportunity to demonstrate their commitment by pledging to protect the planet with socio-economic equality and sustainability. Conscious consumers are turning to products and services that demonstrate environmental and ethical practices that commit to a greener future *'80% of surveyed consumers agree that companies and brands are essential to addressing the current challenges.'*[17] Business leaders must take responsibility as corporate and global citizens to address the uncertainties facing humanity by committing to:

- Reducing carbon footprints
- Sourcing ethical materials
- Decreasing energy consumption
- Creating circular economies of scale
- Forging revolutionary planet-positive innovation

Environmental factors must align themselves to the SDGs viable targets and metrics that not only protect our natural resources but create alternate options. Focussing on the planet is for the welfare of generations to come as they are already acutely aware of the damage done thus far. Greta Thunberg has been championing the urgency of the climate crisis for several years, challenging global leaders as she says that *'the future was sold so that a small number of people could make unimaginable amounts of money. We talk about our future; they talk about their present.'*[18] Today, 67% of 6 to 9-year olds[19] say that saving the planet will be the central mission of their careers in the future. Tracking and measuring the IMPACT can deliver the SDGs by 2030, but time is of the essence.

Profit IMPACT

THE PROGRESSION FROM TRADITIONAL FINANCIAL REPORTING TO TOTAL IMPACT MEASUREMENT

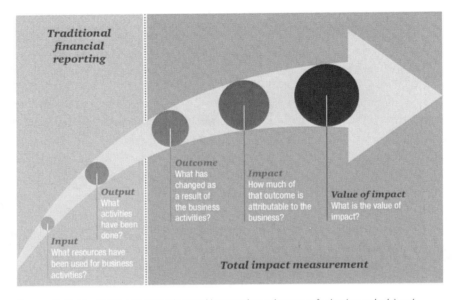

Source: PwC, Measuring and managing total impact: A new language for business decisions[4]

Until recently, a capitalist economy meant that financial performance was the only metric that mattered. Now, purpose-driven leaders are embracing sustainability and socio-economic practices to harness their influence and *become a force for good* in the world. Yet according to PwC, despite 72% of companies publicly citing the SDGs in their corporate reports, only 14% currently translate the SDGs into business strategies and activities.[20] In reality, only 1%[21] actually measure their performance against the targets. It is therefore critical to develop a clear roadmap based on the SDG framework and track progress by hitting the targets with robust metrics in place within a specific time frame. Businesses can assign financial values to measure their IMPACT to the relevant SDGs both within their organisations and their wider industries.

Are businesses and governments truly committed to delivering the SDGs by 2030? Or are they simply re-purposing existing CSR and sustainability policies? Without a comprehensive assessment, many companies will not have the capability to measure the link between the SDG and business growth opportunities to unlock their share of the $12 trillion opportunity. According to Peter Bakker, President, World Business Council for Sustainable Development (WBCSD), *'From a reporting perspective, while many companies already communicate on the topics covered by the SDGs, aligning disclosure with the goals and identifying progress made on targets set against the SDGs, provide an opportunity for businesses to sharpen their existing reporting and to place more focus on the IMPACT of their activities. Integrating the language of the SDGs into reporting also enables companies to ensure that they are engaging in a common dialogue with stakeholders and allows them to clearly articulate the contributions they are making towards this vital global agenda.'* [22]

From a consumer point of view, 88%[23] say that they would boycott a brand due to irresponsible business practices. In fact, 74%[24] believe companies can take actions that both boost profits and improve economic and social conditions at a community level. Purpose-led brand loyalty increases according to 79% of consumers as 67% said that they are more willing to forgive such a company for a mistake.[25] Consumers are even willing to become advocates and influencers of these IMPACT Brands™ as 78% said they would tell others to buy from them.[26] Another 73% would even go so far as share content about a purpose-led company.[27] As the business world is under increasingly greater pressure to put purpose into practice, it must scrutinise existing practices such as:

- Business expenditure and tax laws
- People and planet ethics and practice
- Employment distribution and contribution
- Diversity reward and progression
- Revenue by sector

Today in Britain, 27%[28] of managers would likely accept a salary cut to work for a company that has a clear purpose beyond profit. As many as 32% would actually consider leaving their job if a greater purpose was unclear, and a staggering 53% would leave a company if the values and purpose did not align with their own.[29] Whether businesses like it or not, the EU Non-Financial Reporting Directive requires companies to report on the social and environmental IMPACT of their activities. Negative trust-related issues can erode business market capitalisation anywhere from 20% to 56%, a total loss of $70 billion,[30] so the risks are too great.

The new way of reporting is starting to gain momentum in progressive SMEs and some FTSE 100 organisations. More extensive IMPACT reporting and action will be expected over the coming years, so the days of the traditional Profit and Loss (P&L) financial statement may become a thing of the past. Now is the time to future-proof the business financially, ethically, and sustainably.

Chapter Seven – PERFORMANCE Exercise:

Align and assess your business to the *7 Business Performance Priority Principles* to ensure that your business is ready to scale profit with purpose and IMPACT.

CHAPTER EIGHT: PIVOT

'Don't fear change, change fear.'
– Nelson Mandela

The 2020 Covid-19 pandemic forced many businesses to pivot and defend their livelihoods, protect their brand, or simply survive. A challenging time with nothing but the unknown ahead. Many repurposed their existing assets to re-create value, attract new prospects and deliver innovative solutions:

- Zara, GAP, Nike, and other apparel manufacturers produced masks, gowns, and scrubs
- Luxury perfume brands Dior, Guerlain, LVMH, and Pernod Ricard (makers of Jameson Whiskey and Absolut Vodka) produced hand sanitisers
- Jaguar Land Rover, Ford Motors and Honda stepped up to produce health ventilators

These actions demonstrated their agility to act quickly, galvanise new commercial ventures, and pull together in a time of crisis. Yet one does not need a pandemic to pivot. It tends to come out of a profitability performance assessment, a process that many organisations big or small try to side-step. The numbers either reveal a bleak reality or a healthy performance that the plan is on or off-track. Either way, avoiding it is not going to change the outcome. When you know better, you can do better even against the odds.

Brand positioning, business model paradigms, creation of digital services and product ecosystems can all open up a wealth of untapped opportunities in a changing marketplace. From new routes to market, sales and social entrepreneurship, pivoting can offer a competitive advantage and breathe new life into any organisation culturally, financially, and sustainably.

8.1.   POSITIONING

In the early stages of the planning process, brands have to determine the gap that they are trying to fulfil in the marketplace. This is the white space that they are going after. Yet in the profitability assessment stages, it is key to understand whether the initial plan worked or not. There are some vital questions that need to be answered in order to assess whether one must pivot to re-position the business in the marketplace.

TOP 10 '*WHEN TO PIVOT?*' QUESTIONS™:

1. Is there a strong return on investment (ROI) from the current performance?
2. Have sales performed, plateaued, or declined?
3. Have external market factors changed since the plan was executed?
4. Have competitors upped the ante to steal market share away?
5. Have supply and demand fluctuated?
6. Have pricing and promotions had a positive or negative effect on sales?
7. Has there been enough investment in marketing to drive engagement?
8. Does the proposition purpose still align to customer values? Employees? Shareholders?
9. Is the brand still accurately positioned in the ever-changing landscape?
10. Are contributions being made towards People and Planet?

Take the time to contemplate the many factors that could alter and improve business performance and socio-economic and environmental IMPACT.

Re-Think

The 2020 global disruption left little time for preparation. The world got caught in a chain of events that pushed the boundaries of normality. Everything was being modified for the unknown. Pivoting fundamentally meant changing direction as we knew it.

In business, the main objective to changing course is to improve revenue. It is sometimes seen as a last resort or a proactive step to get ahead of a potential storm. There are numerous ways to develop a pivot strategy, but start with customer, market, and competitor insight to deliver a superior proposition. The communication must be clear and stay true to the company's values and prospects' pain points. This is a golden opportunity to set new goals at great new heights.

Re-Design

Once it is clear that something has changed – macro trends, market forces, competitors, customers, or any other anomaly, then it is time to re-design the proposition and ensure that the business stays ahead of the new tide. Before defaulting to the more obvious tactics, such as pricing and promotions, consider the alternative. Find and align new sources of business growth that would set higher standards for the wider sector instead of falling victim to market cannibalisation.

Re-design as per the current business needs if it will add value to the organisation. By mapping out the industry and category trends, customer behaviours and shifting dynamics, one can begin to see a few emerging patterns. For instance, over the last few years, the Fast-Moving Consumer Goods (FMCG) sector has seen some movements that have forced many brands and businesses to pivot:

- From mass-produced to niche categories
- From orchestrated brand images to transparency and full business disclosure
- From generic products to pre-emptive Internet of Things (IOT) experiences such as digital operating models, data capture and personalised customer relationships
- From standard distribution to seamless omni-channel consumer touch points
- From brand-led to sustainable and society-led

Transformation can take shape in many forms. From minor tweaks to major business reformation. So, start by assessing and spotting opportunities in:

- New categories or networks to deliver long-term value
- Agile supply chains and innovation pipelines
- Mutually beneficial strategic partnerships
- Alternative business models that can deliver new revenue streams
- Option to re-purpose the proposition for existing and new target customers

It is always advisable to test strategic concepts before implementation to ensure traction and long-term success.

Re-Imagine

'Fall in love with the problem, not the solution.'
– Anonymous

Successful entrepreneurs and innovators start with a brilliant insight. They don't just try to sell more copycat products like another ice cream flavour or a product with a better logo design. They see a genuine gap in the world and strive to fulfil it. They identify a problem and attempt to solve it in a new way with a clear mission in mind. Often, the journey not only leads to the discovery of new categories, but unique solutions full of radically new business opportunities as well. That is exactly what Kolibri Co-Founder Kamila Sitwell embraced when she re-imagined her customisable drinks brand.

With a background in insight and category strategy, having worked with some of the world's most recognisable brands, Kamila has always been able to spot lucrative opportunities ahead of the curve. Then in 2016, she had a lightbulb moment. Whilst on a spa retreat, Kamila and her friends were looking to unwind with a celebratory cocktail. Yet each person was looking for a different taste and drink experience. So, they asked the bartender to create something off the menu, bespoke beverages that met their individual needs. Some liked it sweet, some liked it sour and some preferred sparkling.

Kamila began connecting the dots. What if bottled drinks could also offer an element of customisation, just like the skilled bartender? She noted that personalisation was prevalent in many industries from fashion to automobiles to coffee at Starbucks but had yet been offered in packaged drinks. After all, the bottled drinks category is called ready-to-drink (RTD) for a reason. It is comprised of standardised and pre-formulated products – so offering customisable drinks became the founders' mission.

The way to achieve their objective was through radically changing packaging by incorporating technology that would enable customisation. In 2018, Kolibri's *Tailored by You* range of customisable drinks with smart cap closures was launched in the UK. Despite Kolibri's multi-channel success, including landing retail clients such as Harrods, John Lewis and many others, a more serendipitous opportunity was just around the corner.

It soon became apparent that the innovative closure technology had multiple and highly relevant applications for other categories beyond drinks. This range of customised closures could separate ingredients and integrate complementary products that would otherwise be sold separately. Imagine buying one integrated bottle of shampoo with a concentrated conditioner right in the cap that you can dose as needed. Imagine purchasing one integrated bottle of vodka with concentrated flavour shots right in the cap instead of buying multiple bottles. Imagine laundry detergent with a concentrated stain remover right in the cap instead of buying two separate products. Bottled iced coffee you can flavour, sweeten, or whiten to your taste. The possibilities are endless.

The elevated convenience of integrated packaging offers a greater consumer experience, but best of all, in most cases it offers a more sustainable solution. Since Dexos closures integrate two products into one, they can dramatically reduce CO2 emissions. One delivery truck containing Dexos caps is equivalent to 18 trucks[1] of packaging bottles, which means a massive reduction of packaging, storage, transport, water, raw materials, energy in manufacturing, consumer consumption and wastage. The closures are highly compatible and applicable to multiple industries, categories, and brands.

Kamila says that '*The key to Dexos' success was to leverage the data and insight, but then be open to possibilities beyond the plan. We championed the category, we championed the customer, we championed the proposition, but above all, we paid attention to all the little signs on our entrepreneurial journey that pointed to something greater than our business.*'[2] As a result, Dexos has completely re-imagined its business model and is playing bigger by taking this award-winning sustainable solution beyond its brand and category to revolutionise the entire CPG industry with a planet-positive proposition.

'We re-imagine packaging and empower organisations to innovate their circular economy goals': www.dexosclosures.com
Hear Dexos' Story on The IMPACT Game Changers™ Podcast:

www.splitsecondltd.com

8.2. PARADIGMS

Pivoting a business strategy, generating a profit, and making a sustainable IMPACT can be a tricky balancing act. One cannot drive social change on passion alone. Change costs time, effort and yes, money. Aligning the business to one or several of the UN's Sustainable Development Goals (SDGs) directs momentum and energy towards solving some of the world's most meaningful challenges, whilst uncovering some lucrative opportunities. The core business model may require some transformational pivoting to keep up with a renewed strategy.

There are three fundamental types of business paradigms that are at the heart of most organisations, one of them is likely to be the current one in your organisation, whilst the others may be aspirational:

- **The Old Paradigm**: Maximise profits through cost cutting, short-term tactics and the top few leaders benefit from the rewards.
- **The New Paradigm**: Extend beyond monetary value by aligning to people's values - consumers, employees, customers, suppliers, investors, etc. Integrate many accreditations and processes that are highly valued: *Great place to work®, Quality Management*

ISO 9000®, etc. This paradigm has a competitive edge to retain dynamic talent, harness innovation and design, gain consumer and industry credibility.

- **The IMPACT Paradigm™:** Committed to delivering the UN SDGs by 2030 through measurable actions. The SDGs are at the heart of the organisation's commercial and cultural strategy to make a quantifiable IMPACT on People, Planet, and Profit.

The lines between these paradigms are not always clear cut; one business's start point is another's destination. That being said, the key is to define the success criteria, develop a process to execution. Select the relevant options that will deliver the right mix of commercial, innovation, sustainability, and social IMPACT.

Commercial IMPACT

The 2020 lockdown was the catalyst for a new business future. With the commercial world disrupted, governments and industry sectors alike had to find their way through this 'unprecedented' period the world over. Many businesses were asking themselves if they would ever re-open their doors again? If so, would customers return? How many? When?

It is always imperative to stay close to the target prospect and your existing customers to anticipate their next move, especially in a volatile market. Observe, understand, and respond to changing behaviours. For instance, if 57% of consumers say that they would be lost without access to the internet and a business is not set up to cater online, then pivot to the low-hanging fruit. According to E&Y, the pandemic accelerated the e-commerce trend by +74% (vs. a year ago); 44% of consumers now prefer to do their groceries online and 39% purchase more durables online, a trend that is likely to remain or even increase over the next few years.[3]

Many turned to a Direct-to-Consumer (D2C) model as 59%[4] of global consumers preferred this option for easier transactions and better availability. Whether it is D2C, subscription, rental service or resale, different business models can generate new revenue streams and customer experiences. Selecting the right model will depend on existing business infrastructures, logistics, order fulfilment processes, third-party affiliations, and above all the target customer's journey.

However, not all business models or supply channels are digital. Offline distribution expansion can also make a significant commercial IMPACT. More than half of the world's population still does not have access to the internet. The vast majority (80%) of Europe is connected, but some parts of Asia and Africa have the lowest rates of access. The United Nations' research shows that there are also gender disparities in developing countries, especially in Africa where only 11.6% of women have access to the internet vs. 88% in Europe.[5] If a business caters to a local population, then an offline strategy may be more relevant. Geography, demographics, and connectivity will all determine where to focus. Be where your target customer is. Offer them a choice and curate experiences at all the different touch points.

There are other types of models and processes that have appeared when the pressure is on for profit. Many larger organisations often implement zero-based budgeting systems that predominantly focus on cost cutting, often streamlining marketing, research, and innovation initiatives in the hopes of increasing profit, albeit only short-term profit. Mergers and acquisitions have also played an important commercial role among corporates. Yet the level of investment is limited to a few, and the ROI must pay significant dividends. Resist the temptation to automatically default to these practices, as they may not solve the longer-term challenges.

Business models that correspond to the macro trends and market drivers, literally point to where the market is headed. These may be: the circular economy, collaborative consumption, technological innovation, corporate social responsibility, and consumer awareness. By looking outward, organisations can integrate these trends and drivers within their business models to stay commercially ahead of the competition whilst making an environmental and social contribution to *build back better*.

Innovation IMPACT

One of the big positives that came out of 2020, was that when humankind is put to the test *'innovation is where imagination meets ambition'*. The intense activity sparked by governments, businesses, and entrepreneurs to deliver groundbreaking solutions faster than ever before was extraordinary. Businesses worked in partnerships to take bigger risks and reap bigger rewards. From medical breakthroughs to 3-D printing for supply chain self-sufficiency, to AI and all things technology to sustainable living solutions, the demand and race to deliver 21st century innovation is well and truly on.

According to the World Economic Forum (WEF), there are three fundamental innovation pillars[6] of organic growth that will separate the leaders from the laggards:

1. **Invest in Innovation Talent:** The leadership team signals its commitment to innovation with high-profile investments of resources and time.
2. **Adopt an Outside-In Approach:** Innovation that starts by scouring widely for trends and searching for deep insights into customers' emerging needs as well as understanding the inter-dependencies between the key macro trends.
3. **Encourage Prudent Risk-Taking:** Innovative organisations foster a tolerance for risk-taking by endorsing fast-to-fail experiments and learning from their innovation disappointments.

The WEF's research is based on 192 global organisations in which they found that those who applied these pillars more efficiently with speed, had greater competitive advantage than that of their rivals. The new normal is more competitive with a real shift in priorities and spend. For brands to stand out, organisations need to step up the pace of research and development in line with customer-changing needs.

When consumers worry about their lifestyles, the cost of living, health and jobs, businesses have to evolve with them. As we saw in 2020, people prioritised their health and wellbeing, home-based activities, hygiene, ethical and sustainable values. Suddenly, new sanitising brands, masks, test kits and a range of other products sprung up. There was also a resurgence of contactless click-and-collect services and a high-level of demand for functional commodity categories. In today's climate, a fourth innovation pillar should be added to the list, and that is innovation based on the IMPACT Paradigm™. Businesses committed to delivering the UN SDGs by 2030 through measurable actions and innovation where the Sustainable Development Goals are at the heart of the organisation's strategy to make a quantifiable IMPACT on People, Planet, and Profit.

How will your business evolve and innovate to create value?

Creating value, disrupting the category, and making an IMPACT on People and Planet through innovation and design, is exactly what led Co-Founders Josie Harfield and Ryan McSorley to launch their sustainable homecare cleaning brand called Neat. Since inception in April 2020, Neat have been recognised as *'the best soluble product for reducing plastic waste'* by Good Housekeeping magazine.[7] The brand has been listed in national retailers such as Tesco, Waitrose, Ocado, Lakeland and many others, attracted industry investors, and winner of *The Grocer Gold Awards for Best Household Goods Brand of the Year 2022*. Given that Josie and Ryan had previously worked in the homecare cleaning category, they were on a mission to build and pivot from their prior experience in order to create a truly sustainable and innovative concept with purpose.

Homecare shoppers agree that brands should provide more proof of eco-friendly claims. In fact, 70%[8] of them feel quite strongly about it. So, the idea of putting a marketing spin to persuade consumers that some products are environmentally friendly when they are not, is misleading. In other words, *Greenwashing* will not be tolerated. Instead, the Neat brand makes us reconsider our cleaning habits, purchasing repertoire and IMPACT on the planet.

Did you know that most cleaning products are 90%[9] water in single-use plastic? It is not something that one necessarily thinks about, but when presented with the fact, it makes you wonder why? In contrast, Neat offer anti-bacterial concentrates, so they do not unnecessarily ship water around the world. They ask consumers to fill a reusable aluminium spray bottle at home without any plastic waste.

When designing the product, Ryan says, '*A lot of vision was built into the brand. We had a lot of thoughts and ideas on how to make the homecare cleaning category better. Sustainability was a given. Even the name Neat is based on the idea that it's a solution that we are removing unnecessary water and therefore we can create something fundamentally more sustainable. It had to be better for the planet, but the real challenge was how to create a sustainable option that had as much IMPACT as possible as widely as possible?*'[10]

Consumers sometimes have reservations around sustainable solutions involving some sort of compromise. Perceptions range from cost, convenience, and product experience. '*So, we thought if we are going to do this, we are going to have to make products as good, if not better than what already exists. By doing so, we can have a mass IMPACT which we were setting out to do. We didn't want this to be something that was going to be niche, but we wanted to take on the category and the bigger players in the category to create significant change. I think it's fundamental that we create something, knowing what's most important to the people that are going to use it,*'[11] says Ryan.

Neat's Co-Founders have managed to accelerate commercial growth, drive retail engagement, and make it fun for shoppers to shop by bringing purpose to a commodity category. They also learnt to pivot at critical points in their innovation journey: pivoting their brand and design, pivoting their category, pivoting to focus on people and planet. Despite the team's success, Josie says, '*We've got big ambitions! Expanding into different categories, based on the principle of where there is a problem Neat can be a solution. Expanding into other countries. Expanding the team and having a culture that feels as forward-thinking as the products we're making. Being able to break the old rules and the ways of working in what it takes to be successful. Pushing the boundaries from a business perspective is really exciting. I think we can do things quite differently and will be a great case study to show other people that you don't have to do what has been done before to be successful – work smarter not harder.*'[12]

www.splitsecondltd.com

New, emerging and existing categories must innovate to elevate with three IMPACT Principles™ in mind:

- **Invest** in research, customer insight, testing, and an innovative IMPACT Paradigm™
- **Deliver** on quality, sustainability, and purpose to maximise returns
- **Raise the bar** to differentiate, drive demand and make a meaningful difference to the world

'You can have a great product and an average team, and it will never sell. Then the reverse will stand true. If you've got a really strong founding team, they will pivot and react to feedback. They'll change and will eventually get there. It may take them a bit of time, but that is one of the single biggest success factors I see when I come across brands that succeed or fail.'
– Tom Elliott Former Senior Buyer, Sainsbury's Future Brands Team

Sustainability and Social IMPACT

Even if your business has never previously considered addressing sustainability and social challenges, it is not too late. Looking ahead, it is imperative for our survival. Despite some business leaders' apprehension to endorse *green* initiatives for fear of cost and losing competitive advantage, research tells us that sustainability and innovation are inextricably linked to driving incremental profit. In fact, sustainability and social strategies can significantly reduce cost, as part of a circular economy with streamlined processes that put People and Planet at the heart of the business.

The Sustainable Development Goals (SDGs) serve as quantifiable benchmarks for tracking and reporting sustainability and social progress towards 2030. They outline the goals and targets that governments and businesses can directly influence. Making the targets as specific as possible is key to delivering them. Identifying the relevant ones for your business and how they can be galvanised require some investigation across several parts of the organisation. Is the business sustainably and socially compliant in: supply chains, products and services, business models, energy and technology consumption and other areas? By delving into these capacities, the business can start to pinpoint its own IMPACT Drivers™.

TOP 10 SOCIAL AND SUSTAINABILITY IMPACT DRIVERS ™

1 ASSESS INDUSTRY TRENDS AND DISRUPTORS

2 DEFINE THE BUSINESS CASE FOR CHANGE

3 CREATE NEW SOURCES OF GROWTH

4 DRIVE SALES CONVERSION

5 BECOME MORE PROFITABLE LONG-TERM

6 REVIEW CORPORATE SOCIAL GOVERNANCE

7 CHOOSE THE RIGHT PARTNERS

8 EVALUATE GOVERNMENT AND INDUSTRY POLICIES

9 BECOME CARBON NEUTRAL

10 CREATE A MEANINGFUL CHANGE

1. **Assess Industry Trends and Disruptors**: Identify alternative sustainable solutions aligned to industry-specific Sustainable Development Goals (SDGs) and targets.

2. **Define the Business Case for Change**: Adopt a model that creates shared value.

3. **Create New Sources of Growth**: From carbon-positive homes and electric cars to edible cutlery – Sustainability generates new revenue streams.

4. **Drive Sales Conversion:** Align to customer, environmental and social values.

5. **Become More Profitable Long-Term:** Raw materials, supply chains and waste management are just the tip of the iceberg that can ensure financial, environmental, and social sustainability. Discover the socio-economic opportunities in your sector.

6. **Review Corporate Social Governance**: Set environmental and social IMPACT Metrics™.

7. **Choose the Right Partners**: Create affiliations based on values that will make a positive unified IMPACT.

8. **Evaluate Government and Industry Policies:** To align, disrupt and create momentum to deliver the SDGs by 2030.

9. **Become Carbon Neutral:** Invest in renewable energy and offset programs.

10. **Create a Meaningful Change:** Empower people, exceed profits and save the Planet.

Business threats can be planned for, but environmental and social threats are more unpredictable. Every industry will be affected by climate change sooner or later, so control the controllable(s) and incorporate The IMPACT Drivers™ into your IMPACT Roadmap™.

8.3.   PRODUCT ECOSYSTEMS

Pivoting in the *new normal* for digital and traditional businesses can present its own set of challenges. Many will innovate and take a market lead, whilst the laggards will always play catch up. Either way, standing still is not an option. The sooner an organisation can respond to change, the sooner the risks become fuel for a business to become more resilient. This is the time when valuable opportunities are realised.

Like a biological ecosystem, a product equivalent, connects similar organisms to interact as a system. These are a range of products and services that co-exist to best serve the customer and generate different revenue streams. The greater the number of entities, the greater the chances of survival. An ecosystem improves the value of the core proposition as it offers multiple customer solution points. The intention is to draw prospects into the ecosystem then inspire and entice them with a wide range of corresponding products, services, and experiences. Product ecosystems are all around us. We are part of these ecosystems whether we realise it or not.

Develop Digital Assets – *Apples & Orchards*

'*Why sell the apple, when you can sell the orchard*?' is a thought that must have crossed Steve Jobs' mind at some point. Case in point, Apple recently became the first American company valued at $2 trillion (£1.5tn) on the stock market with shares up by more than +50%.[13] This milestone comes just years after becoming the world's first trillion-dollar company in 2018. This astonishing achievement was particularly significant in 2020, as most retail stores were shut during lockdown and political controversies surrounded the giant tech firm.

As an Apple customer, one can seamlessly navigate through the brand's product ecosystem. From the texts and apps on the iPhone®, to the music on the AirPods®, to the notes on the iPad® that instantly show up on the MacBook via the iCloud® – Apple facilitates connectivity. This unified ecosystem delivers greater commercial value than the individual parts. Once customers are within the ecosystem, they are more likely to remain there so that they can benefit from the synergies and convenience. They will only leave if they believe that the ecosystem no longer adds value and the cost exceeds the benefit.

By creating digital assets, one can truly influence purchasing behaviours, generate brand awareness, and keep customers within the ecosystem. Even if one is not a 'techie' or does not have budgets like Apple's, there has never been an easier time to develop a range of assets that engage and entice prospects. Online tools, podcasts, webinars, downloadable content, e-books, customer experiences, the list goes onto endless and almost instantaneous digital assets that can engage potential customers and grow any business.

Create Collaborative Consumption
– *Share and Share Alike*

Whether one is booking an Airbnb or a DogVacay, car-sharing via Zipcar, or investing on Funding Circle – there is no doubt that collaborative consumption has been ignited by some of these digital disruptors. As TechCrunch's Tom Goodwin so accurately observed, *'Uber, the world's largest taxi company, owns no vehicles; Facebook, the world's most popular media owner, creates no content; Alibaba, the most valuable retailer, has no inventory; and Airbnb, the world's largest accommodation provider, owns no real estate – something interesting is happening.'*[14] Indeed, it is.

Collaborative consumption is set to grow to $335 billion in revenue by 2025, with the peer-to-peer rental market alone valued at $26 billion.[15] Some of these industry sectors did not even exist a decade ago. Today, these convenient solutions are well and truly woven into our social fabric. What lies behind their success? At first glance, they appear to generate high business turnover without any notable assets, provide a unique range of products and services and use digital technology to engage their customers. Yet on closer inspection, there is something more intuitive and universal that they have managed to tap into that is connecting people who share common interests. It is breaking with capitalist supply and demand conventions by redefining what and how we consume.

Imagine renting your house to a complete stranger for weeks on end? Sharing your personal life with hundreds of people online? Leaving your beloved pet with someone you have never met before? Or swapping 'nearly new' items based on a one-line description? Today millions of those transactions are taking place because technology has cultivated a sense of trust.

Collaborative consumption has taken us back to our hunter-gatherer instincts, by trading, bartering with a *'share and share alike'* spirit, and serious commercial returns. Financial pundits are predicting that over the next 12 years, companies that have embraced sharing economies will grow by an astronomical 2133%.[16] How is that possible?

This new type of consumption has a direct link to one of the macro trends: instant gratification. Consumers are looking for instant access to information, products, services, and experiences. So give them what they are looking for, by building and connecting people with the right platforms for the right purpose.

The biggest benefit of collaborative consumption is the IMPACT on our environment. Forecasters predict that there will be an additional 5.3 billion middle-class consumers by 2030,[17] adding more pressure on our existing infrastructures, natural resources, and ecological future. *The Sharing Economy, Make it Sustainable* report by Demailly and Novel states that a sharing model can save up to 7% in household budgets and 3.2 million tonnes in waste a year.[18] From redistribution, to rentals, to shared mobility, there are various models that can create a triple-win for People, Planet, and Profit.

Unleash Purpose and Unlock Revenue
– The Age of IMPACT™

'The way the planet is ordered will change. We are now entering the age of meaning.'
– Paul McGillivray, Co-Founder of Remote Online

As we head further into the 21st century, the role of technology is accelerating with pace. Whether you are ambivalent to it or not, technology is here to stay. More and more of our social, educational, and business lives depend on it. Social distancing forced us to connect with one another in imaginative ways that could not have been possible without technology even just a few years ago. Yet communication is just the tip of the iceberg.

Automation is essential in harnessing our creative potential. Some might say that is a contradiction in terms, but the reality is that *'humans were not born to do admin*'[19] according to Paul McGillivray, Co-Founder of Remote (experts in creating new revenue streams through custom digital assets). Paul says that *'humans are linear beings, we imagine tomorrow is going to be pretty similar to yesterday ...'*[20] so by automating some of the everyday tasks, businesses can improve their efficiency and productivity freeing up time and resources to focus on their purpose. *'Computers can work day and night; they don't get sick, tired or take the day off. So, what we're left with is the work we're meant to do, that allows us to express our own uniqueness. You don't often say, 'If I win a million pounds, I will finally fill in those forms I've been dying to fill in...' You say, 'Yeah, now I'm going to learn to play the piano, write a book, or travel the world and meet other cultures.' Human beings are born to be creative. When we're clear on our purpose, we're doing meaningful work.'*[21]

Many organisations take a piece of software, ask themselves how they can use it, install it, and then hope it will make a difference to their businesses. Yet they often end up in a pattern of *'how do I do what I was doing before, but now using this software?'* This may or may not give them a better outcome. The key is to map out the customer's journey and touch points along the way; the process of someone who has an initial awareness of a brand to the point of purchase and experience. Find the customer pain points and identify how the value proposition can fix it. Then and only then, the right technical solution should be sourced and implemented. Technology is a pivotal part of the strategic business engine that ensures faster and greater outcomes.

Technology can offer endless innovation and experiential opportunities beyond packaging, *new and improved* range extensions and other tactics from the standard pivot playbook. The intersection of where product design meets technology opens up new revenue streams. Yet often the initial concerns of most technology projects are around cost and complexity. Once the core assumption that will make the greatest IMPACT to the business is ascertained, the different pieces of work can be executed to test the waters with customers. This provides them with feedback on the usability, preferences, and experience to determine which elements should be part of the wider project scope. Making customers design co-creators will ultimately delight them.

More than 70%[22] of industry leaders say that when automation is deemed as a strategic priority, business objectives are successfully achieved. There is a fine balance between the role of technology and people and the redeployment of responsibilities to ensure that all resources are fully maximised. One can get even greater value out of automation if the operating model is scalable. Even though most smaller organisations tend not to automate internal processes, of those that do, 65% report success with automation vs 55% in larger organisations.[23] It is imperative to connect to one's own purpose first to be able to connect with customers with a little help from technology.

Paul and his wife Jeannie, Co-Founders of Remote, are also on a mission to tackle climate change by connecting purpose and technology. They have developed an app with their client Kanopi, that enables organisations to roll out net zero environmental initiatives to suppliers and customers with key metrics to track climate performance every step of the way. The app streamlines environmental goals throughout a customer's supply chain and supports Small Medium Enterprises (SMEs) struggling to start their green journey. It embeds a collective responsibility and fully automates the progress towards a business's climate ambitions.

As we re-orient ourselves in the *new normal*, we can begin to identify the commercial, innovation and sustainable opportunities that can have a significant socio-economic IMPACT on the world at large. Despite the economic rollercoaster and negative noise out there, remember that out of every recession, new opportunities arise, and new businesses are born. IBM, Burger King, WhatsApp, Airbnb, and Uber are just some of the biggest brands that successfully emerged out of the darkest periods in history. The last economic downturn was *the age of tech start-ups*, so let's ensure that the next one is *The Age of IMPACT*™. Don't panic, just pivot.

'Purpose First': www.remote.online

Hear Remote's Story on The IMPACT Game Changers' Podcast:

www.splitsecondltd.com

Chapter Eight – PIVOT Exercise:

Do your customers still believe that your business's products or services add value to them and/or society? Ask them. If the answer is lukewarm or no, then consider the following:

- Is the value proposition still fulfilling an unmet need?
- Is the target prospect the one who is actually purchasing?
- Is there a clear purpose for the value proposition?
- Could existing assets deliver new value and revenue streams?
- Could pivoting improve sales?
- Could products and services be re-engineered with purpose to deliver IMPACT for People, Planet, and Profit?

CHAPTER NINE: PAY IT FORWARD

'We rise by lifting others.'
– Robert Ingersoll

In the race for success, compassion is sometimes left on the back burner. Of course, many businesses write charitable cheques or support their local communities, but now paying it forward must be more meaningful. It is about a greater purpose, achieving the UN Sustainable Development Goals (SDGs). Our survival depends on it.

Today's bottom line goes beyond our profit and loss (P&L). It is about ensuring *a better and more sustainable future for all.*[1] As good global citizens, we must include other key 'stakeholders' that over time we have taken for granted: our People and our Planet.

By creating mission-driven brands and businesses aligned to the SDGs, we will not only survive, but thrive. Conscience and compassion are integral to purpose-led organisations. They foster trust, build morale, elicit passion and commitment, fuel learning and innovation, and give us the power to pay it forward in unimaginable ways. Thus, paving the way to a brighter, sustainable, and more abundant future.

9.1.   BE HUMAN

*'There is a big difference between a human
being and being human.'*
– Anonymous

Almost every company at some point has either had to re-invent itself or implement a contingency plan to ensure financial, operational, and social continuity. This is much harder in some industry sectors than others. Yet the one thing every business has in common is that people are essential to its survival and, more importantly, to its success. In today's world, business leaders are more conscious than ever of their social, ethical, and environmental responsibilities.

Consumers want companies to be more transparent about their values beyond the numbers in a P&L. According to Edelman research, '*53%[1]of consumers believe that every brand has a responsibility to get involved in at least one social issue*' outside of standard business operations. Adopting and sharing social practices and programs also offer insight into an organisation's people, culture, and their contribution to society.

For most businesses, the term 'people' tends to limit itself to its employees. However, today 'people' often expands to customers, suppliers, and society – extensions of the organisation and beyond. From the individuals where raw materials are sourced, and the vital links in the supply chain, to partnerships with customers and non-profit organisations in the local communities, people are the lifeblood of any business. The more we pay it forward, the greater loyalty, goodwill, and action we inspire, creating a universal ripple effect.

Empower People

People's priorities have shifted for greater alignment to their values, personal development, and flexible life-work balance. People want trust, an enjoyable lifestyle, and an investment in their careers and wellbeing. In return, the employer will attract the most talented and innovative people, a company culture that attracts other like-minded candidates and long-term loyalty. Businesses have to move with the times, otherwise they run the risk of falling behind.

If you have a thriving business, then you will know that the search for high-performing talent is always on. Why? The fact is that high-performing talent in certain sectors can deliver an astounding 800% greater productivity[2] than simply hiring off a standard job board. Steve Jobs once said, '*Go after the cream of the cream. A small team of A+ players can run circles around a giant team of B and C players.*'[3] So how does one define 'A+ talent'? How do we find and attract this talent? What are the key factors affecting the search?

Understanding and staying on top of the trends affecting the market is essential. Newsworthy topics such as the economy, the pandemic, Brexit and politics present certain challenges that can be more difficult to plan for but need to be considered. Adam Gleeson, founder of The TalentPool Company Executive Search, says that '*With the rise of digital, and certain functions becoming obsolete and outdated graduate schemes – the face of recruitment is changing. The focus now is on personal engagement. Millennials are driving the speed of movement because they are more than happy to try something new, until they find the best fit for them.*[4]

The days when employers assumed that the best candidates would simply be lured by compensation packages and fancy job titles are becoming a thing of the past. Candidates are more discerning now. They want to feel valued no matter the size of the organisation; they assess employers just as much as they are being assessed. They expect full transparency, just as it is expected of them. Adam says, *'Companies that cling to and enforce the old school micro-managed culture are not empowering their people, attracting talent is then limited to catchment areas where the talent pool becomes very narrow.'*

Today, many candidates turn to Small and Medium-sized Enterprises (SMEs) to get experience, autonomy, and the buzz they are looking for to make their mark. Ameet Shah, one of Adam's business partners at The TalentPool Company, says, *'In today's society you're being told to be different, more entrepreneurial, create your own dreams, because it is the time of the SME. If we ask ourselves what is happening on the shop shelf, there is greater pressure on businesses to be the first-to-market and have the best product. If you look at food and beverage SMEs, it's the cool young businesses that are doing well, but as a result, the pressure is on to find suitable talent to help these businesses grow.'*[5] The TalentPool Company have strong values and a proposition built on client and candidate needs: energy for high performance, digital, diversity and inclusion, IMPACT and sustainability capability. Finding candidates in the market with these competencies can be a challenge – a real opportunity for universities and companies to educate and upskill talent.

According to an occupation survey of over 600,000 people by Mckinsey,[6] there are four key elements that high-performers evaluate when making career choices:

% Of Employees Satisfied When Their Companies Deliver:

1. **Great Leaders (89%)**: Inspirational, supportive, empowering, focussed on development.
2. **Great Company (81%)**: Reputation, values, culture, business results and contributions made to society.

3. **Great Job (81%)**: Interesting opportunities for growth and advancement with IMPACT and meaning.
4. **Great Rewards (76%)**: Wages, benefits, non-financial forms of recognition.

Source: McKinsey: Attracting and Retaining the right Talent Report

Interestingly, great rewards are not the key driver for high-performers. Identifying and prioritising the most important elements and processes in different markets, business units and functions require ongoing evaluation and updates. For instance, if a role was initially office-based but is now remote, what implications does location have on the responsibilities, capability, and accountability? What IMPACT does it have on the individual?

Why not re-define or surpass the existing set of biased recruitment criteria: skillset, education, cultural fit, and personal preferences. Depending on the role, one may even consider '*open hiring*' similar to an '*open house*' approach. This is an unconventional approach that invites any and all candidates to apply, dispensing formal processes that have little or no regard for someone's background. Companies such as The Body Shop found '*open-hiring*' led to reduction of labour-intensive staff turnover by 60%.[7] Greyston Bakery in the US is another example of this concept as they proudly state, '*We don't hire people to bake brownies, we bake brownies to hire people.*'[8]

Many organisations will be tempted to keep to their traditional working style. However, resist the temptation to force fit *the way we've always done it* if it is no longer relevant. Jake Pacifico at The TalentPool Company says '*The battle for talent is tougher than ever. Candidates have a greater number of options available to them and are more selective when choosing their employer. Having great brands and benefits are no longer enough. Individuals want to work in purpose-led, diverse businesses, who care about more than just profit. An organisation's commitment to people and the planet is absolutely critical when attracting and retaining talent.*'[9] Whether you are an intrapreneur or entrepreneur, people are people, who at the end of the day want to feel empowered. This is an opportunity to re-build a stronger, happier, and loyal workforce.

Empower Culture

There was a time when many felt that a designated workplace was essential to productivity, team building and attracting talent. The bigger and better the office, the bigger and better the prospects. Yet today, expensive empty real estate no longer plays a pivotal role in delivering output. As such, leaders and employees have had to creatively step up to virtual internal and customer-facing collaboration that have had fundamental long-term implications. Is it the end of office life? If so, what IMPACT does it have on company culture?

In some markets, over 62% of employees were working from home at the peak of the 2020 pandemic, as opposed to just 25% in 2018.[10] Once past the initial shock of lockdown, many found that working virtually had some surprising results. Eighty percent said that they preferred to work from home, with 41% saying that they were more productive.[11] No doubt, the absence of a daily commute and working in a home environment, had a positive IMPACT on reducing cost and stress, ultimately increasing productivity. Since most interactions moved online, the brand and customer intersection became even more significant with employees as the linchpins. A positive employee experience results in a better customer experience, giving the workforce a sense of purpose. For many companies, the flexibility of remote working is likely to stay. So, it is imperative to sense the mood and engage the teams to define the culture.

By prioritising what really matters (i.e., the people), there is a real opportunity to break free from the chains holding an organisation back. When you forge a culture that is set up for success, it unearths the possibilities for teams to thrive in.

6 WAYS TO EMPOWER YOUR BUSINESS CULTURE ™

1	2	3
A SHARED PURPOSE	HEALTH AND WELLNESS	DIVERSITY AND EQUALITY

4	5	6
EQUITY-SHARING	CUSTOMER-CENTRICITY	SOCIO-ECONOMIC RESPONSIBILITY

6 WAYS TO EMPOWER YOUR BUSINESS CULTURE™:

1. **A Shared Purpose:** Invite teams to co-create a company mission and vision
2. **Health and Wellness:** Ensure the team's safety, physical and mental wellbeing
3. **Diversity and Equality:** Foster an inclusive culture that values non-conformity
4. **Equity-Sharing:** Create employee-owned cooperatives for business and public benefit
5. **Customer-Centricity**: Empower teams to deliver personalised customer experiences

6. **Socio-Economic Responsibility:** Promote actions that make our world a better place

In an ever-changing business landscape, organisational culture must be nimble and quick to adapt. Don't focus on the past. Empower your tribe and invest in the future.

Empower Society

'We carry inside us, the wonders we seek outside us.'
– Rumi

The United Nations' ambition to create a beautiful global society encompasses these six specific *SDGs: SDG#1 No Poverty, SDG#2 Zero Hunger, SDG#3 Good Health and Wellbeing, SDG#5 Gender Equality, SDG#16 Peace, Justice and Strong Institutions, and SDG#17 Partnerships for the goals.* In other words, *resilient individuals, inclusive communities and a just society.* Sometimes, it is difficult to know how to contribute or make a difference, but every little helps.

The 2020 pandemic brought out a kinder, more generous side of people, brands, and businesses – the best of humanity. When healthcare workers were celebrated as national heroes, brands joined in to show their support. Deliveroo, invited customers to make food donations for doctors and nurses so that 500,000 meals[12] could be delivered to NHS teams across the UK. Allbirds gave away thousands of pairs of their signature Wool Runners to the #healthcareheroes. Pip & Nut called on its community to support food banks to ensure that cupboards were stocked with nutritious necessities with their *'One from you, one from us'* charity drive for those in need.[13] Kleenex tissues relieved stress and anxiety with their #AllTheFeelings campaign by giving 100,000 three-month subscriptions of the Calm app.[14] Companies like Audible and Zoom offered learning tools for education, Google supported small businesses, and Nike promoted safety and fitness with their #playinside #playfortheworld campaigns.[15]

It pays to be kind. The feel-good factor that comes from kindness, empathy and giving is priceless. Instilling these qualities into a company's ethos can empower society and ultimately the world.

However, most people are probably unaware, that every time we indulge in a little of bit of chocolate, we are fuelling a darker world of human exploitation with some startling facts[16]:

- 60% of all global cocoa comes from the Ivory Coast and Ghana
- In those two countries alone, there are 2.5 million cocoa family farms
- Of the 1.56 million children that work on farms, 95% work under illegal and hazardous conditions
- The average cocoa farmer earns 0.78 USD cents a day
- 30,000 people are being trafficked into modern slavery, forced to grow cocoa

Enter Tony's Chocolonely ... a Dutch IMPACT company with a clear roadmap to 100% slave-free chocolate by: driving awareness, leading by example, and inspiring everyone to act. Have they got your attention yet? Read on ...

Tony's Chief Chocolate Officer, Henk Jan Beltman, says, *'We're an IMPACT company that makes chocolate. Not a chocolate company that makes an IMPACT.'* Same thing, right? No. Beltman says it's completely different, because making an IMPACT is the actual goal, while chocolate and making money are the means to make all chocolate 100% slavery-free. That's right: not just their chocolate, but ALL chocolate worldwide.

They urge the entire industry to follow five groundbreaking sourcing principles[17]:

1. **Traceable Cocoa Beans:** Tony's cocoa beans are fully traceable, as they purchase them directly from their partner cooperatives which guaranty that the beans in their bars are slave-free.
2. **Higher Price:** Tony's pay an additional premium for their cocoa, as the standard price keeps farmers in poverty. They believe that every farming household should be able to earn an income for a respectable standard of living.
3. **Strong Farmers:** Tony's invest in farming cooperatives to help them become stronger and drive economies of scale that create commitment and trust.

4. **The Long-Term:** Tony's work with farmers for at least five years to ensure that farmers get a viable return on investment.

5. **Better Quality & Productivity:** Tony's helps farmers in agricultural best practice, which in turn benefits the farmer with higher yields and better quality cocoa. By encouraging crop diversification, farmers are also able to generate other sources of income such as raising chickens and cultivating aubergines, etc.

With revenues of over €110 million,[18] Tony's Chocolonely is the biggest chocolate brand in the Netherlands – with a market share of approximately 19% in bars (in 2020)[19] and growth of 24% as of 2021,[20] with ambitious global expansion plans. Tony's is an IMPACT company first and foremost, so all the SDGs are integrated in everything they do. They focus on seven core SDGs[21] aligned to their mission to ensure that all chocolate is 100% slavery-free: *SDG#1 No Poverty, SDG#2 Zero Hunger, SDG#8 Decent Work & Economic Growth, SDG#10 Reduced Inequalities, SDG#12 Responsible Consumption & Production, SDG#13 Climate Action, SDG#17 Partnerships for the Goals.* You can find their manifesto in every wrapper, along with their delicious chocolate!

'Raise the Bar – Together we make chocolate 100% slavery-free':
www.tonyschocolonely.com
Hear Tony's Chocolonely's Story
on The IMPACT Game Changers™ Podcast:

www.splitsecondltd.com

9.2. BE THE CHANGE

'Be the change you want to see in the world.'
– Mahatma Gandhi

According to the UN, since 1950, 20%[22] of the Amazon rainforest has been lost in the name of cultivation. There has been a 60% decline in vertebrate species since 1970 and six billion tonnes[23] of fish and seafood have been extracted from the world's oceans. Sadly, this bleak state has been accelerated by human activities such as pollution, violence, slavery, poverty, hunger, obesity, and inequality. Drastic measures are needed as there is no planet B.

With a global estimated market size of $15.4 trillion by 2025,[24] the Fast-Moving Consumer Goods (FMCG) sector feeds, clothes, cleans, and entertains us, touching most parts of our lives. Yet this sector has a significant socio-economic and environmental IMPACT on people and the planet. From farming, fishing, to manufacturing, supply chains to energy consumption and waste, the reality is a far cry from glitzy marketing campaigns. The challenge is to create a balance between a rising population set to grow to nearly 10 billion by 2050,[25] achieve the SDGs by 2030 and defeat climate change. This means we must clear the air, clean the oceans, and cool the earth. It's quite a tall order, but still possible ... at this moment in time.

'Plans to protect air and water, wilderness and wildlife, are in fact plans to protect man.'
– Stewart Udall, Advocate for the Planet Earth

Clear the Air

*'The Earth is **4.6 billion** years old. Scaling to **46 years**, humans have been here **4 hours**, The industrial revolution began **1 minute ago**, and in that time, we've destroyed more than half the world's forests. This isn't sustainable. Let's create a better world.'*
– Greenpeace

Traffic levels were down by 35% in 2020, and air pollutants and greenhouse gases dropped by 50%[26] in most global cities. Yet despite the short-term benefits, air pollution SDG targets will still not be met by 2030. Unfortunately, this will also have a direct IMPACT on other SDGs as many of the strategies for waste management, clean energy and socio-economic development are directly linked to air quality. Two billion people are still using carbon-emitting fuels such as coal which will lead to 40% more premature deaths.[27]

Yet according to the National Audit Office, the UK is also not on track to reduce air pollution targets by 2030. Despite the limits on some pollutants and reduced emissions, the government's progress has been very slow. Sadly, air pollution is linked thousands of deaths a year. The report highlights that air pollution is disproportionately emitted across the UK. Low-income and ethnically diverse areas are more severely affected than the rest of the population.[28] To meet all 2030 targets for major air pollutants, most Western governments need to develop robust solutions quickly as existing measures are simply not enough. Businesses must step up to meet the challenges and identify to the opportunities that they represent.

The World Health Organisation recommends the following initiatives that would reduce air pollution deaths by two-thirds by 2030[29]:

- Education and funding to improve urban air quality
- Monitoring via the Global Air Pollution and Health Platform to protect the vulnerable
- Joint action between the financial, health and environmental sectors to deliver clean energy technologies

One brand that has made strides to eliminate their products' carbon footprint is Allbirds. They are the first fashion brand to label every item with their carbon footprint like calories. They are fully transparent with how much CO2 is emitted to produce their trainers. According to their website, '*the average footprint of our products is 7.6 kg CO2e (reminder: that means "carbon dioxide equivalent emissions"—a mouthful, we know), we're saying we're keeping tabs on things like methane emissions, too, a greenhouse gas even more potent than carbon dioxide.*[30] A standard Allbirds' *sneaker* has a carbon footprint of 12.5 kg

CO_2e.[31] Allbirds metrics track greenhouse gases through four key elements: materials, manufacturing, product use, and end of life. Transportation is also measured but reported as part of company-wide emissions. They use natural and recycled materials and offset any remaining elements, thereby making the business carbon neutral. Sandeep Varma, Chief Commercial Officer at Allbirds, believes that it is really important for brands to come together on sustainability. In 2020, at a sustainability transformation conference, he was quoted as saying, *'there are many different ways that brands can work together to share information and share best practice. One of the ways that we are really proud, is the new way of creating a shoe sole from a new material powered by sugar cane. And we actually make that technology open-sourced and have had over a hundred companies globally looking to use it. Sustainability is bigger than any one brand or any industry, it's about coming together to reduce carbon emissions.'*[32] The ambition is to be carbon emission-free and create a more sustainable future.

So how does their average 7.6kg CO_2e footprint stack up? Well, a pair of jeans emits 34kg of CO_2e,[33] a bicycle 240kg CO_2e,[34] and a typical car emits 4.6 metric tons of CO_2e[35] – so you do the maths. Walking, biking, car sharing, or using mass transit can improve our physical health, but also the planet's. Sandeep says that *'our focus has been to reduce our carbon footprint so we can tread more lightly on the planet.'*[36]

> *'We do not inherit the earth from our ancestors,*
> *we borrow it from our children.'*
> – Native American Proverb

Clean the Ocean

> *'If we can't all swim together, we will sink. There is no plan B,*
> *because there is no planet B.'*
> – Ban Ki-Moon, former Secretary-General of the United Nations

Two-thirds of the earth's surface is covered by oceans, which amounts to 97% of the planet's water.[37] The oceans provide livelihoods, coastal resources, tourism, and food to more than three billion people, which is 40% of the global population.[38] They also play a pivotal role in regulating the planet's climate. According to NASA, oceans have a much higher capacity to store heat than our atmosphere. Ninety percent of the extra heat generated from global warming is stored in the ocean.[39]

However, we are drowning the oceans. More than 14 million tonnes of plastic[40] are thought to be on the ocean floor. According to the United Nations Environment Program (UNEP) report, there are more than 51 trillion[41] microplastics in the sea, more than the number of stars in the Milky Way galaxy! UNEP also tells us that plastic accounts for 85% of all marine pollution and *'by 2040, it will nearly triple, adding 23-37 million metric tons of waste into the ocean per year. This means about 50kg of plastic per meter of coastline.'*[42] As a result, *'all marine life – from plankton and shellfish, to birds, turtles and mammals – faces the grave risk of toxification, behavioural disorder, starvation and suffocation.'*[43] Recent studies also show that humans are unknowingly consuming microplastics through the food chain, on average around 5 grams per week[44] resulting in cell death and a variety of allergies.

'By 2050, 99% of earth's seabirds will have ingested plastic.'
– The United Nations

The UNEP insight highlights that one million plastic bottles are purchased every minute and five trillion single-use plastic bags are used every year.[45] We produce 300 million tonnes of single-use plastic waste annually.[46] To put that into perspective, that is nearly the equivalent weight of the entire human population. We must stop our dependency on plastic because 30% of it ends up in natural ecosystems.[47] These alarming figures also point towards a major challenge. Only 14% of plastic[48] is recycled and just 20 companies are responsible for 55%[49] of the world's plastic waste. These state-owned and multinational corporations include oil, gas, and chemical-producing giants.

Pollution, overfishing, and climate change remain key threats to our oceans. According to the World Economic Forum (WEF), the *Ocean Economy* is worth $2.5 trillion[50] a year but is not sustainable unless we radically protect this natural resource. The WEF proposes restorative aquaculture farming, which would absorb CO2 and replenish seafaring stocks. Protection of the Coral Reefs such as the Great Barrier Reef, which is the largest living creature in the world and can be seen from space with the naked eye. Coral Reefs are home to a quarter of all marine life, serve as coastline defences from tropical storms and generate $9 trillion in net benefit a year.[51] We must develop technology that supports marine-protected areas by limiting unregulated ecological exploitation. Scientists believe that 30%[52] of our entire planet should be protected by 2030 or the consequences will be catastrophic. If these initiatives are adopted worldwide, the opportunities could be limitless, and the grim fate of the oceans can be reversed. So how do we tackle such a mammoth task? Start by clearing the plastic where you live.

One morning on his travels, Marius Smit saw the devastating aftermath of a tropical storm that left clean beaches covered in plastic pollution overnight. Marius recognised the problem of plastic in our waters, which he calls 'plastic soup' as an unsustainable challenge, he felt it was time to 'stop talking and start doing.'[53] He had a lightbulb moment. Marius founded and took on the role of Captain and CEO of Plastic Whale, whose mission is to achieve plastic-free waters worldwide.

Inspired by JFK's 1961 'Man on the moon'[54] speech, he set himself a remarkable task to build a boat made out of plastic waste floating in the canals of Amsterdam. He mobilised a team of 450 'whalers' in 2011[55] for their first plastic fishing expedition. He soon began turning PET bottle waste into ship-shape vessels, responding to one of the circular economy's key questions 'what if the goods of today became the resources of tomorrow?'[56] Established on their three pillars We Collect Plastic Waste – We Create Amazing Products – We Educate Those Around Us,[57] Plastic Whale has since become a global plastic fishing movement. They began reeling in key sponsors, talented teams, and shareholders to expand their fishing fleet. Brands like Starbucks, NIKE, ING, Tommy Hilfiger all got on board to go plastic fishing too!

The team also launched the Plastic Whale Foundation, a school program that takes kids fishing and educates them on their mission. Sarah de Beurs, Head of the Plastic Whale Foundation, says, 'After all, making products from plastic waste is a way for us to involve people in our mission and have them change their behaviour in order to use less plastic themselves or make other sustainable choices.'[58] Then in 2017, they had another lightbulb moment. They partnered up with designers LAMA Concept and Vepa office furniture and began converting Amsterdam's canal plastic waste into high-end boardroom circular furniture. Marius believes that plastic soup is a growing global problem, but with all hands on deck, we can do something about it and have a whale of time!

Blue-sky thinking can lead to innovative concepts for any business, even if it is turning trash into treasure. This proves that sustainability and a healthy profit can go hand in hand. In turn, business will grow, society will be educated and empowered, and we will be another step closer to saving the planet. Anchors away!

'Together for plastic-free land and sea – Collect, Create, Educate':
www.plasticwhale.com
Hear Plastic Whale's Story on The IMPACT Game Changers™ Podcast:

www.splitsecondltd.com

Cool the Planet

'I want you to act as if your house is on fire ... because it is.'
– Greta Thunberg

Sunlight hits the earth; energy is reflected back into space and heat is distributed in our atmosphere. That is what used to happen before mankind intervened. Since the mid 20th century, industrial expansion has resulted in the *greenhouse effect* warming the planet as some of the heat gets trapped in the atmosphere rather than being released back into space. The UN and NASA scientists believe that there is a 95% probability that human activities over the last 50 years are responsible for climate change.[59]

Temperatures are rising, fires are burning, ice caps are melting, coral are bleaching, cities are flooding, and the weather is changing. This is not a prediction. This is reality. Today, the Amazon rainforest emits more carbon dioxide than it absorbs. The giant tropical forest known as the *lungs of our planet,* produces 20% of the Earth's oxygen.[60] It is the most biodiverse region in the world, home to three million species of plants and animals. Its billions of trees absorb carbon emissions that mitigate the climate crisis. However, now, mankind is accelerating the catastrophic trajectory and the rainforest is going from CO2 negative to CO2 positive. The cause is deliberate. Deforestation is at a 12-year high, and fires have surged to record levels since 2007,[61] clearing the land for beef and soy production. Such is the sad state of our planet. So how can brands, businesses and individuals activate change? We need to start making the right choices, not just as businesses, but as global citizens.

Food production generates over a quarter of all global greenhouse emissions. It uses 70% of all freshwater resources and occupies 40% of the earth's land surface.[62] With forecasters predicting a population rise to 10 billion by 2050, food manufacturing is set to increase by 60% in order to feed the world.[63] This would tip the scales to dangerous levels of climate change.

One of the biggest contributors of greenhouse emissions are cows. They produce methane and the deforestation for their pastures creates carbon dioxide. Here is some serious food for thought the next time you are tempted to order a steak ... 1.5 billion livestock are responsible for 18% of the greenhouse gases that cause global warming – more than cars and vans combined.[64] Two-thirds of all agricultural land is used for cattle and if released, it would free up space the size of Africa. The current rate of growth suggests that meat consumption will rise by 76% over the next 30 years.[65] There is not enough land to sustain this demand without greater damage to the planet. Making food choices without all the facts can be a challenge. Most of us are unaware that cows generate 2,850 greenhouse gases (GHG) for the production of 1 kg of meat.[66] Pigs stand at 1,130 GHG[67] and chickens at 300 GHG. In the West, reducing our meat intake by 90%[68] is critical to climate change.

Yet what if there was an alternative source of protein that just produced 1 GHG per 1kg?[69] An animal protein that is consumed by over two billion people worldwide as part of a healthy diet. Edible insects are a solution to reducing emissions and global food shortages. Sustainable harvesting is practiced at Eat Grub by Co-Founder Neil Whippey who believes that *'Insects are the original superfood. Eaten throughout the world, insects are enjoyed not only because of their taste but they are also good for you and the environment. They contain all nine essential amino acids and include important minerals like iron and calcium ... not to mention, they can provide up to 69% protein depending on how they are prepared.'*[70]

As more and more people embrace insects as their superfood, these creatures are becoming almost as popular as kale and quinoa. A recent study found that grasshoppers, silkworms, and crickets are five times as rich in healthy antioxidants as fresh orange juice.[71] The trend is definitely catching on. Toasted chili lime grasshoppers have become a hit with Seattle Mariners' baseball fans. The stadium began serving the snack in 2017 and had to impose a per-game order limit as the tasty bugs became a social media sensation. Baseball, beer, and grasshoppers – will we all play ball? Thirty-two percent[72] of British adults believe that worm burgers and cricket snacks will be the norm within the next decade. Bon Appetit!

If insects don't appeal, then perhaps a more plant-based menu may be more mouth-watering. In 2010, on World Animal Day, Jaap Korteweg introduced The Vegetarian Butcher® in the Hague, the Netherlands. According to his team, Jaap who comes from a long line of farmers, *'liked meat so much he decided to make it vegetarian'*.[73] Their mission is to become the biggest butcher in the world by releasing animals from the food chain. That is how The Vegetarian Butcher® was born. Now, with a range of plant-based meat in over 55 countries worldwide,[74] they are driving a food revolution that will make a fundamental IMPACT on the world without ever spilling a drop of blood. And scientists agree. Dr. Marco Springmann from Oxford University says, *'If people opted for a* *predominantly plant-based diet, then food-related emissions could decline by at least three-quarters, and mortality rates could decline by 20%. It would mitigate some of the worst diseases and save over $1 trillion of global healthcare costs.'*[75]

The Netherlands is the world's second biggest food exporter after the US and the leader in sustainable farming.[76] *National Geographic* found that the Dutch have made a commitment to deliver *'twice as much food using half as many resources with most farmers having reduced their dependence on water for key crops by as much as 90%.'*[77] They have almost eliminated the use of pesticides, pushed the boundaries of agriculture through technology and have doubled their crop yields vs the global average. More than 140 countries[78] are in the process of adopting these greener farming methods. *Going Dutch* could literally feed the world!

'Human activity has altered almost 75 per cent of the earth's surface, squeezing wildlife and nature into an ever-smaller corner of the planet,'[79] according to the United Nations. It is a serious challenge as forests are home to 80% of all terrestrial species of animals, plants, and insects.[80] Drought and desertification are the main culprits behind 12 million hectares of land loss every year; 23 hectares per minute.[81] In other words, within one year, 20 million tons of grain could have been grown on the land that was lost.[82] Biodiversity is an intricate web of species and organisms that work together to maintain balance and support life. Yet *The Global Assessment Report on Biodiversity and Ecosystem Service* report found that around 1 million[83] animal and plant species are threatened with extinction – many within decades – which would risk destroying our delicate ecosystems, economies, supply chains, health, and quality of life.

One astonishing fact is that over 80%[84] of the human diet is provided to us by plants. Only three cereal crops – rice, maize, and wheat – offer 60%[85] of energy intake. Ecotone is a food company that has been meeting the biodiversity challenge head on for years. They are Europe's first largest B Corp food business with 9 manufacturing centres in 7 countries, in 6 categories with 16 purposeful brands such as Clipper tea, Whole Earth, Kallo organic snacks and stocks, and many others. Their mission is to provide and promote *'Biodiversity on menus'*.

UK CEO Emma Vass says *'Sustainability and biodiversity are part of the company's DNA of who we are and what the portfolio brand stands for. I'm quite proud of that fact. We are not on a new journey trying to retrofit the challenge that comes to food producers to make more sustainable choices and be more responsible for biodiversity and environment. We've always done that. It's very much been our point of difference.'*[86] Ecotone are fully committed to several Sustainable Development Goals (SDGs): *SDG#2 Zero Hunger, SDG#3 Good Health and Wellbeing, SDG#5 Gender Equality, SDG#12 Responsible Consumption and Production, and SDG#15 Life on Land.* They are pioneers in bringing the SDGs to life via their brands. For instance, Clipper was the first plastic-free teabag, leading the way for other tea brands to follow. They also don't bleach their teabags, unlike most other brands on the market that whiten the product for consumer aesthetics. Points of difference that would shock most consumers and make them reconsider their choices and IMPACT on the planet.

Yet this IMPACT also extends to people. Ecotone recently conducted some research and found that 68% of people believe that the environment is vital to them, but only 30% understand what biodiversity means.[87] Emma believes that there are a lot of opportunities ahead in providing informed choices for consumers and shoppers *'so that they know they are helping stop the climate emergency or stop the devastating IMPACT that the food industry can have.'*[88] *We're always also open to any innovation or working with any partners, whether they are NGOs or other suppliers, who can help us continue providing better choices for shoppers.'*

Ecotone's commitment to restoring and protecting biodiversity goes beyond food and drink. They have also set up a foundation, a charitable body that creates a genuine positive change on their mission to increase biodiversity, restore ecosystems, foster knowledge on how diets and biodiversity are connected, raise public awareness, and give back. From planting trees in the *Forever Forest*, to Fairtrade partnerships that give back to the communities from where the products are sourced from, to protecting orangutangs in their natural habitat – Ecotone can demonstrate actionable IMPACT, build emotional connections with consumers and lead with genuine purpose. Emma says that *'It's a lovely business with an amazing culture and like-minded people that are genuinely passionate about working with purpose for an organisation that cares and wants to do the right thing.'*[89]

'Let's put biodiversity on the menu': www.ecotone.bio
Hear Ecotone's Story on The IMPACT Game Changers™ Podcast:

www.splitsecondltd.com

The clock is ticking, and every business can start right here, right now by identifying and integrating the most pertinent SDGs that can diminish climate change: *SDG#6 Clean Water, SDG#7 Affordable and Clean Energy, SDG#13 Climate Action, SDG#14 Life Below Water, and SDG#15 Life on Land.* By embedding them into business operations, company ethos and team consciousness we can begin to cool the planet.

'For too long, we have been waging a senseless and suicidal war on nature. The result is three interlinked environmental crises: climate disruption, biodiversity loss, and pollution that threaten our viability as a species.'
– António Guterres, Secretary-General of the United Nations

COOL THE PLANET – TOP 10 BUSINESS HACKS ™

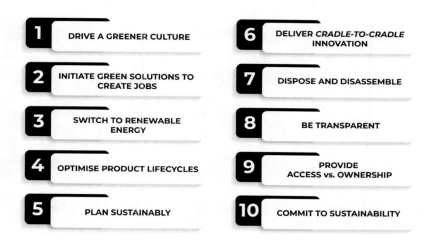

1. DRIVE A GREENER CULTURE
2. INITIATE GREEN SOLUTIONS TO CREATE JOBS
3. SWITCH TO RENEWABLE ENERGY
4. OPTIMISE PRODUCT LIFECYCLES
5. PLAN SUSTAINABLY
6. DELIVER *CRADLE-TO-CRADLE* INNOVATION
7. DISPOSE AND DISASSEMBLE
8. BE TRANSPARENT
9. PROVIDE ACCESS vs. OWNERSHIP
10. COMMIT TO SUSTAINABILITY

COOL THE PLANET – TOP 10 BUSINESS HACKS:

1. **Drive a Greener Culture:** Engage your team to challenge current business operations and brainstorm greener ways of working.

2. **Initiate and Support Green Solutions to Create Jobs**: Reduce carbon pollution, build equity, develop healthy ecosystems and communities through planning and investment, both at business and government levels.

3. **Switch to Renewable Energy:** Many governments, including the UK government aspire to power every home with offshore wind power by 2030. Why wait till then?

4. **Optimise Product Lifecycles:** Review raw materials, CO2e, energy consumption, packaging, and biodegradability to build green products to last.

5. **Plan Sustainably:** Capture and integrate 'green' insights and your SDG targets into your category vision, marketing, and business strategies. Consider greener production, transport, usage, and disposal.

6. **Deliver *Cradle-to-Cradle* Innovation:** Design the next incarnation of new product development by using existing waste in a circular economy.

7. **Dispose and Disassemble:** Where will the product go after usage? Will it be easy to re-use the components to give it a new lease of life?

8. **Be Transparent:** Share and leverage authentic sustainability initiatives and their progress towards the SDGs with your customers as an IMPACT Unique *Solution* Point (USP)™.

9. **Provide Access vs Ownership:** Where possible, provide access to customers rather than selling more 'stuff.' Netflix and Spotify give us access to their movies and music without producing DVDs or CDs.

10. **Commit to Sustainability:** Comply with legislation, get the right certifications, and introduce your own environmental systems supported by the relevant industry bodies.

'It's surely our responsibility to do everything within our power to create a planet that provides a home not just for us, but for all life on earth.'
– Sir David Attenborough

9.3. BE A FORCE FOR GOOD

'If you think you are too small to make a difference,
try sleeping with a mosquito.'
– African Proverb

Responsible companies and individuals are proving that *'doing the right thing'* is essential. Standing up for intrinsic values, standing out to be part of something bigger and standing together to deliver change, actually generate greater commercial profit. These are the principles that ultimately align to the conscious consumer's values. With so many businesses taking steps to act more responsibly towards people, a sustainable planet, and accountable practices to deliver a healthy profit, we can be a force for the greater good.

Stand Up

Today's conscious consumers are not interested in gimmicks and fads. They want to use the power of purchase to make the world a better place. They will stand by you, support you and champion causes as long as you are transparent, sincere, and kind in your mission.

Edelman's *Trust, The New Brand Equity* study suggest that nearly *'two-thirds of respondents say that they are more attracted to brands that focus on making the world a better place while slightly more than a third want brands to focus on individual benefits.'*[90] Taking a stand could make or break a brand. The research found that 63% of consumers believe that they have the power to *'force brands to change'* and 78% feel that they can encourage brands to improve society.[91] In return, brands will be rewarded with trust as 61%[92] are willing to advocate them if they have completely earned their trust. Fifty-seven per cent are willing to purchase them on the trust factor, and 31% are even willing to share their personal data with the brand.[93] Yet if a brand keeps quiet on a key matter, 65%[94] walk away. Until recently, taking the path of least resistance was the primary belief for most brands. Today, it is a deal-breaker because silence is consent. In other words, taking a stand is putting purpose at the heart of a brand.

Since 1978, Ben & Jerry's® ice cream have always promoted a *'values-led mission'*[95] about fairness and equality. The brand has never shied away from controversy. Instead, they have embraced and even stoked political fires in a provocative manner. With a long history of championing social causes and human rights, they have used their voice to stand up for and against issues that don't align with the brand's core values.

In 2018, Ben & Jerry's® launched a limited-edition ice cream called *Pecan Resist* to *'stand up for justice and resist oppression'* under a previous White House administration.[96] The mission-driven ice cream supported some of the causes that the former president did not, from gender equality, immigrants, people of colour, and the environment. A portion of the sales proceeds went to support non-profit partners, thus, promoting brand activism through product innovation. Ben & Jerry's® also teamed up with the Advancement Project National Office, a multi-racial civil rights organisation to raise awareness on criminal justice reform and systemic racism. The brand re-released *Justice ReMix'd 'a flavour and campaign designed to inspire radical change. Just in time for Election Day 2020.'*[97]

More recently, Ben & Jerry's® have been championing the fight against climate change with their UK vegan non-dairy ice cream *Save Our Swirled Now!* The big scoop is to drive awareness on the climate crisis, a portion of each tub will go to *The Climate Coalition*.[98] The flavour's main objective is to urge the UK government to tackle climate change by acting with green solutions as part of their economic recovery plans. The brand believes the way forward is to:

- Unleash a clean energy revolution that boosts UK jobs
- Protect restore and expanding the UK's green spaces
- Increase support to the most vulnerable
- Urge the public to support the cause by signing their declaration: https://www.benjerry.co.uk/values/issues-we-care-about/climate-justice[99]

Ben & Jerry's® also launched the *Un-fudge Our Future* vegan flavour in Australia as part of their sustainable future campaign to petition the leaders to ban fossil fuels. They live and breathe their core values on human rights and dignity, social and economic justice and environmental protection, restoration, and regeneration. There are three parts to their overall mission:

- A product mission drives them to make fantastic ice cream
- An economic mission that manages the company for sustainable financial growth
- A social mission that compels them to use their company in innovative ways to make the world a better place[100]

From a renovated petrol station in Vermont USA, to the global IMPACT Brand™ that it is today, Ben & Jerry's® have put ice cream on the map by doing the world a flavour!

Another brand that has spoken out on elections is California's outdoor wear company Patagonia. They made a very strong political statement of their own against climate change sceptics. The company printed '*Vote the a**holes out*' – a concealed message on the back of some of their 2020 Men's and Women's Stand Up shorts' labels. Thousands questioned if the Twitter post was, in fact, real. Indeed, it was.

The aim was to drive action and awareness. A percentage of the sales went to thousands of grassroots environmental organisations. Company founder Yvon Chouinard said, '*It refers to politicians from any party who deny or disregard the climate crisis and ignore science, not because they aren't aware of it, but because their pockets are lined with money from oil and gas interests.*'[101]

Many individuals have also put their reputations on the line by standing up for what they believe in and using their voices as a force for good. When NFL quarterback Colin Kaepernick remained seated for the American national anthem in the 2016 49'ers third pre-season game, he stood against racial injustice and received a barrage of mixed reactions. He said, '*I am not going to stand up to show pride in a flag for a country that oppresses black people and people of colour. If they take football away, my endorsements from me, I know that I stood up for what is right. This is bigger than football.*'[102] Some were outraged, and others supported his plight against systemic racism and police brutality. Despite risking everything and not playing since New Year's Day 2017, Kaepernick was not left to stand alone.

Nike took a chance and kneeled with the lone athlete to celebrate their 30th anniversary of the *Just Do it* ad. So, even though the campaign was just as divisive as the original protest, it was the right thing to do. Nike's sales grew by +31% and Kaepernick demonstrated that art does indeed imitate life sometimes: '*Believe in something. Even if it means sacrificing everything.*'[103]

'*Be a voice, not an echo.*'
– Albert Einstein

Nike also teamed up with Marcus Rashford as another force for good. The Manchester United forward who launched a parliamentary petition to end food poverty spoke about his own personal experiences of using food vouchers as a child saying, '*I know first-hand what hunger can lead to, so I think enough is enough ...*'[104] He successfully campaigned to extend free school meals during the pandemic summer by writing to ministers to tackle this issue affecting the nation and the world.

According to the UN, more than 700 million people around the world, live in extreme poverty.[105] The Covid-19 pandemic is projected to push that figure up by an additional 70 million over the coming years.[106] One out of five children[107] live in extreme poverty with long-term negative effects. In fact, world hunger has been rising over several consecutive years, and the number of out-of-school primary-age children has been a staggering 60 million in the last decade.[108]

Rashford kept calm and carried on, in spite of a couple of initial setbacks when the UK government rejected his second objective, to extend the free kids' meals program during key holidays including Christmas and Easter. He pleaded, *'Put aside all the noise, the digs, the party politics and let's focus on the reality. A significant number of children are going to bed tonight, not only hungry but feeling like they don't matter ...'*[109] Rashford's spotlight on the issue garnered enough attention that created a coalition of supermarkets, charities, local businesses, and councils banded together to support his mission. He said he was *'Blown away by news of local businesses stepping up to fill the voucher scheme deficit during the October half-term. Selflessness, kindness, togetherness, this is the England I know.'*[110] Rashford is determined to push the boundaries, influence decision-makers and end child food poverty for good. *'If you have things that you care about keep them close to your heart; I'd always encourage to speak about them,'*[111] he said. The government eventually made another U-turn and spent £400 million to support 1.7 million poor children and their families.[112] Where there is a will, there is a way. Rashford says, *'I am fully committed to this cause, and I will fight for the rest of my life for it.'*[113]

Some may feel that it is easier for celebrities and big brands to stand up for what they believe in. They have a strong share of voice and marketing support that is likely to get media attention and promote their proposition value. However, driving change takes courage, patience, and a purpose. So, whether you are an individual, entrepreneur or intrapreneur, stand up and:

1. BE Kind
2. BE Honest
3. BE Bold
4. BE Informed
5. BE An Example

6. BE United
7. BE Inclusive
8. BE Committed
9. BE A Community
10. BE A Force for Good

And the rest will follow...

> *'When we practice loving kindness and compassion, we are the first ones to profit.'*
> – Rumi

Stand Out

IMAGINE *a world where everything we do makes a life-changing IMPACT.*
IMAGINE for every email we send, a day's access to education is provided.
IMAGINE for every product we sell, a tree is planted.
IMAGINE for every new client we acquire, a social entrepreneur is funded.
IMAGINE for every cup of coffee we buy, access to life-saving water is given.
IMAGINE for every takeaway we order, food waste is rescued.
IMAGINE for every bouquet we buy, sustainable farming is practised.
IMAGINE for every glass of water we drink, sea turtles are protected.
IMAGINE for every birthday we celebrate, orphans are fed.
IMAGINE for every trading goal we hit, a family business is backed.

Now it is all possible.

The universal law of cause and effect states that for every action there is a reaction. By aligning our intentions and actions, is where the magic begins. We can all create an IMPACT that can make the world a better place. This is when we suddenly go from being good global citizens to creating great global communities. Every business is an opportunity to create a need, solve a problem and follow a passion. So how does purpose fit in when running a business when there are so many other priorities?

B1G1 Founder Masami Sato says, *'I think every business starts with a sense of aspiration, but often many business owners feel that they are not ready to do great things yet. One day, a simple idea came to me.*

What if every business could make a difference in their own way, just by doing what they normally do?"[114] That is how the *Buy1Give1* concept was born in 2007.

Unlike conventional compassion models, B Corp certified B1G1 is a global giving movement that brings a community of nearly 3,000 SMEs together that are changing the world in a big way, one IMPACT at a time. Businesses can now make an instantaneous social IMPACT by embedding giving activities into everyday commercial operations. This can be achieved for even as little as just one cent. Unlike traditional philanthropy where substantial donations are made to a single cause, now one can select from over +450 carefully vetted high-IMPACT projects in over +30 countries. There is complete transparency of where 100% of the giving goes. B1G1 is about creating *Giving Stories* aligned to a business's mission and vision of the world. These *IMPACTS* can celebrate company wins, build team rapport, or just to do some good in the world ... so giving does not have be taxing.

Co-Founder Paul Dunn says that *'60-70% of people have a negative reaction to the word 'charity' because it makes them feel guilty. We shouldn't give from a place of guilt – it's not sustainable. We believe that the beneficiary is not just the person receiving it, but it's actually about all of us. It's about sharing the joy of giving and making an IMPACT. Every second, every day and in every way.'*[115]

With over 250 million IMPACTS made to date, B1G1 also serves as a business conduit to the UN SDGs based on personal, company, and community values. The organisation handpicks IMPACT projects from around the world to support all 17 SDGs. The *Giving Stories* can be directly linked to an *SDG IMPACT Plan*™. These align the company strategy, stakeholders, and innovation pipeline – providing solutions that will address some of the biggest challenges facing our world today such as climate change, poverty, health, and other issues. Start small and grow from there in realising the SDGs by 2030 and becoming a business for good.

www.splitsecondltd.com

Stand Together

> *'United we stand, divided we fall.'*
> – Aesop

Since 2007, more than half of humanity – 3.5 billion people – live in cities, and this number is expected to rise to 60% by 2030 and 70% by 2050.[116] Even though cities only take up 3% of the planet's land, they account for 60-80% of energy consumption and 75% of carbon emissions, putting pressure on local infrastructures, economies, resources, and public health.[117]

Why does this matter? Because the paradox is that cities generate 80%[118] of the global economy. Socio-economic sustainable societies can be the catalysts of positive change and equality that can unlock the $12 trillion opportunity.

Past pandemics suggest that the public health, economic, political, and social implications will be felt for years to come. On top of rising inflation, conflict, inequality, and climate change, we need to address the rapid dominance of urbanisation and its implications on our fragile Earth. The Sustainable Development Goals are the world's collective commitment to 'end poverty, protect the planet, and ensure that all people enjoy peace and prosperity by 2030.'[119] In the words of the United Nations, this call to action is designed to 'leave no one behind and member countries have pledged to fast-track progress for those furthest behind first.'[120] As we stand up to be better global citizens, stand out as global communities, we can hopefully stand together in sustainable societies.

The UN's urban vision is to create SDG cities. Translating this concept into living, breathing, vibrant municipalities is an ambitious target. It requires strong partnerships and collaboration between governments, communities, and businesses. These hubs would accelerate the SDGs through strategic planning, governance, policy, and investment. Once a city demonstrates a standard of excellence, it can be certified as an official SDG city from the UN's flagship programme. The ambition is to have 900 cities in over 100 countries participate in this groundbreaking programme with over a billion people to accelerate the progress in achieving the SDGs by 2030.[121]

Matti Siemiatycki, Professor of the School of Cities at the University of Toronto, says, 'Future cities play on our ideas of technology, our ideas of how societies are structured and our ideas of how transformations can happen to achieve some of the goals that we're going to need to reach if we're going to avoid a real climate disaster and some of the social challenges that come along with these rapid and dramatic transformations. Businesses that will ultimately be the most ethical will succeed in the long run. The ones that can align their core values and underpin technological and ecological transformation in big data or shared mobility, are the ones used for good.'[122]

'The School of Cities – Where diverse communities come together to spark new insights and design creative ways for cities and their citizens to thrive.': www.schoolofcities.utoronto.ca

**Hear the School of Cities' Story
on The IMPACT Game Changers™ Podcast:**

www.splitsecondltd.com

Chapter Nine – PAY IT FORWARD Exercise:

How will your organisation PAY IT FORWARD?

1. Be Human – Empower your people? Empower your culture? Empower society?
   (For example: Reward and recognition, employee surveys, charity, etc.)
2. Be the Change – Clear the air? Clean the ocean? Cool the planet?
   (For example: Recycling, save electricity, car-sharing, etc.)
3. Be a Force for Good – Stand up? Stand out? Stand together?
   (For example: Support worthy causes, launch your mission, engage your community)

A HUMAN RACE ... TO 2030

'At present, we are moving farther away from our SDG goals that can and must be turned around. We have the knowledge, the science, the technology, and the resources. What we need is unity of purpose, effective leadership from all sectors and urgent, ambitious action. If we combine forces now, we can avert climate catastrophe ... but there is no time for delay and no room for excuses.'
– António Guterres, Secretary-General of the United Nations

At the time of writing these words, there are still 7 years: 20 days: 2 hours: 46 minutes on the Climate Clock to 2030, counting down to the rise of global temperatures above 1.5°C. This is the point of no return that scientists say could be catastrophic (https://climateclock.world).[1] A stark reminder that humankind is not invincible, and that the world is at an inflection point. We must #ActinTime.

The Climate Clock represents the urgency of our mission, the crucial action we must all take to transition to a safe climate. The business case for socio-economic growth and sustainability has finally come of age and every second counts. By setting sustainable targets in isolation or without action, we risk losing human civilisation as we know it by 2050.

The UN's Intergovernmental Panel on Climate Change (IPCC) landmark '*Code Red*' report based on the contributions of 750 authors, 14,000 studies and over 78,000 comments from governments and climate change experts which was approved by 195 nations, confirmed that our planet is in the middle of a climate crisis.[2] Humans are responsible for changing the climate like never before. There is more C02 in the atmosphere right now than at any point in the last two million years. Meeting a 1.5°C target is still possible, but requires '*deep emissions reductions*' and '*rapid, far-reaching, and unprecedented changes in all aspects of society*.'[3] The report also found that '*limiting global warming to 1.5°C compared to 2°C would reduce challenging IMPACTS on ecosystems, human health and wellbeing*.'[4]

Sadly, Earth Overshoot Day is becoming the most critical day in the diary. It marks the date when '*humanity's demand for ecological resources* and services in a given year exceed what the Earth can regenerate in that year.'[5] Over the last 20 years, the date has moved forward by three months. In 2020, Earth Overshoot Day fell on 22 August, partly brought on by the COVID-19 pandemic, in 2021, it fell on July 29, the earliest ever calculated, which means that we are literally living beyond our means.[6] This timeline is getting shorter and shorter every year due to unsustainable human activity such as rapid deforestation, ocean and atmospheric pollution, intensive food agriculture and overall disregard for our planet. We have increased our global carbon footprint by +6.6% from 2020, and reduced our global forest biocapacity, mainly due to the year-on-year deforestation of the Amazon Rainforest by +43%.[7] This date is a vivid reminder that we are depleting the world's natural resources 1.75 times[8] faster than the planet's ecosystem can generate. In other words, we don't have 1.75 Earth (s). We only have one planet, and we must protect it. #Movethedate.

Even if every country around the globe drastically cuts their carbon emissions, we are still likely to experience extreme weather for decades to come. So, we must act now:

- To reduce carbon emissions that will keep global warming down
- To collectively reach net zero emissions long before 2050
- To redefine how we use and produce energy
- To limit our consumption of natural resources and drive a circular economy
- To educate all global citizens on the actions they can take to protect the planet
- To deliver the Sustainable Development Goals (SDGs) by 2030

'If you're feeling comfortable about climate change, you're not acting fast enough.'[9] One of the key messages that was echoed at the *Climate Innovation Forum 2022*, a key stepping stone to COP27. The UN is urging everyone to put pledges into practice as the window to the climate catastrophe is closing. Let's not make this humankind's '*Don't Look Up*'[10] moment.

However, the good news is that we can still turn this fate around and thrive in a better world. Unlike most governments that are financially and politically restricted to act with pace, the business sector is more equipped and agile to deliver the fine balance between economic growth and sustainable ethical societies. As highlighted in the *Better Business Better World* report, the Sustainable Development Goals represent a \$12 trillion opportunity (an estimated 10% of global GDP in 2030), 380 million jobs and a formidable responsibility for a greener, more peaceful world.[11] Sixty of the fastest-growing market opportunities are in four key areas that can generate the greatest economic IMPACT in food and agriculture, cities, energy and materials, and health and well-being. They represent around 60%[12] of the real economy and are crucial to delivering the SDGs. Businesses must prioritise and pursue sustainability with the same rigour and relentless focus that they pursue profit because the two are inextricably linked, but time is of the essence.

Even though sustainability has become part of our everyday language, what can brands, businesses and global citizens do? Everyone can mobilise change. In June 2022, more than 400 CEOs from every sector urged G7 leaders to step up their efforts to tackle climate change. In an open letter, they asked for '*greater clarity and stability*' on climate policies. They said '*Restoring our planetary, human and economic health is vital, as is adapting to those impacts that cannot be avoided. This is going to require trillions of dollars, much of which can be met by the private sector. We call on governments to put in place the market signals that will stimulate and channel this investment.*'[13] This coalition is known as the Sustainable Markets Initiative with the Terra Carta, A Charter for Change. The Charter promotes:

- A dramatic shift in corporate strategies and operations
- A reformed global financial system
- An enabling environment that attracts investment and incentivises action[14]

The letter also says '*Tackling climate change is complex and expensive. But our companies and many others within the Sustainable Markets Initiative are already taking major strides in that direction. If the G7, G20, Commonwealth and others can act on this plan, can work with the private sector to help accelerate our progress, we can do this.*'[15] Yet throughout this process, we must keep the United Nations '*leave no one behind*' pledge in mind and in our actions.

At the UN Climate Talks in Bonn in June 2022, it was apparent broken promises from many wealthy countries stand in the way of climate action for all. These nations are blocking progress by reneging on their financial pledges and support to developing countries that would enable them to tackle climate change. The World Wildlife Fund for Nature (WWF) says, '*Broken promises and unfulfilled commitments on climate finance and action by rich countries stand in the way of progress for all. Countries are falling back into old habits of holding one issue hostage to further another issue dear to them. So, when some countries block progress on loss-and-damage finance and respond to increasing impacts of climate change, others block progress on mitigation. As a consequence, developing countries are deeply concerned that the burden of fighting climate change is increasingly being pushed onto them, without sufficient financial and other support, while many of them are also bearing the brunt of the impacts the world is already feeling.*'[16] It is a fact that climate change affects people of colour the most. UN research[17] tells us that the racial and social disparity is based on who *caused* climate change, as opposed to who are *feeling* its IMPACT. The developed countries caused climate change, but greater IMPACT is being felt by the developing nations, even though their own carbon footprints are generally quite low. The reality is that ultimately climate change affects all living beings on earth. We are one race, the human race against time ... a race we can still win.

Despite the global energy crisis, cost of inflation, geo-political conflicts, standing still is not an option. If businesses don't embrace the new normal and the Sustainable Development Goals, they will be left behind. It's not a question of if, but when. From entrepreneurs, Small Medium Enterprises (SMEs) to global conglomerates, it is every global citizen's responsibility and opportunity to make themselves accountable to the United Nations Sustainable Development Goals. Many businesses have already started to reconsider how they can realign their proposition, practices, and innovation with purpose. They are also the ones to successfully scale Profit for People and Planet. The race to collectively deliver the Sustainable Development Goals by 2030 is well and truly on. It starts right here, right now and the clock is ticking.

Embedding the SDGs into business strategy allows any business to:

- Provide a sustainable business framework for all stakeholders to align strategic priorities and mitigate risk for People, Planet, and Profit
- Identify where the SDG commercial opportunities are for value creation, innovative solutions, and conscious consumers
- Have a shared purpose that enables people to become mindful global citizens that shape businesses for good and make a lasting positive IMPACT

However, it is not just the world of business that needs to change. We, as global citizens need to act as well. There is good news. People want change:

- 72% want to see greater change after the pandemic
- 9 out of 10 people want to live in a fairer world
- 86% want a more sustainable planet[18]

Every split second decision we make, has a negative or positive IMPACT – You decide.

Together, we can design businesses for good, build a sustainable and just society and reverse the current fate of the planet. By making changes not only will we ensure our long-term survival, but we can generate 380 million jobs by 2030 and unlock the $12 trillion and open the door to a sustainable future. The IMPACT Roadmap™ enables businesses to PLAN with Purpose™, PERSUADE with Promise™ and PROFIT with IMPACT™.

Be Part of the Solution. Start an IMPACT Revolution™.

www.splitsecondltd.com

'As human beings, equipped with marvellous intelligence and the potential for developing a warm heart, each of us can become a force for good.'
– The Dalai Lama

ENDNOTES

Dedication:

*Quotation:

Mead, Margaret. Available from:
https://www.brainyquote.com/quotes/margaret_mead_100502 (Accessed 4 May 2022).

The Clock is Ticking:

1. Reuters Events. (14 October 2016) *Making the SDGs a force for good in business.* Available from: https://www.reutersevents.com/sustainability/making-sdgs-force-good-business (Accessed 15 February 2020).
2. Caulkin, Simon. Financial Times. (24 January 2016) *Companies with a purpose beyond profit tend to make more money.* Available from: https://www.ft.com/content/b22933e0-b618-11e5-b147-e5e5bba42e51 (Accessed 1 March 2020). Original source: Collins, Jim and Porras, Jerry. (2005) *Built to Last, Successful habits of visionary companies.* Random House Business (Accessed 14 August 2021).
3. Edelman. (2020) *Edelman Brand Trust Report 2020.* Available from: https://www.edelman.com/sites/g/files/aatuss191/files/2020-03/2020%20Edelman%20Trust%20Barometer%20Brands%20and%20the%20Coronavirus.pdf (Accessed 10 December 2020).
4. Wikipedia. (2020) *Amazon.* Available from: https://en.wikipedia.org/wiki/History_of_Amazon (Accessed 17 December 2020).
5. Social Media Today. (19 December 2019) *Eight Year-Old Ryan Kaji Leads YouTube's Top Earners for 2019.* Available from: https://www.socialmediatoday.com/news/eight-year-old-ryan-kaji-leads-youtubes-top-earners-for-2019/569373/ (Accessed 9 January 2020).
6. Social Media Today. *Eight Year-Old Ryan Kaji Leads YouTube's Top Earners for 2019.*
7. Social Media Today. *Eight Year-Old Ryan Kaji Leads YouTube's Top Earners for 2019.*
   *Quotation:
   Obama, Barack. (23 September 2014) *Remarks by the President at U.N. Climate Change Summit.* The White House. Available from: https://obamawhitehouse.archives.gov/the-press-office/2014/09/23/remarks-president-un-climate-change-summit (Accessed 4 November 2020).
8. Elkington, John. (25 June 2018) *25 Years Ago I Coined the Phrase "Triple Bottom Line." Here's Why It's Time to Rethink It.* Harvard Business Review. Available from: https://hbr.org/2018/06/25-years-ago-i-coined-the-phrase-triple-bottom-line-heres-why-im-giving-up-on-it (Accessed 23 December 2020).
   *Quotation:
   Attenborough, David. (1 October 2020) *David Attenborough leads call for world to invest $500 billion a year to protect nature.* World Economic Forum. Available from: https://www.weforum.org/agenda/2020/10/david-attenborough-global-invest-500-protectnatureiodiversity/?fbclid=IwAR3PLOKu5U97pkg5GXJBf7yxAdGvbeMGTeofMt7qAp-s03OrsRIB-NT092I (Accessed October 4, 2020). By permission of DLA Piper law firm (10 December 2021).
9. United Nations Foundation. (2019) *2019 In Review: The year the world began to wake up to the climate emergency.* Available from: https://unfoundation.org/blog/post/2019-in-review-year-world-began-wake-up-climate-emergency/ (Accessed 7 February 2021). By permission (21 April 2022).
10. World Business Council for Sustainable Development. (2020) *CEO Guide to the Sustainable Development Goals.* Available from: https://sdghub.com/ceo-guide/ (Accessed 28 December 2020).
11. World Business Council for Sustainable Development. *CEO Guide to the Sustainable Development Goals.*

12. World Business Council for Sustainable Development. *CEO Guide to the Sustainable Development Goals.*

13. United Nations Development Programme. (2022) *Sustainable Development Goals Accelerator* Denmark. Available from: https://www.sdg-accelerator.org/content/sdg-accelerator/en/home/sdg-presa/SDGbiz.html (Accessed 29 December 2020). By permission (21 April 2022).
* The Sustainable Development Goals Chart:
United Nations. Department of Economic and Social Affairs, Sustainable Development. *The 17 Goals.* Available from: https://sdgs.un.org/goals (Accessed 1 May 2020). By permission (21 April 2022).

14. United Nations Global Compact. (2020) *Uniting Business in the Decade of Action, Building on 20 Years of Progress.* Available from: https://ungc-communications-assets.s3.amazonaws.com/docs/publications/UN-Global-Compact-Progress-Report-2020.pdf (Accessed 30 December 2020). By permission (21 April 2022).

15. Business & Sustainable Development Commission. (2017) *Sustainable Business can Unlock at lease US $12 Trillion in New Market Value, and Repair Economic System.* Available from: http://businesscommission.org/news/release-sustainable-business-can-unlock-at-least-us-12-trillion-in-new-market-value-and-repair-economic-system (Accessed 2 July 2021).
*Quotation:
Annan, Kofi. (15 March 2001) *Secretary-General Calls for Break in Political Stalemate over Environmental Issues.* United Nations Information Service. Available from: https://unis.unvienna.org/unis/en/pressrels/2001/sgsm7739.html (Accessed 2 November 2021). By permission (21 April 2022).

16. World Business Council for Sustainable Development (WBCSD). (2019). *Better Business, Better World.* Available from:
https://sustainabledevelopment.un.org/content/documents/2399BetterBusinessBetter World.pdf (Accessed 28 December 2021).
*6 Areas of Systematic Transformations Chart:
World Business Council for Sustainable Development (WBCSD) and PWC. (2019) *Creating a Strategy for a Better World.* Available from:
https://sustainabledevelopment.un.org/content/documents/2399BetterBusinessBetter World.pdf and https://www.pwc.com/gx/en/sustainability/SDG/sdg-2019.pdf (Accessed 28 December 2021).

17. PwC. (2019) *Creating a Strategy for a Better World.* Available from: https://www.pwc.com/gx/en/sustainability/SDG/sdg-2019.pdf (Accessed 28 December 2021).

18. PwC. *Creating a Strategy for a Better World.*

19. PwC. *Creating a Strategy for a Better World.*

20. PwC. *Creating a Strategy for a Better World.*
*Quotation:
Kingo, Lise. (2020) United Nations Global Compact. Available from: https://unglobalcompact.org/library/5746 (Accessed 8 January 2021). By permission (21 April 2022).

21. Edelman. (2021) *21st Annual Edelman Trust Barometer Global Report.* Available from: https://www.edelman.com/sites/g/files/aatuss191/files/2021-01/2021-edelman-trust-barometer.pdf (Accessed 12 February 2021).

22. Caulkin, Simon. Financial Times. *Companies with a purpose beyond profit tend to make more money.*

23. PwC. (June 2016) *Putting Purpose to Work: A study of purpose in the workplace.* Available from: https://www.pwc.com/us/en/about-us/corporate-responsibility/assets/pwc-putting-purpose-to-work-purpose-survey-report.pdf (Accessed 10 January 2021).

24. Edelman. *21st Annual Edelman Trust Barometer Global Report.*

25. PwC. (2015) *Make it your Business: Engaging with the Sustainable Development Goals.* Available from: https://www.pwc.com/gx/en/sustainability/SDG/SDG%20Research_FINAL.pdf (Accessed 21 January 2021)

*Quotation:
Beltman, Henk Jan – Chief Chocolate Officer. Tony's Chocolonely. (March 2019) The Impact Game Changers™ podcast. Available from: www.splitsecondltd.com. By permission (19 May 2022).

The IMPACT Roadmap™:

    *Quotation:
    Anonymous. Twitter. (Accessed 15 December 2021).

1.   Caulkin, Simon. Financial Times. *Companies with a purpose beyond profit tend to make more money.*

2.   Deloitte. (2021) Purpose is Everything. Available from: https://www2.deloitte.com/us/en/insights/topics/marketing-and-sales-operations/global-marketing-trends/2020/purpose-driven-companies.html (Accessed 1 March 2021).
    *Quotation:
    Branson, Sir Richard. (15 August 2016) Twitter. Available from: https://twitter.com/richardbranson/status/765116560541220864?lang=en-GB (Accessed November 2020). By permission (December 17, 2021).

3.   United Nations. (2020) *Leave No One Behind.* Available from: https://unsdg.un.org/2030-agenda/universal-values/leave-no-one-behind (Accessed March 1, 2021). By permission (21 April 2022).

4.   Unilever. (May 2020) *Unilever celebrates 10 years of the Sustainable Living Plan.* Available from: https://www.unilever.co.uk/news/press-releases/2020/unilever-celebrates-10-years-of-the-sustainable-living-plan.html (Accessed August 31, 2021). By permission (May 2022).

5.   Unilever. *Unilever celebrates 10 years of the Sustainable Living Plan.*

6.   Unilever. *Unilever celebrates 10 years of the Sustainable Living Plan.*

7.   Unilever. *Unilever celebrates 10 years of the Sustainable Living Plan.*

8.   Unilever. *Unilever celebrates 10 years of the Sustainable Living Plan.*

9.   Unilever. *Unilever celebrates 10 years of the Sustainable Living Plan.*

10.   Business & Sustainable Development Commission. (2017) *New Paper: Valuing the SDG Prize.* Available from: http://businesscommission.org/our-work/valuing-the-sdg-prize-unlocking-business-opportunities-to-accelerate-sustainable-and-inclusive-growth (Accessed March 2, 2021).

STEP 1 - PLAN with PURPOSE™:

    *Quotation:
    De Saint-Exupery, Antoine. Quotespedia. Available from: https://www.quotespedia.org/authors/a/antoine-de-saint-exupery/a-goal-without-a-plan-is-just-a-wish-Antoine-de-Saint-Exupery/ (Accessed 25 April 2021).

1.   Harvard Business Review. (6 October 2020) *Why is Strategic Planning Important?* Available from: https://online.hbs.edu/blog/post/why-is-strategic-planning-important (Accessed 25 April 2021).

2.   Harvard Business Review. *Why is Strategic Planning Important?*

3.   Harvard Business Review. *Why is Strategic Planning Important?*

4.   Harvard Business Review. *Why is Strategic Planning Important?*

CHAPTER ONE: PRIZE:

    *Quotation:
    Maeztu, Juvencio – Deputy CEO of Ingka Group. Ikea Retail. *The Ikea Point of View.* Available from: https://about.ikea.com/en/about-us/our-view-on (Accessed 23 March 2022). By permission (11 April 2022).

*Industry Selection of Sustainable Development Goals Chart:
PwC. (2019) *Creating a Strategy for a Better World*. Available from:
https://www.pwc.com/gx/en/sustainability/SDG/sdg-2019.pdf (Accessed 12 March 2021).

1. World Business Council for Sustainable Development (WBCSD). (2019) *Better Business, Better World*. Available from:
https://sustainabledevelopment.un.org/content/documents/2399BetterBusinessBetter
World.pdf (Accessed 10 March 2021).
*60 Biggest Market Opportunities Related to Delivering the Global Goals:
World Business Council for Sustainable Development (WBCSD). (2019) *Better Business, Better World*. Available from:
https://sustainabledevelopment.un.org/content/documents/2399BetterBusinessBetter
World.pdf (Accessed 10 March 2021).

2. World Business Council for Sustainable Development (WBCSD). *Better Business, Better World*.

3. World Business Council for Sustainable Development (WBCSD). *Better Business, Better World*.

4. United Nations. (2020) *Sustainable Development Goals*. Available from:
https://www.un.org/sustainabledevelopment/sustainable-consumption-production/
(Accessed 14 March 2021). By permission (21 April 2022).

5. Ringstrom, Anna. Reuters. (2 September 2020) *IKEA stores owner Ingka accelerates investments to cut emissions*. Available from: https://www.reuters.com/article/us-ikea-emissions-idUSKBN25T20B (Accessed 28 February 2021).

6. Ringstrom, Anna. Reuters. *IKEA stores owner Ingka accelerates investments to cut emissions*.

7. Sweden Culture. (2020) *The World's First IKEA Second-hand Store Opens in Sweden*. Available from: https://www.swedenhk.com/the-worlds-first-ikea-second-hand-store-opens-in-sweden/ (Accessed 1 March 2021).

8. Anderson, Deonna. Green Biz. (25 November 2020) *More Pieces of IKEA's Sustainability Puzzle Come Together*. Available from: https://www.greenbiz.com/article/more-pieces-ikeas-sustainability-puzzle-come-together (Accessed 1 March 2021).

9. Ingka Group IKEA Press Office. By permission (11 April 2022).

10. Sweden Culture. *The World's First IKEA Second-hand Store Opens in Sweden*.

11. The Good Shopping Guide. (16 March 2018) *IKEA Sees Growth in Sales for Sustainable Products*. Available from: https://thegoodshoppingguide.com/ikea-sees-growth-in-sales-for-sustainable-products/ (Accessed 1 March 2021).

12. Ingka Group IKEA Press Office. By permission (11 April 2022).

13. BBC News. (5 May 2021) *Ikea Starts Buy-back Scheme Offering Vouchers for Old Furniture*. Available from: https://www.bbc.co.uk/news/business-56981636 (Accessed 8 March 2021).

14. The Good Shopping Guide. *IKEA Sees Growth in Sales for Sustainable Products*.

15. IKEA.com. *Think What 170 Million Could Do*. Available from:
https://www.ikea.com/ms/en_JO/the_ikea_story/people_and_the_environment/a_more
_sustainable_life_at_home.html (Accessed 1 March 2021).
*Quotation:
Zeitz, Jochen – CEO and Chairman. Harley-Davidson Inc. Allgreatquotes.com. Available from: https://www.allgreatquotes.com/quote-210706/ (Accessed 15 December 2021).

CHAPTER TWO: PROSPECT:

*Quotation:
Anonymous. NA (Accessed 26 October 2021).

1. Inman, Paul. 75 Media. (10 February 2022) *How Many Ads Do You See in One Day?* Available from: https://75media.co.uk/blog/how-many-ads-seen-one-day/ (Accessed 15 February 2022).

2. Inman, Paul. 75 Media. *How Many Ads Do You See in One Day?*

3. Beard, Randall. Nielsen (13 January 2015). Available from: https://www.nielsen.com/ca/en/insights/article/2015/make-the-most-of-your-brands-20-second-window/ (Accessed 2 May 2021).

4. Ogilvy, David. Ogilvy & Mather. (1963). Available from: https://www.goodreads.com/quotes/7740616-first-study-the-product-you-are-going-to-advertise-the (Accessed 20 March 2021).

5. Opielka, Kathrin. Stormid. (13 June 2016) *How to be Successful in Content Marketing: The Art of Finding and Delighting the Right Audience.* Available from: https://blog.stormid.com/finding-and-delighting-the-right-audience/ (Accessed 20 March 2021).
    * Quotation:
    Reberga, Simon. By permission (February 2020).

6. Poynter, Tom. The Drum. (5 February 2020) *The conscious consumer part II - What will we buy into in 2030?* Available from: https://www.thedrum.com/opinion/2020/02/05/the-conscious-consumer-part-ii-what-will-we-buy-2030 (Accessed 1 May 2021).

7. Smurfit Kappa. (26 May 2020) *New research reveals Conscious Consumerism will keep sustainability a top priority for businesses.* Available from: https://www.smurfitkappa.com/newsroom/2020/new-research-reveals-conscious-consumerism-will-keep-sustainability-a-top-priority-for-businesses (Accessed 21 March 2021).

8. Smurfit Kappa. *New research reveals Conscious Consumerism will keep sustainability a top priority for businesses.*

9. Niazi, Luq. Forbes. (11 January 2020) *How Retailers Can Thrive in The Era of the "Conscious Consumer.* Available from: https://www.forbes.com/sites/ibm/2020/01/11/how-retailers-can-thrive-in-the-era-of-the-conscious-consumer/?sh=46b673dc2416 (Accessed 21 March 2021).

10. Edelman. *Edelman Trust Barometer Special Report: Brand Trust in 2020.*

11. Aziz, Afdhel. Forbes. (15 April 2020) *LEGO Donates $50 Million To Support Families During COVID-19.* Available from: https://www.forbes.com/sites/afdhelaziz/2020/04/15/lego-donates-50-million-to-support-families-during-covid19/?sh=5b072f7c5794 (Accessed 21 March 2021).

12. Aziz, Afdhel. Forbes. (*LEGO Donates $50 Million To Support Families During COVID-19.*

13. LEGO.com. *The first LEGO® plants made from plants have arrived!* Available from: https://www.lego.com/en-us/campaigns/plantsfromplants (Accessed 21 March 2021). By permission (31 May 2022).

14. LEGO.com. *Sustainability.* Available from: https://www.lego.com/en-gb/aboutus/news/2020/september/sustainability (Accessed 30 May 2022). By permission (31 May 2022).

15. Aziz, Afdhel. Forbes. *LEGO Donates $50 Million To Support Families During COVID-19.*

16. Aziz, Afdhel. Forbes. (*LEGO Donates $50 Million To Support Families During COVID-19.*

17. LEGO.com. *Sustainability.*

18. LEGO.com. *Sustainability.*

19. LEGO.COM. (2021) *The LEGO Group Sustainability Progress 2021.* Available from: https://www.lego.com/cdn/cs/aboutus/assets/blt15f6010332752196/The_LEGO_Group_SustainabilityProgressReport2021.pdf (Accessed 30 May 2022). By permission (31 May 2022).

20. LEGO.COM. *The LEGO Group Sustainability Progress 2021.*
    *Quotation:
    Vig Knudstorp, Jørgen – Executive Chairman. The LEGO Group. Reeves, Martin. BCG Henderson Institute. (14 April 2020) *Lessons from the COVID Crisis: Jørgen Vig Knudstorp, Chairman of LEGO Brand Group* Available from: https://bcghendersoninstitute.com/lessons-from-the-covid-crisis-jørgen-vig-knudstorp-chairman-of-lego-brand-group-ab10ea135c60 (Accessed 21 March 2021). By permission (31 May 2022).

CHAPTER THREE: PROPOSITION:

*Quotation:
Jobs, Steve. Mui, Chunka. Forbes. (17 October 2011) *Five Dangerous Lessons to Learn from Steve Jobs*. Available from: https://www.forbes.com/sites/chunkamui/2011/10/17/five-dangerous-lessons-to-learn-from-steve-jobs/?sh=6ed49913a95c (Accessed 6 May 2021).

1. Robinson, Phil Alden and Kinsella, W. P. Kinsella. Universal Pictures. *Field of Dreams* (5 May 1989). Available from: https://en.wikipedia.org/wiki/Field_of_Dreams (Accessed 17 June 2020).

2. McKinsey & Company. McKinsey Quarterly. (1 January 2009) *The Consumer Decision Journey*. Available from: https://www.mckinsey.com/business-functions/marketing-and-sales/our-insights/the-consumer-decision-journey (Accessed 31 March 2020).

3. McKinsey & Company. McKinsey Quarterly. *The Consumer Decision Journey*.

4. Brown, Marcel. This Day in Tech History. (23 October 2001) *1000 Songs in Your Pocket*. Available from: https://thisdayintechhistory.com/10/23/1000-songs-in-your-pocket/ (Accessed 29 March 2021).

5. Harrington, Rebecca. Business Insider. (26 January 2017) *By 2050, the oceans could have more plastic than fish*. Available from: https://www.businessinsider.com/plastic-in-ocean-outweighs-fish-evidence-report-2017-1?r=US&IR=T (Accessed 4 April 2020).

6. Greenpeace Instagram. (14 April 2021) *It All Starts with Oil*. Available from: https://www.instagram.com/p/CNpOCWwFSjq/?utm_medium=copy_link (Accessed 21 August 2021).

7. Greenpeace Instagram. *It All Starts with Oil*.

8. Ellen McArthur Foundation. (2016) *The Circular Economy Solution to Plastic Pollution*. Available from: https://plastics.ellenmacarthurfoundation.org/breaking-the-plastic-wave-perspective?gclid=EAIaIQobChMImK_O0-L99wIVmt_tCh1gsQ7HEAAYASAAEgI_A_D_BwE (Accessed 21 August 2021). By Permission (8 April 2022).

9. Ellen McArthur Foundation. By permission (8 April 2022).

10. The Explorer. (12 March 2020) *How the Circular Economy is Changing Business*. Available from: https://www.theexplorer.no/stories/renewable-resources/an-introduction-to-the-circular-economy/?gclid=EAIaIQobChMIs52f_5nP6AIVGeDtCh221A-DEAAYASAAEgKfrPD_BwE (Accessed 4 April 2020).

11. Edelman. *Edelman Trust Barometer Special Report: Brand Trust in 2020*.

12. Edelman. *Edelman Trust Barometer Special Report: Brand Trust in 2020*.

13. Edelman. *Edelman Trust Barometer Special Report: Brand Trust in 2020*.

14. Pursuitthelabel.com. *Our Purpose*. Available from: https://www.pursuitthelabel.com/pages/our-purpose (Accessed 4 April 2020). By permission (4 April 2022).

15. Dopper_Official Instagram. (2020). Available from: https://www.instagram.com/dopper_official/ (Accessed 31 August 2021). By permission (29 December 2020).

16. Branson, Sir Richard LinkedIn. Virgin.com. (April 2021) *Five Environmentally Friendly Start-ups*. Available from: https://www.virgin.com/about-virgin/latest/five-environmentally-friendly-start-ups?utm_medium=social&utm_source=linkedin&utm_author=richard&utm_type=editorial (Accessed 31 August 2021). By permission (17 December 2021).

17. Daykin, Hannah & Humphrey, Annabel – Founders. Pursuit the Label. (November 2019) The Impact Game Changers™ podcast. Available from: www.splitsecondltd.com. By permission (4 April 2022).
   *Quotation:
   Priestley, Daniel. Instagram. By permission (11 April 2020).

18. Morgan, Blake. Forbes. (24 September 2019) *50 Stats That Prove the Value of Customer Experience*. Available from: https://www.forbes.com/sites/blakemorgan/2019/09/24/50-stats-that-prove-the-value-of-customer-experience/#106a470a4ef2 (Accessed 4 May 2020).

19. United Nations. *Tackling Climate Change*. Available from: https://www.un.org/sustainabledevelopment/climate-action/ (Accessed 6 May 2021). By permission (21 April 2022).

20. Tesla.com. Available from: https://www.tesla.com (Accessed 4 May 2020).

21. Vlaskovits, Patrick. Harvard Business Review. (29 August 2011) *Henry Ford, Innovation, and That "Faster Horse" Quote*. Available from: https://hbr.org/2011/08/henry-ford-never-said-the-fast (Accessed 5 April 2022).

22. Lambert, Fred. Electrek.com. (16 February 2021) *Tesla owns 79% of the electric car market in the US, and that needs to change*. Available from: https://electrek.co/2021/02/16/tesla-owns-electric-car-market-us/ (Accessed 4 May 2021).

23. Statista.com. (9 February 2021) *Size of the global market for electric vehicles in 2020 and 2026*. Available from: https://www.statista.com/statistics/271537/worldwide-revenue-from-electric-vehicles-since-2010/ (Accessed 4 May 2021).

24. Brook, Giles – CEO, Entrepreneur, Mentor, Investor. Vita Coco & White Space. (March 2019) The Impact Game Changers™ podcast. Available from: www.splitsecondltd.com. By permission (26 April 2022).

25. Evans, Peter. The Times. (10 June 2018) *Q&A with Angel Investor Giles Brook*. Available from: https://www.thetimes.co.uk/article/q-a-with-angel-investor-giles-brook-mc76pxqqp (Accessed 22 May 2020).

26. Brook, Giles – CEO, Entrepreneur, Mentor, Investor. Vita Coco & White Space. (March 2019) The Impact Game Changers™ podcast. Available from: www.splitsecondltd.com. By permission (26 April 2022).

27. Brook, Giles – CEO, Entrepreneur, Mentor, Investor. Vita Coco & White Space. (March 2019) The Impact Game Changers™ podcast. Available from: www.splitsecondltd.com. By permission (26 April 2022).

28. Vita Coco.com. Available from: https://www.vitacoco.co.uk/?gclid=EAIaIQobChMIwKv5w9qC-AIV2YBQBh3kSQePEAAYASAAEgIEOfD_BwE&gclsrc=aw.ds (Accessed 22 February 2021).

29. Brook, Giles – CEO, Entrepreneur, Mentor, Investor. Vita Coco & White Space. (March 2019) The Impact Game Changers™ podcast. Available from: www.splitsecondltd.com. By permission (26 April 2022).

30. Vita Coco.com. Available from: https://vitacoco.com/pages/impact (Accessed 25 April 2022).

31. Brook, Giles – CEO, Entrepreneur, Mentor, Investor. Vita Coco & White Space. (March 2019) The Impact Game Changers™ podcast. Available from: www.splitsecondltd.com. By permission (26 April 2022).

32. Vita Coco.com. Available from: https://vitacoco.com/pages/impact (Accessed 25 April 2022).

33. Accenture. (2018) *To Affinity and Beyond – From Me to We, The Rise of the Purpose-led Brand*. Available from: https://www.accenture.com/_acnmedia/thought-leadership-assets/pdf/accenture-competitiveagility-gcpr-pov.pdf (Accessed 1 June 2020).

34. Accenture. *To Affinity and Beyond – From Me to We, The Rise of the Purpose-led Brand*.

35. Accenture. *To Affinity and Beyond – From Me to We, The Rise of the Purpose-led Brand*.

36. Accenture. *To Affinity and Beyond – From Me to We, The Rise of the Purpose-led Brand*.

37. Accenture. *To Affinity and Beyond – From Me to We, The Rise of the Purpose-led Brand*.
    *Pursuit the Label Instagram. (2021). Available from: https://www.instagram.com/p/CNpOCWwFSjq/?utm_medium=copy_link (Accessed 8 December 2021).

38. Townsend, Solitaire. Forbes. (6 September 2018*) How Brands Can Serve Social Movements*. Available from: https://www.forbes.com/sites/solitairetownsend/2018/09/06/how-to-make-a-movement/#22cf0ef97eea (Accessed 3 June 2020).

39. Google. Available from:
https://www.google.co.uk/search?ei=5XfXXqu5E5Gx8gL30LC4Ag&q=millennials+share+
of+population+uk&oq=millennials+share+of+population+uk&gs_lcp=CgZwc3ktYWIQAzI
GCAAQFhAeOgcIABBHELADOggIABAWEAoQHIDZDFjMEWDwF2gBcAB4AIABPYgBjA
GSAQEzmAEAoAEBqgEHZ3dzLXdpeg&sclient=psy-
ab&ved=0ahUKEwjrv9vJtOXpAhWRmFwKHXcoDCcQ4dUDCAs&uact=5 (3 June 2020).
40. Google. Available from:
https://www.google.co.uk/search?ei=5XfXXqu5E5Gx8gL30LC4Ag&q=millennials+share+
of+population+uk&oq=millennials+share+of+population+uk&gs_lcp=CgZwc3ktYWIQAzI
GCAAQFhAeOgcIABBHELADOggIABAWEAoQHIDZDFjMEWDwF2gBcAB4AIABPYgBjA
GSAQEzmAEAoAEBqgEHZ3dzLXdpeg&sclient=psy-
ab&ved=0ahUKEwjrv9vJtOXpAhWRmFwKHXcoDCcQ4dUDCAs&uact=5 (3 June 2020).
41. United Nations. (2021). Available from: https://www.un.org/en/fight-
racism/background/the-road-to-fight-racism (Accessed 4 June 2020). By permission (21
April 2022).
42. Levine, Stuart R. Forbes. (15 January 2020) *Diversity Confirmed to Boost Innovation and
Financial Results.* Available from:
https://www.forbes.com/sites/forbesinsights/2020/01/15/diversity-confirmed-to-boost-
innovation-and-financial-results/?sh=77e905efc4a6 (Accessed 16 September 2021).
43. Rocio, Voigt, Tsusaka, Krentz, Abouzahr. BCG. (23 January 2018) *How Diverse Leadership
Teams Boost Innovation.* Available from: https://www.bcg.com/publications/2018/how-
diverse-leadership-teams-boost-innovation (Accessed 16 September 2021).
44. Rocio, Voigt, Tsusaka, Krentz, Abouzahr. BCG. *How Diverse Leadership Teams Boost
Innovation.*
45. Rocio, Voigt, Tsusaka, Krentz, Abouzahr. BCG. *How Diverse Leadership Teams Boost
Innovation.*
46. Levine, Stuart R. Forbes. *Diversity Confirmed to Boost Innovation and Financial Results.*
47. Levine, Stuart R. Forbes. *Diversity Confirmed to Boost Innovation and Financial Results.*
48. Credit Suisse. (28 September 2021) *Credit Suisse Gender 3000 report shows women
hold almost a quarter of board room positions globally.* Available from:
https://www.credit-suisse.com/about-us-news/en/articles/media-releases/credit-suisse-
gender-3000-report-shows-women-hold-almost-a-quart-202109.html (Accessed 17
September 2021).
*Quotation:
Gandhi, Mahatma. UN Geneva Twitter. (24 October 2020). Available from:
https://twitter.com/ungeneva/status/1320100500596031488?lang=en-GB (Accessed 8
April 2021).
49. Rogers, E.M. Wikipedia. (1962) *Diffusions of Innovations.* Available from:
https://en.wikipedia.org/wiki/Diffusion_of_innovations (Accessed 6 June 2020).
50. Rogers, E.M. Wikipedia. *Diffusions of Innovations.*
51. Impact Hub. Available from: https://impacthub.net/ (Accessed 31 March 2021).
52. Glad, Tatiana – Co-founder and Executive Director. Impact Hub. (March 2019) The
Impact Game Changers™ podcast. Available from: www.splitsecondltd.com. By
permission (16 May 2022).
53. Glad, Tatiana – Co-founder and Executive Director. Impact Hub. (March 2019) The
Impact Game Changers™ podcast. Available from: www.splitsecondltd.com. By
permission (16 May 2022).
54. Glad, Tatiana – Co-founder and Executive Director. Impact Hub. (March 2019) The
Impact Game Changers™ podcast. Available from: www.splitsecondltd.com. By
permission (16 May 2022).

STEP 2 - PERSUADE with PROMISE™:

*Quotation:
Jobs, Steve. Kirirom Institute of Technology. (Feb 22, 2019) *"The people who are crazy
enough to think they can change the world are the ones who do."* Available from:
https://medium.com/@kirirom_instituteoftechnology/the-people-who-are-crazy-

enough-to-think-they-can-change-the-world-are-the-ones-who-do-187d2e08a0a8 (Accessed 2 September 2021).

CHAPTER FOUR: PITCH:

*Quotation:
Anonymous. YouTube (NA) (Accessed 2021).

1. Mahoney, Manda. Harvard Business School. (13 January 2003) *The Subconscious Mind of the Consumer (And How to Reach It)*. Available from: https://hbswk.hbs.edu/item/the-subconscious-mind-of-the-consumer-and-how-to-reach-it (Accessed 8 March 2021).
   *Quotation:
   Elliott, Tom – Former Senior Buyer. Sainsbury's. (1 May 2019) The Impact Game Changers™ podcast. Available from: www.splitsecondltd.com. By permission (28 April 2022).
2. Gartner. (2021) *The B2B Buying Journey - The B2B buying process has changed, has your sales strategy?* Available from: https://www.gartner.com/en/sales/insights/b2b-buying-journey (Accessed 22 May 2021).
3. Gartner. *The B2B Buying Journey - The B2B buying process has changed, has your sales strategy?*
4. Carrington, Damian. The Guardian. (4 March 2021) *People Wasting Almost 1bn Tonnes of Food a Year, UN Report Reveals*. Available from: https://www.theguardian.com/environment/2021/mar/04/people-wasting-almost-billion-tonnes-food-year-un-report (Accessed 24 May 2021).
5. Carrington, Damian. The Guardian. *People Wasting Almost 1bn Tonnes of Food a Year, UN Report Reveals*.
6. Carrington, Damian. The Guardian. *People Wasting Almost 1bn Tonnes of Food a Year, UN Report Reveals*.
7. Carrington, Damian. The Guardian. *People Wasting Almost 1bn Tonnes of Food a Year, UN Report Reveals*.
8. Carrington, Damian. The Guardian. *People Wasting Almost 1bn Tonnes of Food a Year, UN Report Reveals*.
9. Cooked Best. (30 September 2020) *Food Waste Facts, Figures & Statistics 2021*. Available from: https://cookedbest.com/food-waste-facts/ (Accessed 24 May 2021).
10. Toast Ale. (2021) *Toast Ale Impact Report*. Available from: https://www.toastale.com/uploads/files/1585947098ToastAle2019ImpactReport.pdf (24 May 2021).
11. Toast Ale. *Toast Ale Impact Report*.
12. Wilson, Rob – Chief Toaster. Toast Ale. (November 2019) The Impact Game Changers™ podcast. Available from: www.splitsecondltd.com. By permission (28 April 2022).
13. United Nations. *Sustainable Development Goals*. Available from: http://www.fao.org/sustainable-development-goals/indicators/1231/en/ (Accessed 31 2021).
14. Toast Ale. (2019) *Toast Ale Impact Report*.
15. Toast Ale. (2019) *Toast Ale Impact Report*.
16. Wilson, Rob – Chief Toaster. Toast Ale. (November 2019) The Impact Game Changers™ podcast. Available from: www.splitsecondltd.com. By permission (28 April 2022).
17. Elliott, Tom – Former Senior Buyer. Sainsbury's. (1 May 2019) The Impact Game Changers™ podcast. Available from: www.splitsecondltd.com. By permission (28 April 2022).

CHAPTER FIVE: PARTNERSHIP:

*Quotation:
Ki-Moon, Ban. SDG Compass. (2020) *The Guide for Business Action on the SDGs*. Available from: https://sdgcompass.org/wp-

content/uploads/2015/12/019104_SDG_Compass_Guide_2015.pdf (Accessed 4 April 2022). By permission (21 April 2022).

*Quotation:

The CEO Magazine. (10 June 2021) *How François-Henri Pinault is leading Kering's sustainable mission.* Available from: https://www.theceomagazine.com/business/coverstory/kering-francois-henri-pinault/ (Accessed 15 June 2021).

1. Cap Gemini. (2020) *Why purpose-led organisations are winning consumers' hearts Driven to a higher purpose.* Available from: https://www.capgemini.com/gb-en/research/why-purpose-led-organisations-are-winning-consumers-hearts/ (Accessed 8 June 2021). By permission (15 September 2021).

2. Dopper. *Our Mission.* Available from: https://dopper.com/our-mission (5 June 2021).

3. Grostern, Joey. The Guardian. (5 August 2021) *Environmental Impact of Bottled Water 'Up to 3,500 Times Greater than Tap Water'.* Available from: https://www.theguardian.com/environment/2021/aug/05/environmental-impact-of-bottled-water-up-to-3500-times-greater-than-tap-water (Accessed 12 April 2022).

4. Grostern, Joey. The Guardian. *Environmental Impact of Bottled Water 'Up to 3,500 Times Greater than Tap Water'.*

5. Dopper. Dopper Blog. (21 January 2021) *Dopper's Sustainable Seafaring with GoodShipping.* Available from: https://dopper.com/blog/doppers-sustainable-seafaring-with-goodshipping (Accessed 8 June 2021).

6. GoodShipping. Available from: https://goodshipping.com (Accessed 8 June 2021).

7. Dopper. Dopper Blog. *Dopper's Sustainable Seafaring with GoodShipping.*

8. World Health Organisation. (12 July 2017) *2.1 Billion People Lack Safe Drinking Water at Home, More Than Twice as many Lack Safe Sanitation.* Available from: https://www.who.int/news/item/12-07-2017-2-1-billion-people-lack-safe-drinking-water-at-home-more-than-twice-as-many-lack-safe-sanitation (Accessed 7 June 2021).

9. World Health Organisation. *2.1 billion People Lack Safe Drinking Water at Home, More Than Twice as many Lack Safe Sanitation.*

10. Everaarts, Merijn – Founder & Owner. Dopper. (December 2020) The Impact Game Changers™ podcast. Available from: www.splitsecondltd.com. By permission (December 2020).

11. Cartner-Morley, Jess. The Guardian. (5 February 2022) *Brands are Moving from Fast to 'Forever Fashion' – but are New Clothes ever Sustainable?* Available from: https://www.theguardian.com/fashion/2020/jul/14/fast-fashion-20-ways-stop-buying-new-clothes-fair-wage-wardrobes (Accessed 15 February 2022).

12. Cartner-Morley, Jess. The Guardian. *Brands are Moving from Fast to 'Forever Fashion' – but are new Clothes ever Sustainable?*

13. Wicker, Alden. Vox.com. (31 January 2022) *Fashion has a Misinformation Problem. That's Bad for the Environment.* Available from: https://www.vox.com/the-goods/2020/1/27/21080107/fashion-environment-facts-statistics-impact (Accessed 14 June 2021).

14. Wicker, Alden. Vox.com. *Fashion has a Misinformation Problem. That's Bad for the Environment.*

15. United Nations. (2021) *Act Now: Towards a Net-Zero Future - The UN Campaign for Individual Action.* Available from: https://www.un.org/actnow (Accessed 14 June 2021).

16. United Nations. *Act Now: Towards a Net-Zero Future - The UN Campaign for Individual Action.*

17. Kering.com. (2021). Available from: https://www.kering.com/en/group/ (Accessed 14 June 2021).

18. Kering.com.

19. Patel, Chetna – Founder. Chillies and Clothes. (June 2021) The Impact Game Changers™ podcast. Available from: www.splitsecondltd.com. By permission (28 May 2022).

20. Kering.com.

21. Patel, Chetna – Founder. Chillies and Clothes. (June 2021) The Impact Game Changers™ podcast. Available from: www.splitsecondltd.com. By permission (28 May 2022).

22. Devenyns, Jessi. Fooddive.com. (8 September 2020) *Oatly faces boycott backlash for its investment from Blackstone*. Available from: https://www.fooddive.com/news/oatly-faces-boycott-backlash-for-its-investment-from-blackstone/584778/ (Accessed 19 October 2020).

23. Devenyns, Jessi. Fooddive.com. *Oatly faces boycott backlash for its investment from Blackstone*.

24. Devenyns, Jessi. Fooddive.com. *Oatly faces boycott backlash for its investment from Blackstone*.

25. Dummett, Gottfried, Chung. The Wall Street Journal. (14 July 2020) *Oat-Milk Company Oatly Draws Investment from Blackstone-Led Group Including Oprah*. Available from: https://www.wsj.com/articles/oat-milk-company-oatly-draws-investment-from-blackstone-led-group-including-oprah-11594701001 (Accessed 19 October 2020).

26. Devenyns, Jessi. Fooddive.com. *Oatly faces boycott backlash for its investment from Blackstone*.

27. Chiorando, Maria. Plant Based News. (4 September 2020) *Oatly Cancelled? Plant-Based Brand Responds to Backlash Over Controversial Investor*. Available from: https://plantbasednews.org/news/oatly-backlash-controversial-investor/ (Accessed 9 September 2020).

28. Oatly. Instagram. (2020). Available from: https://www.instagram.com/oatly/?hl=en (Accessed August 2020).

29. Chiorando, Maria. Plant Based News. *Oatly Cancelled? Plant-Based Brand Responds to Backlash Over Controversial Investor*.

30. Oatly.com. (2020). Available from: https://www.oatly.com/uploads/attachments/ckpmjybkq0x9rcbgi6tot8590-oatly-uk-2sidedfactsheet-uk-june2021-web.pdf (Accessed 14 June 2021).

31. H&M.com. (2022) *Conscious Collection*. Available from: https://www.hm.com/entrance.ahtml?orguri=%2F (Accessed 15 June 2021). By permission (19 May 2022).

32. Deacetis, Joseph. Forbes. (6 May 2021) *H&M Drives Innovation in Sustainability with 2021 Style*. Available from: https://www.forbes.com/sites/josephdeacetis/2021/05/06/hm-drives-innovation-in-sustainability-with-2021-style/ (Accessed 15 June 2021).

33. Ernest-Jones, Sam. GWI. (2 April 2019) *42% of U.S. and UK Consumers Say Products that use Sustainable Materials are Important in their Day-to-Day Purchasing*. Available from: https://blog.gwi.com/marketing/sustainable-brands/ (17 June 2021).

34. H&M.com. (2022) *Conscious Collection*.

35. H&M.com. (2022) *Conscious Collection*.

36. Brun, Pascal. H&M.com. Available from: https://www2.hm.com/en_gb/life/culture/inside-h-m/looop-it-like-maisie-williams.html (Accessed 15 June 2021). By permission (19 May 2022).
     * Quotation:
     The United Nations Partnering Initiative. (2021) *Maximising the impact of partnerships for the SDGs*
     A practical guide to partnership value creation. Available from: https://sustainabledevelopment.un.org/content/documents/2564Maximising_the_impact_of_partnerships_for_the_SDGs.pdf (Accessed 21 June 2021). By permission (29 April 2022).

37. Isle of Wight Distillery.com. *Sustainability*. (2021). Availability: https://isleofwightdistillery.com/sustainability (Accessed 21 June 2021).

38. Isle of Wight Distillery.com. *Sustainability*.

39. Isle of Wight Distillery.com. *Sustainability*.

40. Spring Wise. (2021) *Net-Zero Liquor Company Offsets Emissions Through Blue Carbon Projects*. Available from: https://www.springwise.com/sustainability-innovation/food-drink/net-zero-gin-mermaid (Accessed 22 June 2021).

41. Smart, Sarah – UK & Europe CEO. The Collective Dairy. (March 2022) The Impact Game Changers™ podcast. Available from: www.splitsecondltd.com. By permission (15 May 2022).

42.   Smart, Sarah – UK & Europe CEO. The Collective Dairy. (March 2022) The Impact Game Changers™ podcast. Available from: www.splitsecondltd.com. By permission (15 May 2022).

43.   ClimatePartner. (2022) *Success Stories*. Available from: https://www.climatepartner.com/en/success-stories (Accessed 14 February 2022). By permission (24 May 2022).

44.   Smart, Sarah – UK & Europe CEO. The Collective Dairy. (March 2022) The Impact Game Changers™ podcast. Available from: www.splitsecondltd.com. By permission (15 May 2022).

45.   Prasad, Ashwin – Chief Commercial Officer. Tesco. By permission (29 May 2022).

46.   Nazir, Sahar. Retail Gazette. (17 May 2022). *Tesco launches new campaign to help Brits make better food choices.* Available from: https://www.retailgazette.co.uk/blog/2022/05/tesco-launches-new-campaign-to-help-brits-make-better-food-choices/ (Accessed 25 May 2022).

47.   Nazir, Sahar. Retail Gazette. *Tesco launches new campaign to help Brits make better food choices.*

48.   Tesco.com. (2022) *Better Baskets*. Available from: https://www.tesco.com/groceries/en-GB/zone/better-baskets (Accessed 25 May 2022).

49.   Tesco.com. *Better Baskets*.

50.   Tesco.com. *Better Baskets*.

51.   Tesco.com. *Better Baskets*.

52.   The Collective Dairy. Available from: https://www.thecollectivedairy.com (Accessed 6 March 2022).

53.   Smart, Sarah – UK & Europe CEO. The Collective Dairy. (March 2022) The Impact Game Changers™ podcast. Available from: www.splitsecondltd.com. By permission (15 May 2022).

54.   Mizuiro Inc.com. (2021). Available from: https://mizuiroinc.com/en (Accessed 22 June 2021).

55.   Zuckerman, Arthur. (7 May 2020) *48 Food Waste Statistics 2020/2021: Causes, IMPACT & Solutions.* Available from: https://comparecamp.com/food-waste-statistics/ (Accessed 22 June 2021).

56.   Zuckerman, Arthur. *48 Food Waste Statistics 2020/2021: Causes, IMPACT & Solutions.*

57.   Zuckerman, Arthur. *48 Food Waste Statistics 2020/2021: Causes, IMPACT & Solutions.*

58.   Zuckerman, Arthur. *48 Food Waste Statistics 2020/2021: Causes, IMPACT & Solutions.*

59.   Zuckerman, Arthur. *48 Food Waste Statistics 2020/2021: Causes, IMPACT & Solutions.*

60.   Zuckerman, Arthur. *48 Food Waste Statistics 2020/2021: Causes, IMPACT & Solutions.*
        *Quotation:
        African Proverb. (2021) Google. Available from: Google (Accessed 5 June 2021).

61.   Spring Wise. (2021) *Water-saving, Salon-Quality Haircare Set-up for the Home.* Available from: https://www.springwise.com/sustainability-innovation/fashion-beauty/l-oreal-water-saver-hair-washing (Accessed 22 June 2021).

62.   Spring Wise. *Water-saving, Salon-Quality Haircare Set-up for the Home.*

63.   Spring Wise. *Water-saving, Salon-Quality Haircare Set-up for the Home.*

64.   UN Water. United Nations. (2021) *Water Quality and Wastewater.* Available from: https://www.unwater.org/water-facts/quality-and-wastewater/ (Accessed 22 June 2021). By permission (21 April 2022). By permission (21 April 2022).

65.   Spring Wise. *Water-saving, Salon-Quality Haircare Set-up for the Home.*

CHAPTER SIX: PURCHASE:

        *Quotation:
        Anonymous. NA (Accessed 23 June 2021).

1.   Sularia, Sanjeev. Forbes. (8 September 2020) *2020 Consumer Purchasing Behaviour and The Pivotal Events That Shaped It.* Available from: https://www.forbes.com/sites/forbestechcouncil/2020/09/08/2020-consumer-purchasing-behavior-and-the-pivotal-events-that-shaped-it/?sh=2d9dad3f3450 (Accessed 3 January 2021).

2.   Edelman. *21st Annual Edelman Trust Barometer Global Report*.

3.   Accenture. (2018) *To Affinity and Beyond – From Me to We, The Rise of the Purpose-led Brand*. Available from: https://www.accenture.com/_acnmedia/thought-leadership-assets/pdf/accenture-competitiveagility-gcpr-pov.pdf (Accessed 1 June 2020).

4.   Accenture. *To Affinity and Beyond – From Me to We, The Rise of the Purpose-led Brand*.

5.   AC Nielsen. (13 January 2015) *Make the Most of Your Brand's 20-Second Window*. Available from: https://www.nielsen.com/us/en/insights/article/2015/make-the-most-of-your-brands-20-second-window/ (Accessed 5 January 2021).

6.   Think with Google. (2011) *Zero Moment of Truth*. Available from: https://www.thinkwithgoogle.com/marketing-strategies/micro-moments/zero-moment-truth/ (Accessed 3 June 2020).

7.   Lecinski, Jim. Think with Google. (2011) *ZMOT Winning the ZERO Moment of Truth*. Available from: https://www.thinkwithgoogle.com/marketing-strategies/micro-moments/zero-moment-truth/ (Accessed 3 June 2020).

8.   Think with Google. (2015) *Micro-Moments*. Available from: https://www.thinkwithgoogle.com/marketing-strategies/micro-moments/ (Accessed 4 June 2020).

9.   Malyon, Jane – Founder. The English Cream Tea Company. (21 August 2015) *How Afternoon Tea Could Save the World*. Available from: https://www.youtube.com/watch?v=vaDquLlxDsI (Accessed 4 June 2020).

10.   Malyon, Jane – Founder. The English Cream Tea Company. (March 2019) The Impact Game Changers™ podcast. Available from: www.splitsecondltd.com. By permission (4 May 2022).

11.   Accenture. *To Affinity and Beyond – From Me to We, The Rise of the Purpose-led Brand*.

12.   Accenture. *To Affinity and Beyond – From Me to We, The Rise of the Purpose-led Brand*.

13.   Accenture. *To Affinity and Beyond – From Me to We, The Rise of the Purpose-led Brand*.

14.   Watson, Imogen. The Drum. (22 April 2021) *Earth Day 2021: brands from P&G to Apple take action on climate change*. Available from: https://www.thedrum.com/news/2021/04/22/earth-day-2021-brands-pg-apple-take-action-climate-change (Accessed 5 July 2021).

15.   Accenture. *To Affinity and Beyond – From Me to We, The Rise of the Purpose-led Brand*.

16.   Accenture. *To Affinity and Beyond – From Me to We, The Rise of the Purpose-led Brand*.

17.   Faelli, Van den Branden, Davis-Peccoud, Deryckere. Bain & Company. (11 December 2020) *The Sustainable Brands in Your Future - Consumers demand sustainable goods, but why are so many brands late to the game?* Available from: https://www.bain.com/insights/sustainable-brands-in-your-future/ (Accessed 5 July 2021).

18.   Mooney & Johnsmeyer. Think with Google. (2015) *I-want-to-buy moments: How mobile has reshaped the purchase journey*. Available from: https://www.thinkwithgoogle.com/consumer-insights/consumer-trends/i-want-to-buy-moments/ (Accessed 5 July 2021).

19.   Mooney & Johnsmeyer. Think with Google. *I-want-to-buy moments: How mobile has reshaped the purchase journey*.

20.   Think with Google. (June 2018) *Study reveals the complexity of modern consumer paths to purchase and how brands can make inroads*. Available from: https://www.thinkwithgoogle.com/intl/en-cee/consumer-insights/consumer-journey/study-reveals-complexity-modern-consumer-paths-purchase-and-how-brands-can-make-inroads/ (Accessed 5 July 2021).

21.   E-consultancy. (4 March 2022) *Stats Roundup: The Impact of Covid-19 on Ecommerce*. Available from: https://econsultancy.com/stats-roundup-the-impact-of-covid-19-on-ecommerce/ (Accessed 6 July 2021).

22. Wtorek. OC&C Strategy Consultants. 27 Lutego Press Release. (2018) *Voice shopping in the UK to be worth £3.5bn by 2022*. Available from: https://www.occstrategy.com/pl/about-occ/news-and-media/article/id/1938/2018/02/voice-shopping-in-the-uk-to-be-worth-35bn-by-2022 (Accessed 6 July 2021).

23. Wtorek. OC&C Strategy Consultants. 27 Lutego Press Release. *Voice shopping in the UK to be worth £3.5bn by 2022*.

24. Wtorek. OC&C Strategy Consultants. 27 Lutego Press Release. *Voice shopping in the UK to be worth £3.5bn by 2022*.

25. Wtorek. OC&C Strategy Consultants. 27 Lutego Press Release. *Voice shopping in the UK to be worth £3.5bn by 2022*.

26. Selfridges.com. (17 August 2020) *Project Earth*. Available from: https://www.selfridges.com/GB/en/features/project-earth/ (Accessed 14 September 2021).

27. Butler, Sarah. The Guardian. (17 August 2020) *Selfridges Launches Project Earth to Connect with its Ethical Consumers*. Available from: https://www.theguardian.com/business/2020/aug/17/selfridges-launches-project-earth-to-connect-with-its-ethical-consumers (Accessed 6 July 2021).

28. Internet Retailing.Net. (2021) *John Lewis and IKEA Accelerate their Focus on Sustainable Future*. Available from: https://internetretailing.net/sustainability/sustainability/john-lewis-and-ikea-accelerate-their-focus-on-sustainable-future-18505 (Accessed 8 July 2021).

29. Internet Retailing.Net. *John Lewis and IKEA Accelerate their Focus on Sustainable Future*.

30. Internet Retailing.Net. *John Lewis and IKEA Accelerate their Focus on Sustainable Future*.

31. Internet Retailing.Net. *John Lewis and IKEA Accelerate their Focus on Sustainable Future*.

32. Cap Gemini Research Institute. Cap Gemini. (July 2020) *Consumer Products and Retail: How sustainability is fundamentally changing consumer preferences*. Available from: https://www.capgemini.com/gb-en/research/how-sustainability-is-fundamentally-changing-consumer-preferences/ (Accessed 14 September 2021). By permission (15 September 2021).

33. Cap Gemini Research Institute. Cap Gemini. *Consumer Products and Retail: How sustainability is fundamentally changing consumer preferences*.

34. Cap Gemini Research Institute. Cap Gemini. *Consumer Products and Retail: How sustainability is fundamentally changing consumer preferences*.

35. Cap Gemini Research Institute. Cap Gemini. *Consumer Products and Retail: How sustainability is fundamentally changing consumer preferences*.

36. Hargreaves, Paul – CEO. Cotswold Fayre & Flourish. (1 July 2021) The Impact Game Changers™ podcast. Available from: www.splitsecondltd.com. By permission (3 May 2022).

37. Hargreaves, Paul. LinkedIn Blog. (13 September 2021) *Better Planet = Better Profits*. Available from: https://www.linkedin.com/pulse/better-planet-profits-paul-hargreaves/?trackingId=M0wgGK8%2FS4SXZHoctoPjOg%3D%3D (Accessed 14 September 2021). By Permission (3 May 2022).

38. Accenture. (April 2020) *How COVID-19 will Permanently Change Consumer Behaviour*. Available from: https://www.accenture.com/_acnmedia/PDF-134/Accenture-COVID19-Consumer-Behaviour-Survey-Research-PoV.pdf#zoom=40 (Accessed 8 July 2021).

39. Cap Gemini Research Institute. Cap Gemini. *Consumer Products and Retail: How sustainability is fundamentally changing consumer preferences*.

40. Cap Gemini Research Institute. Cap Gemini. *Consumer Products and Retail: How sustainability is fundamentally changing consumer preferences*.

41. Schwartz, Ariel. The Centre for Social Impact Strategy. (17 August 2017) *Social IMPACT Fundamentals*. Available from: https://csis.upenn.edu/news/what-is-social-impact-anyways/ (Accessed 9 July 2021).

42. Accenture. *How COVID-19 will Permanently Change Consumer Behaviour*.

43. Accenture. (2018) *To Affinity and Beyond – From Me to We, The Rise of the Purpose-led Brand*. Available from: https://www.accenture.com/_acnmedia/thought-leadership-assets/pdf/accenture-competitiveagility-gcpr-pov.pdf (Accessed 1 June 2020).

44. Accenture. *To Affinity and Beyond – From Me to We, The Rise of the Purpose-led Brand*.

45. Murray, Pippa – Founder/Chief Squirrel. Pip & Nut. (29 May 2019) The Impact Game Changers™ podcast. Available from: www.splitsecondltd.com. By permission (29 May 2019).

46. Pip&Nut.com. Pip & Nut. (2019). Available from: https://www.pipandnut.com (Accessed 4 June 2019).
    *Quotation:
    Lavoisier, Antoine. Available from: https://www.azquotes.com/quote/720158 (Accessed 6 June 2020).

47. Stenzel, Tess. Fashion United. (8 March 2021) *United Colors of Benetton debuts sustainable store concept*. Available from: https://fashionunited.uk/news/retail/united-colors-of-benetton-debuts-sustainable-store-concept/2021030854219 (Accessed 11 July 2021).

48. Benetton Group. (2021) Press Release *The New Sustainable Concept Store*. Available from: https://gb.benetton.com/inside/article_florence-sustainable-store.html (Accessed 16 July 2021).

49. Mintel. (2021) *Future Forward Leadership Strategic Brief: Purpose*. Available from: https://www.mintel.com/future-forward-leadership-strategic-brief (Accessed 13 July 2021).

50. Starostinetskaya, Anna. Veg News. (24 May 2021) *World's First Meatless Burger King to Open in Germany*. Available from: https://vegnews.com/2021/5/meatless-burger-king-germany (Accessed 13 July 2021).

51. Webber, Jemima. Live Kindly. (9 November 2019) *Burger King's Earnings Skyrocket Nearly 30% Since Vegan Whopper Launch*. Available from: https://www.livekindly.co/burger-kings-earnings-skyrocket-nearly-30-since-vegan-whopper-launch/ (Accessed 13 July 2021).

52. Webber, Jemima. Live Kindly. *Burger King's Earnings Skyrocket Nearly 30% Since Vegan Whopper Launch*.
    *Quotation:
    Gandhi, Mahatma. Walia, Neha. Tribune of India. Tribune News Service. (10 June 2022) *Remembering Mahatma, his philosophy on environment*. Available from: https://twitter.com/ungeneva/status/1320100500596031488?lang=en-GB (Accessed 11 June 2022).

STEP 3 - PROFIT with IMPACT™:

*Quotation:
Greenfield, Jerry – Founder. Ben & Jerry's. Unilever. Hadden, Joey. Business Insider. (14 June 2020) *Meet the founders of Ben & Jerry's, Who Started their Company in a Converted Gas Station and Built it up into an Ice cream empire*. Available from: https://www.businessinsider.com/meet-ben-cohen-jerry-greenfield-founders-of-ben-and-jerrys-2020-6?r=US&IR=T (Accessed 15 July 2021).

1. Caulkin, Simon. Financial Times. *Companies with a purpose beyond profit tend to make more money*.

2. Harvard Business Review. (2015) *The Business Case for Purpose*. Available from: https://hbr.org/resources/pdfs/comm/ey/19392HBRReportEY.pdf (Accessed 20 July 2021).

3. Harvard Business Review. *The Business Case for Purpose*.

CHAPTER SEVEN: PERFORMANCE:

*Quotation:
Fachie, Neil - Paralympic Gold Medal Cyclist. (April 2020) The Impact Game Changers™ podcast.
Available from: www.splitsecondltd.com. By Permission (4 May 2022).

1. Interbrand. (2017) *Grow. Change. Grow.* Available from: http://interbrand.com/wp-content/uploads/2018/02/Best-Global-Brands-2017.pdf. By Permission (27 July 2021).

2. Kantar. (2020) *Purpose 2020.* Available from: https://www.kantar.com/Inspiration/Brands/The-Journey-Towards-Purpose-Led-Growth (Accessed 27 July 2021).

3. DDI World. (2018) *Global Leadership Report 2018.* Available from: https://www.ddiworld.com/research/global-leadership-forecast-2018 (Accessed 27 July 2021).

4. Business of Purpose. (2020) *Statistics.* Available from: https://www.businessofpurpose.com/statistics (Accessed 27 July 2021).

5. Business of Purpose. *Statistics.*

6. United Nations. (June 2016) *Final list of Proposed Sustainable Development Goal Indicators.* Available from: https://sustainabledevelopment.un.org/content/documents/11803Official-List-of-Proposed-SDG-Indicators.pdf (Accessed 28 July 2021). By permission (21 April 2022).

7. United Nations. *Final list of Proposed Sustainable Development Goal Indicators.*

8. United Nations. *Final list of Proposed Sustainable Development Goal Indicators.*
    *Quotation:
    Guterres, António. United Nations. UNDP. (2021) *The SDGs in Action.* Available from: https://www.undp.org/sustainable-development-goals?utm_source=EN&utm_medium=GSR&utm_content=US_UNDP_PaidSearch_Brand_English&utm_campaign=CENTRAL&c_src=CENTRAL&c_src2=GSR&gclid=EAIaIQobChMIuvXcqK6q-AIVEbrtCh1GpAxEEAAYBCAAEgJNAvD_BwE (Accessed 26 July 2021). By permission (21 April 2022).

9. PwC. (2017) *SDG Reporting Challenge 2017.* Available from: https://www.pwc.com/gx/en/sustainability/SDG/pwc-sdg-reporting-challenge-2017-final.pdf (Accessed 29 July 2021).

10. Elkington, John. (25 June 2018) *25 Years Ago I Coined the Phrase "Triple Bottom Line." Here's Why It's Time to Rethink It.* Harvard Business Review. Available from: https://hbr.org/2018/06/25-years-ago-i-coined-the-phrase-triple-bottom-line-heres-why-im-giving-up-on-it (Accessed 23 December 2020).

11. B Corp (2018). Business of Purpose. (2020) *Statistics.* Available from: https://www.businessofpurpose.com/statistics (Accessed 27 July 2021).

12. *Great Place to Work Survey.* Business of Purpose (2020) *Statistics.* Available from: https://www.businessofpurpose.com/statistics (Accessed 27 July 2021).
    *Quotation:
    Shakespeare, William. Allauthor.com Available from: https://allauthor.com/quotes/273986/ (Accessed 26 August 2021).

13. Schoenwaelder, Mennel, Silverstein, Beery. Deloitte. (2021) *The Purpose Premium - Why a Purpose-Driven Strategy is Good for Business.* Available from: https://www2.deloitte.com/content/dam/Deloitte/us/Documents/process-and-operations/purpose-premium-pov.pdf (Accessed 5 August 2021).

14. Miller, Kelsey. Harvard Business School Online. (8 December 2020) *The Triple Bottom Line: What it is & Why it's Important.* Available from: https://online.hbs.edu/blog/post/what-is-the-triple-bottom-line (Accessed 2 August 2021).

15. Miller, Kelsey. Harvard Business School Online. *The Triple Bottom Line: What it is & Why it's Important.*

16. Schoenwaelder, Mennel, Silverstein, Beery. Deloitte. *The Purpose Premium - Why a Purpose-Driven Strategy is Good for Business.*

17. Schoenwaelder, Mennel, Silverstein, Beery. Deloitte. *The Purpose Premium - Why a Purpose-Driven Strategy is Good for Business.*

18. Thunberg, Greta. Walsh, Grace. Goodto.com. (21 April 2021). Who is Greta Thunberg, How Old is She and What did She Do? Available from: https://www.goodto.com/family/who-is-greta-thunberg-595368 (Accessed 3 August 2021).
19. Business of Purpose. *Statistics.*
20. PwC. (2017) *SDG Reporting Challenge 2017.* Available from: https://www.pwc.com/gx/en/sustainability/SDG/pwc-sdg-reporting-challenge-2017-final.pdf (Accessed 29 July 2021).
21. PwC. *SDG Reporting Challenge 2017.*
22. Schoenwaelder, Mennel, Silverstein, Beery. Deloitte. *The Purpose Premium - Why a Purpose-Driven Strategy is Good for Business.*
23. Schoenwaelder, Mennel, Silverstein, Beery. Deloitte. *The Purpose Premium - Why a Purpose-Driven Strategy is Good for Business.*
24. Edelman. (21 January 2018) *2018 Edelman Trust Barometer.* Available from: https://www.edelman.com/sites/g/files/aatuss191/files/2020-03/2020%20Edelman%20Trust%20Barometer%20Brands%20and%20the%20Coronavirus.pdf (Accessed 10 December 2020).
25. Business of Purpose. *Statistics.*
26. Business of Purpose. *Statistics.*
27. Business of Purpose. *Statistics.*
28. Business of Purpose. *Statistics.*
29. Business of Purpose. *Statistics.*
30. Schoenwaelder, Mennel, Silverstein, Beery. Deloitte. *The Purpose Premium - Why a Purpose-Driven Strategy is Good for Business.*

CHAPTER EIGHT: PIVOT:

*Quotation:
Mandela, Nelson. United Nations. (2020) *Nelson Mandela International Day 18 July.* Available from: https://www.un.org/en/events/mandeladay/legacy.shtml (Accessed 5 May 2022). By permission (21 April 2022).
*Quotation:
Anonymous.
*Quotation:
Anonymous.
1. Dexosclosures.com. (2021) *Sustainability.* Available from: https://www.dexosclosures.com/sustainability (Accessed 1 November 2021).
2. Sitwell, Kamila – Co-Founder. Kolibri & Dexos Closures. (May 2019) The Impact Game Changers™ podcast. Available from: www.splitsecondltd.com. By permission (5 May 2022).
3. Buchanan, Laurence. EY. (2020) *How to Accelerate Online Direct to Consumer Strategies Beyond Covid 19.* Available from: https://www.ey.com/en_gl/consumer-products-retail/how-to-accelerate-online-direct-to-consumer-strategies-beyond-covid-19 (Accessed 2 August 2020).
4. Buchanan, Laurence. EY. *How to Accelerate Online Direct to Consumer Strategies Beyond Covid 19.*
5. International Telecommunications Union. (September 2017) *The State of Broadband: Broadband Catalyzing Sustainable Development September 2017.* Available from: https://www.itu.int/dms_pub/itu-s/opb/pol/S-POL-BROADBAND.18-2017-PDF-E.pdf (Accessed 12 August 2020).
*Quotation:
Anonymous.
6. World Economic Forum. (19 June 2020) *COVID-19: 3 Ways Businesses can Find Growth Opportunities During the Crisis.* Available from: https://www.weforum.org/agenda/2020/06/innovation-rethink-wharton-covid19-coronavirus/ (Accessed 3 August 2020). By permission (12 October 2020).

7.   Denham, Jess. Good Housekeeping. (18 February 2022) *10 Best Soluble Cleaning Products for Reducing Plastic Waste*. Available from: https://www.goodhousekeeping.com/uk/product-reviews/house-garden/g37775038/best-soluble-cleaning-products/ (Accessed 6 February 2022).

8.   Mintel. (2021) *The UK Green Household Care Consumer Market Report 2021*. Available from: https://reports.mintel.com/display/1049549/?fromSearch=%3Ffreetext%3DThe%2520UK%2520Green%2520Household%2520Care%2520Consumer%2520Market%2520Report%25202021 (25 January 2022).

9.   Harfield, Josie and McSorley, Ryan – Co-Founders. NEAT. (20 January 2022) The Impact Game Changers™ podcast. Available from: www.splitsecondltd.com. By permission (10 May 2022).

10.   Harfield, Josie and McSorley, Ryan – Co-Founders. NEAT. (20 January 2022) The Impact Game Changers™ podcast. Available from: www.splitsecondltd.com. By permission (10 May 2022).

11.   Harfield, Josie and McSorley, Ryan – Co-Founders. NEAT. (20 January 2022) The Impact Game Changers™ podcast. Available from: www.splitsecondltd.com. By permission (10 May 2022).

12.   Harfield, Josie and McSorley, Ryan – Co-Founders. NEAT. (20 January 2022) The Impact Game Changers™ podcast. Available from: www.splitsecondltd.com. By permission (10 May 2022).
      *Quotation:
      Elliott, Tom – Former Senior Buyer. Sainsbury's. (1 May 2019) The Impact Game Changers™ podcast. Available from: www.splitsecondltd.com. By permission (28 April 2022).

13.   BBC News. (20 August 2020) *Apple first US company to be valued at $2tn*. Available from: https://www.bbc.co.uk/news/business-53840471 (Accessed 20 August 2020).

14.   Goodwin, Tom. TechCrunch. (3 March 20215) *The Battle is for Customer Interface*. Available from: https://techcrunch.com/2015/03/03/in-the-age-of-disintermediation-the-battle-is-all-for-the-customer-interface/ (Accessed 14 May 2019). By permission (5 May 2022).

15.   Petrov, Christo. Spendmenot. (5 November 2021). *25+ Sharing Economy Statistics to Share in 2021*. Available from: https://spendmenot.com/blog/sharing-economy-statistics/ (Accessed 21 August 2021).

16.   Petrov, Christo. Spendmenot. (5 November 2021). *25+ Sharing Economy Statistics to Share in 2021*. Available from: https://spendmenot.com/blog/sharing-economy-statistics/ (Accessed 21 August 2021).

17.   The European Commission. (2018) *Developments and Forecasts of Growing Consumerism*. Available from: https://knowledge4policy.ec.europa.eu/foresight/topic/growing-consumerism/more-developments-relevant-growing-consumerism_en (Accessed 22 August 2021).

18.   Demailly & Novel. IDDRI (Institut du Développement Durable et des Relations Internationales). (14 July 2014) *The Sharing Economy: Make it Sustainable*. Available from: https://www.iddri.org/sites/default/files/import/publications/st0314_dd-asn_sharing-economy.pdf (Accessed 22 August 2020).
      *Quotation:
      McGillivray, Paul – Co-Founder. Remote Online. (1 April 2020) The Impact Game Changers™ podcast. Available from: www.splitsecondltd.com. By permission (10 May 2022).

19.   McGillivray, Paul – Co-Founder. Remote Online. (1 April 2020) The Impact Game Changers™ podcast. Available from: www.splitsecondltd.com. By permission (10 May 2022).

20.   McGillivray, Paul – Co-Founder. Remote Online. (1 April 2020) The Impact Game Changers™ podcast. Available from: www.splitsecondltd.com. By permission (10 May 2022).

21.   McGillivray, Paul – Co-Founder. Remote Online. (1 April 2020) The Impact Game Changers™ podcast. Available from: www.splitsecondltd.com. By permission (10 May 2022).

22. McKinsey & Company. (25 August 2020) *The Imperatives for Automation Success*. Available from: https://www.mckinsey.com/business-functions/operations/our-insights/the-imperatives-for-automation-success/ (Accessed 27 August 2020).

23. McKinsey & Company. *The Imperatives for Automation Success*.

CHAPTER NINE: PAY IT FORWARD:

*Quotation:
Ingersoll, Robert. Available from: https://www.forbes.com/quotes/8067/ (Accessed 19 May 2022).

1.   United Nations. (2015) *The Sustainable Development Goals* (SDGs). Available from: https://sdgs.un.org/goals (Accessed 12 January 2018).
*Quotation:
Anonymous. Available from: https://allauthor.com/quotes/18784/ (Accessed 2 February 2020).

2.   McKinsey & Company. (24 November 2017) *Attracting and Retaining the Right Talent*. Available from: https://www.mckinsey.com/business-functions/organization/our-insights/attracting-and-retaining-the-right-talent (Accessed 7 September 2020).

3.   Zippia Blog. (5 August 2014) Steve Jobs' Top Hiring Tip: "Hire the Best". Available from: https://www.zippia.com/employer/steve-jobs-top-hiring-tip-hire-the-best/ (Accessed 12 November 2020).

4.   Gleeson, Adam – Founder. The TalentPool Company Executive Search. (3 June 2019) The Impact Game Changers™ podcast. Available from: www.splitsecondltd.com. By permission (4 May 2022).

5.   Shah, Ameet – Business Partner. The TalentPool Company Executive Search. (3 June 2019) The Impact Game Changers™ podcast. Available from: www.splitsecondltd.com. By permission (4 May 2022).

6.   McKinsey & Company. *Attracting and Retaining the Right Talent*.

7.   Peters, Adele. Fast Company. (2 December 2020*) The Body Shop Will Start Hiring the First Person who Applies for any Retail Job*. Available from: https://www.fastcompany.com/90462746/the-body-shop-will-start-hiring-the-first-person-who-applies-for-any-retail-job (Accessed 17 September 2020).

8.   Peters, Adele. Fast Company. *The Body Shop Will Start Hiring the First Person who Applies for any Retail Job*.

9.   Pacifico, Jake – Business Partner. The TalentPool Company Executive Search. By permission (4 May 2022).

10. McKinsey & Company. (8 June 2020) *Reimagining the Office and Work Life After COVID-19*. Available from: https://www.mckinsey.com/business-functions/organization/our-insights/reimagining-the-office-and-work-life-after-covid-19/ (Accessed 7 September 2020).

11. McKinsey & Company. *Reimagining the Office and Work Life After COVID-19*.
*Quotation:
Rumi. Available from: https://quotefancy.com/quote/903910/Rumi-We-carry-inside-us-the-wonders-we-seek-outside-us (Accessed 19 May 2020).

12. Barnett, Dale. Influencer Intelligence. (2020) *11 Consumer Brands Giving Back for COVID-19 Relief*. Available from: https://www.influencerintelligence.com/blog/Ttb/11-consumer-brands-giving-back-for-covid-19-relief (Accessed 22 September 2020).

13. Barnett, Dale. Influencer Intelligence. *11 Consumer Brands Giving Back for COVID-19 Relief*.

14. Barnett, Dale. Influencer Intelligence. *11 Consumer Brands Giving Back for COVID-19 Relief*.

15. Barnett, Dale. Influencer Intelligence. *11 Consumer Brands Giving Back for COVID-19 Relief*.

16. Tony's Chocolonely Global Press Office (2022). By permission (19 May 2022).

17. Tony's Annual Fair Report 2019. (Accessed 24 September 2020).

18. Van Gelder, Koen. Statista. (10 February 2022) *Revenue of Tony's Chocolonely in the Financial Year 2020/2021, by Region*. Available from:

https://www.statista.com/statistics/942652/revenue-of-tony-s-chocolonely-by-region/ (Accessed 15 February 2022).

19. Tony's Chocolonely Global Press Office (2022). By permission (19 May 2022).
20. Tony's Chocolonely Global Press Office (2022). By permission (19 May 2022).
21. Tony's Chocolonely Global Press Office (2022). By permission (19 May 2022).
     *Quotation:
     Gandhi, Mahatma. Available from:
     https://www.brainyquote.com/quotes/mahatma_gandhi_109075 (Accessed 2 June 2020).
22. United Nations Global Compact. (2020) *Uniting Business in the Decade of Action.* Available from: https://ungc-communications-assets.s3.amazonaws.com/docs/publications/UN-Global-Compact-Progress-Report-2020.pdf (Accessed 13 June 2021).
23. United Nations Global Compact. (2020) *Uniting Business in the Decade of Action.*
24. United Nations Global Compact. (2020) *Uniting Business in the Decade of Action.*
25. United Nations Global Compact. (2020) *Uniting Business in the Decade of Action.*
     *Quotation:
     Udall, Stewart. Available from:
     https://www.brainyquote.com/quotes/stewart_udall_142796 (Accessed 8 May 2022).
     *Quotation:
     Greenpeace. Available from:
     https://twitter.com/GreenpeaceUK/status/1496479280221634565 (8 May 2022).
26. McGrath, Matt. BBC News. (19 March 2020) *Coronavirus: Air pollution and CO2 Fall Rapidly as Virus Spreads.* Available from: https://www.bbc.co.uk/news/science-environment-51944780 (Accessed 4 October 2020).
27. Science Direct. (2018) *Global Environmental Change.* Available from: https://www.sciencedirect.com/science/article/pii/S0959378018304035 (Accessed 4 October 2020).
28. Rannard, Georgina. BBC News. (17 June 2022) *Government Set to Miss Air Pollution Goals – Report.* Available from: https://www.bbc.co.uk/news/science-environment-61825379 (Accessed 17 June 2022).
29. IISD SDG Knowledge Hub. (8 November 2018) *WHO Global Conference Recommends Reducing Deaths from Air Pollution by Two-Thirds by 2030.* Available from: https://sdg.iisd.org/news/who-global-conference-recommends-reducing-deaths-from-air-pollution-by-two-thirds-by-2030/ (Accessed 1 October 2020).
30. Allbirds.com. (2021) *Sustainability.* Available from: https://www.allbirds.co.uk/pages/sustainability (Accessed 24 May 2021).
31. Allbirds.com. *Sustainability.*
32. Kantar. (25 November 2020) *Future-Proof Your Brand's Sustainable Transformation Goals* webinar.
33. FashionRevolution.org. (2020) *What my Jeans Say about the Garment Industry.* Available from: https://www.fashionrevolution.org/wp-content/uploads/2017/02/What-My-Jeans-Say-About-the-Garment-Industry.pdf (Accessed 4 October 2020).
34. London, Lela. Forbes. (15 April 2020) *Allbirds Is the First Fashion Brand to Label Its Carbon Footprint Like Calories.* Available from: https://www.forbes.com/sites/lelalondon/2020/04/15/allbirds-is-the-first-fashion-brand-to-label-its-carbon-footprint-like-calories/ (Accessed 4 October 2020).
35. Carbon Independent. (4 October 2020) Emissions from Cars. Available from: https://www.carbonindependent.org/17.html (Accessed 4 October 2020).
36. Kantar. *Future-Proof Your Brand's Sustainable Transformation Goals* webinar.
     *Quotation:
     Native American Proverb. Available from: https://www.facebook.com/unesco/posts/we-do-not-inherit-the-earth-from-our-ancestors-we-borrow-it-from-our-children-am/10156425995373390/ (Accessed 8 May 2022).
     *Quotation:
     Ki-Moon, Ban – Former Secretary-General. The United Nations. (15 November 2016) *Remarks to the Press at COP22 Marrakech, 15 November 2016.* Available from:

https://www.un.org/sustainabledevelopment/blog/2016/11/secretary-generals-remarks-to-the-press-at-cop22/ (Accessed 19 August 2020). By permission (21 April 2022).

37. United Nations Environment Programme (UNEP). (8 June 2018) *World Oceans Day 2018 to Focus on Cleaning up Plastic in Oceans.* Available from: https://www.un.org/sustainabledevelopment/blog/2018/06/world-oceans-day-2018-to-focus-on-cleaning-up-plastic-in-oceans/ (Accessed 5 October 2020). By permission (21 April 2022).

38. United Nations Environment Programme (UNEP). *World Oceans Day 2018 to Focus on Cleaning up Plastic in Oceans.*

39. Buis, Alan. NASA Global Climate Change. (12 July 2019) *Nope, Earth Isn't Cooling.* Available from: https://climate.nasa.gov/ask-nasa-climate/2893/nope-earth-isnt-cooling/ (Accessed 7 October 2020).

40. Redfearn, Graham. The Guardian. (5 October 2020) *More than 14m Tonnes of Plastic Believed to be at the Bottom of the Ocean.* Available from: https://www.theguardian.com/environment/2020/oct/06/more-than-14m-tonnes-of-plastic-believed-to-be-at-the-bottom-of-the-ocean (Accessed 19 October 2020).

41. United Nations Environment Programme (UNEP). (23 February 2017) *'Turn the tide on plastic' urges UN, as Microplastics in the Seas Now Outnumber Stars in our Galaxy.* Available from: https://news.un.org/en/story/2017/02/552052-turn-tide-plastic-urges-un-microplastics-seas-now-outnumber-stars-our-galaxy (Accessed 27 August 2021). By permission (21 April 2022).

42. United Nations Environment Programme (UNEP). (21 October 2021) *Plastic Pollution on Course to Double by 2030.* Available from: https://news.un.org/en/story/2021/10/1103692 (Accessed 22 November 2021). By permission (21 April 2022).

43. United Nations Environment Programme (UNEP). *Plastic Pollution on Course to Double by 2030.*

44. Carrington, Damian – Environment Editor. The Guardian. (8 December 2021) *Microplastics Cause Damage to Human Cells, Study Shows.* Available from: https://www.theguardian.com/environment/2021/dec/08/microplastics-damage-human-cells-study-plastic (Accessed 22 November 2021).
*Quotation:
United Nations Environment Programme (UNEP). *'Turn the tide on plastic' urges UN, as Microplastics in the Seas Now Outnumber Stars in our Galaxy.*

45. United Nations Environment Programme (UNEP). *World Oceans Day 2018 to Focus on Cleaning up Plastic in Oceans.*

46. United Nations Environment Programme (UNEP). *World Oceans Day 2018 to Focus on Cleaning up Plastic in Oceans.*

47. United Nations Environment Programme (UNEP). *World Oceans Day 2018 to Focus on Cleaning up Plastic in Oceans.*

48. World Economic Forum (WEF) & The Ellen McArthur Foundation. (2020) *Ocean Clean Up.* Available from: https://www.weforum.org/projects/ocean-clean-up (Accessed 5 October 2020). By permission (2022).

49. Laville, Sandra. The Guardian. (18 May 2021) *Twenty Firms Produce 55% of World's Plastic Waste, Report Reveals.* Available from: https://www.theguardian.com/environment/2021/may/18/twenty-firms-produce-55-of-worlds-plastic-waste-report-reveals (Accessed 27 August 2021).

50. World Economic Forum (WEF). (28 September 2020) *These are the 4 Biggest Challenges Facing the Ocean.* Available from: https://www.weforum.org/videos/these-are-the-4-biggest-challenges-facing-the-ocean (Accessed 13 October 2020). By permission (12 October 2020).

51. World Economic Forum (WEF). *These are the 4 Biggest Challenges Facing the Ocean.*

52. World Economic Forum (WEF). *These are the 4 Biggest Challenges Facing the Ocean.*

53. Plastic Whale. (2020) *Our Story.* Available from: https://plasticwhale.com/our-story/ (Accessed 11 November 2020). By permission (12 May 2022).

54. Plastic Whale. *Our Story.*

55. Plastic Whale. *Our Story.*

56. Ellen MacArthur Foundation. (2020) *Towards the Circular Economy Vol. 1: an Economic and Business Rationale for an Accelerated Transition*. Available from: https://www.ellenmacarthurfoundation.org/assets/downloads/publications/Ellen-MacArthur-Foundation-Towards-the-Circular-Economy-vol.1.pdf (Accessed 11 November 2020). By permission (8 April 2022).

57. Ellen MacArthur Foundation. *Towards the Circular Economy Vol. 1: an Economic and Business Rationale for an Accelerated Transition*.

58. Strategy& (Part of PwC). (2020) *Turning Plastic into Hope - How Plastic Whale has set Itself the Mission of Achieving Plastic-Free Waters, Worldwide*. Available from: https://www.strategyand.pwc.com/nl/en/who-we-are/corporate-responsibility/plastic-whale.html (Accessed 12 November 2020).
*Quotation:
Thunberg, Greta. The Guardian. (25 January 2019) *'Our House is on Fire': Greta Thunberg, 16, Urges Leaders to Act on Climate*. Available from: https://www.theguardian.com/environment/2019/jan/25/our-house-is-on-fire-greta-thunberg16-urges-leaders-to-act-on-climate (Accessed 9 May 2021).

59. NASA. (2020) *The Causes of Climate Change*. Available from: https://climate.nasa.gov/causes/ (Accessed 7 October 2020).

60. Wikipedia. Available from: https://en.wikipedia.org/wiki/Amazon_rainforest (Accessed 26 August 2021).

61. Carrington, Damian. The Guardian. (14 July 2021) *Amazon Rainforest now Emitting More CO2 than it Absorbs*. Available from: https://www.theguardian.com/environment/2021/jul/14/amazon-rainforest-now-emitting-more-co2-than-it-absorbs (Accessed 26 August 2021).

62. The Economist. YouTube. (27 November 2018) *How Veganism could Change the World*. Available from: https://youtu.be/hwoL6hWd4l0 (Accessed 13 October 2020).

63. The Economist. YouTube. *How Veganism could Change the World*.

64. Harvey, Fiona. The Guardian. (22 September 2020) *EU's Farm Animals 'Produce more Emissions than Cars and Vans Combined'*. Available from: https://www.theguardian.com/environment/2020/sep/22/eu-farm-animals-produce-more-emissions-than-cars-and-vans-combined-greenpeace (Accessed 13 October 2020).
Milman, Oliver. The Guardian. (13 September 2020) *Meat Accounts for Nearly 60% of All Greenhouse Gases from Food Production, Study Finds*. Available from: https://www.theguardian.com/environment/2021/sep/13/meat-greenhouses-gases-food-production-study (Accessed 13 October 2020).
Lean, Geoffrey. The Independent. (2006) *Cow 'Emissions' more Damaging to Planet than CO2 from Cars*. Available from: https://www.independent.co.uk/environment/climate-change/cow-emissions-more-damaging-to-planet-than-co2-from-cars-427843.html (Accessed 13 October 2020).

65. Greenpeace Instagram. (Accessed 27 August 2021).

66. EatGrub.co.uk. *Why Eat Insects?* Available from: https://www.eatgrub.co.uk/why-eat-insects/ (Accessed 14 October 2020). By permission (October 2019).

67. EatGrub.co.uk. *The Original Superfood - Why Eat Insects?* Available from: https://www.eatgrub.co.uk/why-eat-insects/ (Accessed 14 October 2020). By permission (October 2019).

68. Brown, Jessica. The Guardian. (15 October 2018) *Would You Eat Insects to Save the Planet from Global Warming?* Available from: https://www.theguardian.com/commentisfree/2018/oct/15/edible-insect-save-planet-global-warming-tasty-trendy (Accessed 14 October 2020).

69. EatGrub.co.uk. *The Original Superfood - Why Insects?* Available from: https://www.eatgrub.co.uk/why-eat-insects/ (Accessed 14 October 2020). By permission (October 2019).

70. Whippey, Neil – Co-Founder. Eat Grub. (November 2019) The Impact Game Changers™ podcast. Available from: www.splitsecondltd.com. By permission (November 2019).

71. Hampson, Laura. The Evening Standard. (15 July 2019) *Edible Insects like Crickets and Grasshoppers have more Antioxidants than Orange Juice, says Study*. Available from:

https://www.standard.co.uk/lifestyle/health/insects-antioxidants-study-a4190061.html (Accessed 14 October 2020).

72. Hampson, Laura. The Evening Standard. *Edible Insects like Crickets and Grasshoppers have more Antioxidants than Orange Juice, says Study.*

73. The Vegetarian Butcher. LinkedIn. (World Animal Day 2020). Available from: https://www.linkedin.com/posts/devegetarischeslager_thevegetarianbutcher-10ytvb-foodrevolution-activity-6718406213652004864-7Sm7 (Accessed 9 October 2020).

74. The Vegetarian Butcher Global Press Office. Unilever. By permission (31 May 2022).

75. Dr. Springmann, Marco. The Economist. YouTube. (27 November 2018) *How Veganism could Change the World.* Available from: https://youtu.be/hwoL6hWd4I0 (Accessed 13 October 2020).

76. World Economic Forum. (27 November 2019) *These Dutch Tomatoes Can Teach the World About Sustainable Agriculture.* Available from: https://www.weforum.org/agenda/2019/11/netherlands-dutch-farming-agriculture-sustainable/ (29 March 2022).

77. National Geographic. (17 September 2017) *How This Tiny Country Feeds the World.* Available from: https://www.nationalgeographic.com/magazine/article/holland-agriculture-sustainable-farming (Accessed 13 October 2020).

78. National Geographic. *How This Tiny Country Feeds the World.*

79. United Nations. (2022) *Sustainably Manage Forests, Combat Desertification, Halt and Reverse Land Degradation, Halt Biodiversity Loss.* Available from: https://www.un.org/sustainabledevelopment/biodiversity/ (Accessed 7 February 2022). By permission (21 April 2022).

80. United Nations. *Sustainably Manage Forests, Combat Desertification, Halt and Reverse Land Degradation, Halt Biodiversity Loss.*

81. United Nations. *Sustainably Manage Forests, Combat Desertification, Halt and Reverse Land Degradation, Halt Biodiversity Loss.*

82. United Nations. *Sustainably Manage Forests, Combat Desertification, Halt and Reverse Land Degradation, Halt Biodiversity Loss.*

83. United Nations. *Sustainably Manage Forests, Combat Desertification, Halt and Reverse Land Degradation, Halt Biodiversity Loss.*

84. United Nations. *Sustainably Manage Forests, Combat Desertification, Halt and Reverse Land Degradation, Halt Biodiversity Loss.*

85. United Nations. *Sustainably Manage Forests, Combat Desertification, Halt and Reverse Land Degradation, Halt Biodiversity Loss.*

86. Vass, Emma – UK CEO. Ecotone. (July 2021) The Impact Game Changers™ podcast. Available from: www.splitsecondltd.com. By permission (10 May 2022).

87. Vass, Emma – UK CEO. Ecotone. (July 2021) The Impact Game Changers™ podcast. Available from: www.splitsecondltd.com. By permission (10 May 2022).

88. Vass, Emma – UK CEO. Ecotone. (July 2021) The Impact Game Changers™ podcast. Available from: www.splitsecondltd.com. By permission (10 May 2022).

89. Vass, Emma – UK CEO. Ecotone. (July 2021) The Impact Game Changers™ podcast. Available from: www.splitsecondltd.com. By permission (10 May 2022).

*Quotation:
Guterres, António. United Nations. (18 February 2021) Press Conference by Secretary-General António Guterres at United Nations Headquarters. Available from: https://www.un.org/press/en/2021/sgsm20585.doc.htm (Accessed 15 February 2022). By permission (21 April 2022).

*Quotation:
Attenborough, David. WWF Australia. (18 November 2022) *10 best nature quotes from Sir David Attenborough.* Available from: https://www.wwf.org.au/news/blogs/10-best-nature-quotes-from-sir-david-attenborough (Accessed 8 December 2021). By permission of DLA Piper law firm (10 December 2021.

*Quotation:
African Proverb. Available from: https://quotlr.com/quotes-about-mosquito (Accessed 12 May 2020).

90. Edelman, Richard. Edelman. (23 June 2021) *Edelman Trust Barometer Special Report - Trust, The New Brand Equity*. Available from: https://www.edelman.com/trust/2021-brand-trust/brand-equity (Accessed 10 November 2021).

91. Edelman, Richard. Edelman. *Edelman Trust Barometer Special Report - Trust, The New Brand Equity*.

92. Edelman, Richard. Edelman. *Edelman Trust Barometer Special Report - Trust, The New Brand Equity*.

93. Edelman, Richard. Edelman. *Edelman Trust Barometer Special Report - Trust, The New Brand Equity*.

94. Edelman. *2018 Edelman Trust Barometer*.

95. Ben & Jerry's. Unilever. (May 2020) *Driving Superior Performance with Our Purpose-Led, Future-fit Business*. Available from: https://www.unilever.com/Images/making-purpose-pay-inspiring-sustainable-living-170515_tcm244-506419_en.pdf (Accessed August 31, 2021). By permission (May 2022).

96. Ben & Jerry's.co.uk. Unilever. (2021) *Values – Issues We Care About*. Available from: https://www.benjerry.co.uk/values/issues-we-care-about/climate-justice (Accessed 21 August 2021). By permission (May 2022).

97. Ben & Jerry's.co.uk. Unilever. *Values – Issues We Care About*.

98. Ben & Jerry's.co.uk. Unilever. *Values – Issues We Care About*.

99. Ben & Jerry's.co.uk. Unilever. *Values – Issues We Care About*.

100. Ben & Jerry's.co.uk. Unilever. *Values – Issues We Care About*.

101. Chouinard, Yvon – Founder. Patagonia. Evans, Jonathan. Esquire. (19 September 2020) The Full Story Behind Patagonia's 'Vote the Assholes Out' Tags. Available from: https://www.esquire.com/style/mens-fashion/a34078539/patagonia-vote-the-assholes-out-shorts-tag-meaning/ (Accessed 19 October 2020).

102. Kaepernick, Colin. New York Times. (15 February 2019) *A Timeline of Colin Kaepernick vs. The NFL*. Available from: https://www.nytimes.com/2019/02/15/sports/nfl-colin-kaepernick-protests-timeline.html (Accessed 20 October 2020).

103. The Guardian. (16 September 2019) *Nike's 'Dream Crazy' advert starring Colin Kaepernick wins Emmy*. Available from: https://www.theguardian.com/sport/2019/sep/16/nikes-dream-crazy-advert-starring-colin-kaepernick-wins-emmy (Accessed 10 May 2022).
    *Quotation:
    Einstein, Albert. (2021) Facebook.

104. Rashford, Marcus. Instagram. (Accessed 23 October 2020).

105. United Nations. (2021) *Goal 1: End Poverty in all its Forms Everywhere*. Available from: https://www.un.org/sustainabledevelopment/poverty/ (Accessed 11 June 2021). By permission (21 April 2022).

106. United Nations. *Goal 1: End Poverty in all its Forms Everywhere*.

107. United Nations. *Goal 1: End Poverty in all its Forms Everywhere*.

108. Brown, Kaysie and Rasmussen, Krista. United Nations Foundation. (9 July 2019) *The Sustainable Development Goals in 2019: People, Planet, Prosperity in Focus*. Available from: https://unfoundation.org/blog/post/the-sustainable-development-goals-in-2019-people-planet-prosperity-in-focus/ (21 October 2020).

109. Rashford, Marcus. Instagram. (Accessed 23 October 2020).

110. Rashford, Marcus. Twitter. (Accessed 23 October 2020).

111. Rashford, Marcus. Instagram. (Accessed 11 December 2020).

112. Richardson, Hannah. BBC News. (8 November 2020) *Marcus Rashford Welcomes School Holiday Support Climbdown*. Available from: https://www.bbc.co.uk/news/education-54841316 (Accessed 9 November 2020).

113. Richardson, Hannah. BBC News. *Marcus Rashford Welcomes School Holiday Support Climbdown*.
    *Quotation:
    Rumi. Available from: https://quotefancy.com/quote/904574/Rumi-When-we-practice-loving-kindness-and-compassion-we-are-the-first-ones-to-profit (Accessed 10 May 2021).

114. Sato, Masami – Founder. B1G1. *The Story of B1G1* video. Available from: B1G1.com. (Accessed 2018). By permission (9 November 2021).

115. Dunn, Paul – Co-Founder. B1G1. (April 2020) The Impact Game Changers™ podcast. Available from: www.splitsecondltd.com. By permission (10 May 2022).
*Quotation:
Aesop. Google. (Accessed April 2020).

116. United Nations. SDGs. *Goal 11: Make Cities inclusive, Safe, Resilient and Sustainable*. Available from: https://www.un.org/sustainabledevelopment/cities/ (Accessed 31 October 2020). By permission (21 April 2022).

117. United Nations. SDGs. *Goal 11: Make Cities inclusive, Safe, Resilient and Sustainable*.

118. UN Habitat. *Sustainable Development Goal Cities*. Available from: https://unhabitat.org/programme/sustainable-development-goals-cities (Accessed 3 November 2020). By permission (21 April 2022).

119. United Nations Development Programme (UNDP). *The SDGs in Action*. Available from: https://www.undp.org/content/undp/en/home/sustainable-development-goals.html (Accessed 3 November 2020). By permission (21 April 2022).

120. United Nations Development Programme (UNDP). *The SDGs in Action*.

121. UN Habitat. *UN Habitat, For a Better Urban Future. Flagship Programme, SDG Cities*. Available from: https://unhabitat.org/sites/default/files/2020/01/fp5-sdg_cities_v261119.pdf (Accessed March 2021).

122. Siemiatycki, Matti – Professor of the School of Cities. University of Toronto. (2 September 2019) The Impact Game Changers™ podcast. Available from: www.splitsecondltd.com. By permission (2 September 2019).

A HUMAN RACE ... TO 2030:

*Quotation:
Guterres, António – Secretary-General. United Nations News. (13 July 2021) *UN Chief Says Race to Reach SDGs 'Can and Must' be Turned Around*. Available from: https://news.un.org/en/story/2021/07/1095792 (Accessed 17 February 2020). By permission (21 April 2022).

1. The Climate Clock. Available from: https://climateclock.world (Accessed June 2022).

2. Intergovernmental Panel on Climate Change (IPCC). (2021) *Global Warming of 1.5 °C Special Report*. Available from: https://www.ipcc.ch/sr15/ (Accessed 19 December 2021).

3. United Nations. Business and Sustainable Development Commission. (2017) *Better Business, Better World*. Available from: https://sustainabledevelopment.un.org/index.php?page=view&type=400&nr=2399&menu=1515
(Accessed 6 September 2020). By permission (21 April 2022).

4. UN, *Better Business, Better World*.

5. Geneva Environment. (20 May 2022) *Earth Overshoot Day 2022*. Available from: https://www.genevaenvironmentnetwork.org/resources/updates/earth-overshoot-day/ (Accessed May 2022).

6. Geneva Environment. *Earth Overshoot Day 2022*.

7. IPCC. *Global Warming of 1.5 °C*.

8. IPCC. *Global Warming of 1.5 °C*.

9. Climate Innovation Forum. (28 June 2022) Westminster, London.

10. Netflix. (2021) *Don't Look Up*. Available from: https://www.netflix.com/gb/title/81252357 (Accessed June 2022).

11. UN, *Better Business, Better World*.

12. UN, *Better Business, Better World*.

13. Sustainable Markets Initiative. (26 June 2022) *Flipping the Switch*. Available from: https://www.sustainable-markets.org/news/flipping-the-switch/ (Accessed 28 June 2022).

14. Sustainable Markets Initiative. *Flipping the Switch*.

15. Sustainable Markets Initiative. *Flipping the Switch*.

16. Lutes, Mark. World Wildlife Fund (WWF). (16 June 2022) *Undelivered Climate Finance and Action by Rich Countries Stand in the Way of Future Action by All*. Available from: https://wwf.panda.org/wwf_news/?5843441/WWF-SB56-Bonn-climate-talks (Accessed 20 June 2022).

17. United Nations. (2017) *Climate Change and Social Inequality*. Available from: https://www.un.org/esa/desa/papers/2017/wp152_2017.pdf (Accessed 26 September 2021).

18. Broom, Douglas. World Economic Forum. (18 September 2020) *An Overwhelming Majority of People want Real Change after COVID-19*. Available from: https://www.weforum.org/agenda/2020/09/sustainable-equitable-change-post-coronavirus-survey/ (Accessed 9 September 2021).

     *Quotation:

     The Dalai Lama. Available from: https://wisdomquotes.com/dalai-lama-quotes-tenzin-gyatso/ (Accessed 2020).

Be Part of the Solution. Start an IMPACT Revolution™.

www.splitsecondltd.com

ACKNOWLEDGEMENTS

Thank you to everyone who shared their insight, creativity, and inspiration to make this book happen. It's been a labour of love putting pen to paper, connecting the dots, and collaborating with some of the most dynamic leaders, conscious global citizens, and businesses for good:

Giles Brook (Vita Coco & Whitespace), Henk Jan Beltman (Tony's Chocolonely), Rob Wilson (Toast Ale), Pippa Murray (Pip & Nut), Emma Vass (Ecotone), Tatiana Glad (Impact Hub), Merijn Everaarts (Dopper), Paul Hargreaves (Cotswold Fayre), Sarah Smart (The Collective Dairy), Paul Dunn & Masami Sato (B1G1), Tom Elliott (formerly at Sainsbury's), Hannah Daykin & Annabel Humphrey (Pursuit the Label), Professor Matti Siemiatycki (University of Toronto), Chetna Patel (Chillies & Clothes), Josie Harfield & Ryan McSorley (Neat Clean), Neil Fachie (Paralympic Gold Medal Cyclist and Author), Jane Malyon (The English Cream Tea Company), Neil Whippey (Eat Grub), Amanda Freeland (Manufacturing Growth Hub). **Business Accountability Peer Group:** Paul & Jeannie McGillivray (remote.online), Adam Gleeson, Ameet Shah, Jake Pacifico (thetalentpoolcompany.com).

Special Thank You to the Teams at:
The United Nations, B Lab Europe & B Corp, Impact Hub, Tony's Chocolonely, Unilever, IKEA, Ellen MacArthur Foundation, ClimatePartner, Kamila & Vincent Sitwell (Dexos Closures & Kolibri Drinks), Daniel Priestley (Founder & Author) and Dent Global, Sir Richard Branson and the team at Virgin, and Sir David Attenborough and his team.

Book Cover, Graphics and All Creative by Suraaj Nakil:
www.suraajnakil.com

Editing, Insight & Design Contributions: Rosalind Stefanac, Neelu Lamba, Simon Reberga, Alex Meadows, Ishani Abdoelgafoer, Gloria Vidovich, Manjula Shukla, Alexandra Dunsmuir.

Additional Support: Christelle Sigre, Clare Bucknall, Divya Gururaj, Debbie Russeth, Nina Saxena, Jasmine Lamba, Bonnie Hamilton, George Triantafillou, Daniel Zuidema, Shalini Sinha, Nick Brookes, Beena Goel, Diwaker Srivastava, Angela Morgan, Zoe Nash, Kiera Schoenemann.

Massive thank you to all other family and friends who cheered me onto the finish line, your encouragement has been invaluable!

THE AUTHOR

NUPUR SAXENA

Think global, act local is the mantra that best describes Nupur's perspective of the world. It is a way of life that embodies the diversity of cultures, communities and collaboration that open up limitless opportunities. It is the most valuable lesson she has learnt to date, and nowhere is it more epitomised than in the world of business.

Nupur is a passionate advocate for cultural values that centre on diversity and inclusion, energy for performance, wellbeing, and sustainability. She is multi-lingual and has lived in several countries. Her international track record of accelerating business growth has delivered lucrative financial returns, formed strategic partnerships, and embedded capability in 30+ industry channels. Her corporate and consulting career includes some of the most recognised brands and retailers in the world such as: Coca-Cola, GlaxoSmithKline, Bacardi, Tesco, Sainsbury's, PepsiCo, Starbucks and many other UK, Pan-European, Asian, and North American organisations.

Today, Nupur is the founder of Split Second Ltd., an IMPACT growth strategy consultancy committed to scaling profit with purpose to deliver the UN Sustainable Development Goals by 2030. She believes that businesses need to abandon a one-size-fits-all approach. Instead, they must take urgent responsibility for global challenges such as the climate crisis, rising inequality and socio-economic issues that ultimately affect us all.

Nupur is also the host of The IMPACT Game Changers™ podcast which offers real-life insight and examples from CEOs, founders, and business leaders. She collaborates with B Corp certified, Fortune 500, and challenger brands who are on a mission to make a positive IMPACT on People, Planet and Profit. Every second counts.

Contact Details:
http://uk.linkedin.com/in/nupursaxena/
nsaxena@splitsecondltd.com

Manufactured by Amazon.ca
Acheson, AB